PEKING TO LHASA

PEKING TO LHASA

THE NARRATIVE OF JOURNEYS IN THE CHINESE EMPIRE MADE BY THE LATE BRIGADIER - GENERAL GEORGE PEREIRA, C.B., C.M.G., D.S.O., COMPILED BY SIR FRANCIS YOUNGHUSBAND, K.C.S.I., K.C.I.E., FROM NOTES AND DIARIES SUPPLIED BY MAJOR - GENERAL SIR CECIL PEREIRA, K.C.B., C.M.G.

WITH MAPS AND ILLUSTRATIONS

GYAN

Published by

Gyan Publishing House
5, Ansari Road
Daryaganj, New Delhi-110002
Phone: 011-47034999, 9811692060
E-mail: books@gyanbooks.com

Distribution Network
gyanbooks.com
India, USA, Canada, UK, Australia, France

ISBN : 978-81-212-2905-0 (PB)
First Published, 1925

2nd Impression 2021

Printed at: Gyan Press, Delhi.

Peking to Lhasa
Author: General George Pereira

PEKING TO LHASA

THE NARRATIVE OF JOURNEYS IN THE CHINESE EMPIRE MADE BY THE LATE BRIGADIER-GENERAL GEORGE PEREIRA, C.B., C.M.G., D.S.O., COMPILED BY SIR FRANCIS YOUNGHUSBAND, K.C.S.I., K.C.I.E., FROM NOTES AND DIARIES SUPPLIED BY MAJOR-GENERAL SIR CECIL PEREIRA, K.C.B., C.M.G.

WITH MAPS AND ILLUSTRATIONS

LONDON
CONSTABLE AND COMPANY LTD.
1925

Brigadier General George Pereira
C.B., C.M.G., D.S.O.

PREFACE

General Pereira, nearly up to the last day of his life, kept a diary of his travels, and literally up to the last day of his life made observations for his map. He was exceptionally methodical in his observations, and no illness or discomfort was ever allowed to stand in the way of making his record.

From his survey maps have been compiled in the War Office, and copies may be seen at the rooms of the Royal Geographical Society; and it is from these that the map accompanying this book has been compiled. And to make the story of his travels available for the general public, his brother, Sir Cecil Pereira, placed the diaries at my disposal. With so much detail available it has been possible to describe with great accuracy the route followed on his journeys. But General Pereira was singularly restrained in the expression of those feelings which every traveller has: it is not possible, therefore, to describe what he felt. But how concentrated and intense his feelings must have been we may conclude from the single fact that these journeys were made at all—made in the face of physical disabilities so grave that they cost him his life. His feelings he expressed in his journeys: if he had put them into his diaries he might not have made the journeys.

F. E. Y.

July 1925.

CONTENTS

LIST OF ILLUSTRATIONS

MAPS

Potala Lhasa.

face p. 1.

CHAPTER I

GEORGE PEREIRA

George Pereira died in 1923 on the borders of China and Tibet at almost the close of the third of three remarkable journeys made in succession through the Chinese Empire. The first and most important was from Peking across Tibet to Lhasa and India. This was a great enough journey in itself to satisfy most men; but no sooner had he completed it than he started off back again—this time from west to east instead of from east to west—across the Chinese Empire from Burma to Shanghai. And even this was not enough: not content with travelling from east to west and west to east, he must needs now travel from south to north. And it was on his way from Yūnnan to Kansu that he finally succumbed.

Before the War he had travelled much in China; but the present record is of this series of journeys which he had undertaken after the War from 1921 to 1923. And the journeys are all the more remarkable because they were made by a man nearer sixty than fifty years of age, and partially lame from a riding accident he had had in his youth. Physically he was a weak man. But his spirit was indomitable. And before the account of his journeys is begun it is well to say something of the man who made them.

By profession he was a soldier. In 1883, at the age of eighteen, he entered the Grenadier Guards; and like most Guardsmen he was incessantly working to get on active service. It was the days of campaigns in Egypt; and when preparations were being made for the advance on Khartum he went to Egypt, studied and passed an examination in Arabic and applied for an appointment with the Expeditionary Force; but Kitchener, considering his lameness from his hunting accident would be a disqualification, rejected the application.

Baulked in Egypt, Pereira turned to China. In 1900 he joined the Chinese Regiment which was being raised by the British Government in the recently annexed port of Wei-hai-wei. And with this regiment he took part in the operations for the relief of the Legations in Peking during the Boxer Rising, and was slightly wounded.

Meanwhile his battalion of the Grenadier Guards had proceeded on active service in South Africa, and he was only able to get away from the Chinese Regiment in time to reach South Africa a few months before the end of the war. Then back again he went to China; and in 1904 was appointed Military Secretary in Korea and was present at Chemulpho at one of the first actions in the Russo-Japanese War. In the following year he was appointed Military Attaché with the Third Japanese Army and was present at the Battle of Mukden. In October 1905 he was appointed Military Attaché at Peking, and after holding this appointment for four years he rejoined his Regiment; but peace soldiering had no attractions for him and he resigned his commission.

This, however, was not the end of his military service; for in August 1914 he was posted to the Staff of the 47th Division and went to France with them. Then he was appointed to the command of the 4th Battalion Royal Welsh Fusiliers, and led them in the battle of Loos, where he was slightly wounded. In 1916 he was appointed to the command of the 47th Infantry Brigade and captured Guillemont during the Battle of the Somme. In 1918 he commanded the 43rd Brigade during the final advance of the Allies. And on his Brigade being demobilised he joined General Knox's Mission to General Kolchak in Siberia and was with the Russian force until it withdrew.

This is but the bare record of his military service, but it is sufficient to show the variety of his professional experience and the keenness with which he sought active service. It may be added that on active service he was distinguished for his courage and his care of his men. Utterly fearless and ever thoughtful of the welfare of his men, he was regarded by his comrades as a good man, a good fellow, and a good Guardsman.

Apart from his keenness for active service two passions ruled him: one was racing; the other was travel. And while he was at home racing he would be thinking of the journeyings which were to follow; and all through his journeys he would be thinking of the next Derby, and be asking his brother for all the racing news. Racing and travel were his ruling passions whenever he was at leisure, and perhaps in his mind the two were one. Perhaps attaining a goal—stretching oneself out to the very utmost—was the dominating idea which connected the two. For, in a sense, his journey from Peking to Lhasa *was* a race. Others there were who were striving for the same end. And always he had in his mind the idea of getting there first. " Englishman first " is what he telegraphed from Lhasa on his arrival.

Having then seen the Derby in 1920 he withdrew into the wilds to indulge his other passion, meaning to get back for the Derby of 1924. He returned to China to carry out his great ambition of reaching Lhasa from the east. In 1848 two daring French missionaries, Pères Huc and Gabet, had reached the Holy City of the Grand Lama from China. But since then no European had followed in their steps. Many had tried—Russians, French, English, Danes, Swedes, Norwegians, Americans—but none had succeeded. Pereira meant to make the attempt.

And for this enterprise he was peculiarly qualified. For his passion for travel had possessed him during all his military service in China. Missionaries travel extensively in China; but few even of them can have travelled as much as Pereira. He had visited every Province. He had travelled over the whole of Korea and right across Manchuria, Mongolia and Chinese Turkestan. He must have travelled 50,000 miles in the Chinese Empire if he had travelled a yard. And he had travelled not only as a private individual but as an official. When Military Attaché he had made a point of going about visiting the various units of the Chinese Army. And his tact, his understanding of Chinese etiquette and his conversational ability enabled him to make personal friendships with many of the Viceroys and high officials. So he had a knowledge of Chinese of all degrees, from the soldiers of his Wei-hai-wei Regiment and from peasants and carters to the highest in the land.

Such were Pereira's qualifications for the task he had before him when he arrived in Peking in January 1921. And all this experience he needed. For the obstacles which lay between him and his goal were not so much physical as human. And to overcome human obstacles, capacity for dealing with men is the chief need. The most determined and pertinacious man in the world would never succeed if he had not also the knack of winning over men to his own side.

The first obstacle he would meet would be the famine in North China. Poor China is subject to many calamities. And the great plains of the north are liable to both floods and famine: to floods from an excess of rainfall and to famine from a deficiency. When Pereira planned his journey to Lhasa there had been a deficiency of rainfall. The crops had not matured. The wretched inhabitants were starving. And through a starving population it is not easy for a stranger to find his way.

Famine, however, was not so serious an obstacle as civil war. China was in chaos. One Province was at war with another. And all were more or less at war with the Central Government. The ancient monarchy had been swept away. The

Republic had not yet established itself. There was no order in the country. The various armies were not paid. And the soldiery, to support themselves, were driven to looting; or they would break up into bands of brigands and scour the country.

And if and when Pereira had made his way through the famine-stricken peoples and through the warring factions and bands of brigands, and had reached the borders of Tibet, still greater obstacles might meet him. On the establishment of the Republic in China the Tibetans had evicted the Chinese from Tibet. And, as a consequence, all along the border between Tibet and China, where it is difficult to state exactly at what line Chinese authority ends and Tibetan begins, there was disorder. Many of the border people owe only a loose allegiance to Lhasa. Many others owe only a loose allegiance to China. And when Tibet and China are at variance, these try to be independent of both. Pereira, on arrival at the fringe of China Proper, might find it impossible to get through disorderly frontier peoples.

And supposing he did get through these wild border tribesmen there was still the Central Government of Tibet to reckon with. Since the British Mission to Lhasa of 1904 they had been well-disposed towards travellers coming from India. But so far they had allowed no European to enter Lhasa from the side of China. Would they show any favour towards Pereira? If not, his aims would be thwarted at their very climax.

These were the obstacles he had to expect. And in addition there were of course the ordinary hardships of travel—poor food, unhealthy accommodation, rain, heat, cold, etc.—which to a man fifty-six years of age when he started, and with an injured spine, were in themselves sufficiently serious.

CHAPTER II

THE START FROM PEKING

FULLY aware of the difficulties which lay before him, but conscious also of his ability to deal with them, Pereira, after a visit to Peking, left Tientsin on February 15, 1921. And wisely he travelled alone—that is to say, alone as regards European companionship. For it is much easier for a solitary European to find his way through such obstacles as he was likely to meet with than for even a couple of Europeans. A single European is viewed with much less suspicion. He may be only a stray lunatic. If there are two there must be some design behind. Moreover, when transport and supplies are difficult to procure, one European is more easily provided for than two. Pereira was, therefore, wise to set out on his journey by himself.

But, of course, he took Chinese servants—"boys"—with him. Each of the two had his bundle of bedding containing all his worldly goods. His wages were to be drawn at the Tientsin bank, and two dollars each a week sufficed for food and other necessities of the way.

It will not be necessary to follow Pereira very closely over the first part of his journey, for he covered well-known ground. He first of all traversed the dreary, densely populated plain of Chihli, now in the winter time devoid of a vestige of colour. At Tsang Chow, 79 miles, normally reckoned as a town of 40,000 or 50,000 inhabitants, while some had fled from the famine more had come in from the stricken areas. Continuing across the plain to Hochien Fu he found the whole land given up to cultivation and thickly populated, studded with many villages surrounded by trees and sometimes by orchards of pear or Chinese dates. The cart tracks were fair in fine weather, but dusty, for they were unmade. The plain was indeed all alluvial. There were practically no stones. The houses were usually built of mud, single-storied, with flat roofs. Only the better class houses were constructed of brick.

At Hochien Fu were a Church of England and a Roman Catholic Mission. Pereira called on the magistrate and found the same old ceremonies observed of putting the visitor into the place of honour, sitting down together, producing tea when it was time to go, and accompanying the guest to the third gate. The only difference from old times was that the magistrate wore no official robes and wore no queue. The latter need not be regretted; but the substitution of imitation European clothes for the beautiful silks and fur of the old regime is a change which most will deplore. The magistrate put the average size of a family in China at six. Adults, he thought, predominated in the towns and children in the country. On the average there are six men to four women, and consequently there is a difficulty in finding wives.

With all his experience of travel in China

Pereira was still annoyed at the vexatious inquisitiveness of Chinese crowds. At meals or a halt in a village the crowds would close in to watch him eating and pester him with inquiries. On arriving at an inn the traveller alights in a filthy courtyard which has never been swept out. He then proceeds to his chamber, on the north side of which is the kang or raised platform, beneath which runs a flue which is heated by burning long millet stalks. Lying on the kang the traveller is roasted when the millet stalks are burning and frozen when the fire dies out. The walls are of mud, with the accumulated dirt of ages. The wooden door never fits the doorway, so admits plenty of fresh air. The windows are of paper.

Such inns Pereira found a poor refuge after a long day's journey. In the winter time the traveller is frozen, but free of insects. In summer time the walls are the refuge of countless bugs, who issue forth at night in legions to attack their unfortunate victim. And if they cannot reach him on his bed they climb on to the ceiling and drop on him from above. If he sleeps on the kang without a bed he becomes a victim to lice. And on the cart, too, he must be careful not to get near the wadded clothes of the carters for fear of these pests.

At Chengting Fu, which has a population of about 90,000, he found a large French Lazarist Mission with schools for 150 boys, orphanages where boys are taught various trades, and a convent with sixteen Sisters of Charity who usually look after about a thousand orphans and destitute women, but who during the famine had to succour twice that number.

The plains of Chihli were soon after left behind, and Pereira entered the more hilly Province of Shansi. Here a railway ascends some bare, treeless hills to a height of 4400 feet and then gradually descends to the Taiyüan plain 2625 feet above sea-level. In the city of Taiyüan he found many improvements. Good streets had been laid out. A university and several foreign-looking school buildings had been erected. Electric light had been installed. There were three motors, two motor cycles, a motor lorry and eight hundred rickshaws all licensed and with European numbers. The European community now numbered between fifty and sixty.

Pereira stayed with Mr. Ross, the Postal Commissioner, and records that, ably run by foreigners, the Chinese Post Office is year by year improving. New offices are constantly being opened and old ones improved. Notwithstanding the bad roads and brigands he invariably received his mail in all sorts of places throughout the Empire punctually and without loss.

Shansi has the reputation of being the home of Chinese bankers, but in general it is one of the poorest Provinces. Twenty years previously it was perhaps the most opium-soaked Province in China. With the suppression of opium it improved for a while. But now again, owing to the connivance of Chinese officials, morphia and morphine are being smuggled in, and people are taking to bad habits again. The people make poor soldiers and are a quiet race. The governor (Yen-shih-shah) ten years before was a sergeant. He had risen more by luck than through any real capacity. But he had been able to preserve his Province from internal risings, and was therefore popular. He is honest according to his lights, and he has done much good in his Province by allowing no squeezes, establishing girls' schools and paying high salaries to good teachers. But he is a weak man, unable to cope with the corruption round him, afraid of the students and ready for the sake of peace and for fear of their power to give in to their absurd demands.

The President of the local assembly with very proper foresight bought up a huge supply of grain when he saw that famine was imminent. But he sold it at more than twice the price he gave for it and made for himself a huge profit.

A model prison is one of the features of Taiyüan. It is run on modern lines and has over nine hundred male prisoners and thirty female in a separate part. The cells are warmed with kangs and are clean. There are twelve workshops, and the prisoners are usefully employed in making carpets, carpentry, etc. They get three meals a day, and according to the warder they come in thin and go out plump. The majority (those with long sentences) wear chains round their ankles. The chief offences were brigandage and consuming morphia. In this model prison there is no corporal punishment. But a stranger coming to China and only visiting this prison would get a very erroneous impression of Chinese prison administration. The state of the old-fashioned yamen prisons is very different.

The Chief Justice of the Shansi Province was an enlightened man of forty, trained in America.

In the face of the old official opposition, he had established law courts on the modern system. In the higher court at least five trained judges sit, whilst in two minor courts for lesser offences there are three judges. Altogether there are in the Province nine judges trained on modern lines, and they form a court of appeal.

The court-houses are on modern lines, with raised benches for the judges, tables on either side for the opposing advocates, and railed-in seats on either side for the spectators. And instead of having to kneel, as in old times, the defendant is allowed to stand.

There are law courts in other Provinces, but few have such an enlightened Chief Justice as Mr. Hsü to direct them. If only all courts in China were directed like this, one of the greatest scandals in the country would be removed.

Another innovation at Taiyüan is a small modern garden with a lake and a building like a church, in which moral lectures were given weekly on Sundays. Officials from the governor downwards used to come to these lectures, but the practice has been gradually falling off.

Leaving this progressive city on March 7 with one four-mule open cart and two two-mule Peking carts, Pereira was delayed one and a half hours at the start because carts were not allowed to go over the modern roads of the city. Eventually leave from the Police Commissioner was obtained and he proceeded on his way. On the following day he was able to do 35¾ miles. The mules did not look much and were uncared for and dirty. But even on the wretched Chinese roads they cover great distances. The carters also are a stout set of men: nothing daunts them and they are always cheerful. The carter uses no reins: he either walks alongside directing by word of mouth or with his whip, or he sits on the left-hand side of the cart and directs from there. Much traffic was passed: it included many carts, wheelbarrows drawn by donkeys, coolies carrying loads, donkeys with packs, and one string of camels.

At Fenchow Fu, which has from 60,000 to 70,000 inhabitants, he found the American Board Mission established in a fine compound with two-storied schools, a church and a very fine two-storied hospital in process of construction.

At Ping-yang Fu on March 14, Pereira stayed with Doctor and Mrs. Carr of the China Inland Mission. Dr. Carr runs an excellent hospital, assisted by a properly qualified Chinese assistant. These hospitals are kept up for the benefit of the poor, and too much praise, Pereira thought, could not be given to the noble band of men who devote their lives and labour ungrudgingly to alleviate the ills of suffering humanity.

The sad case of a Scotch girl who married a fairly well-to-do Chinese in a neighbouring village was related by Dr. Carr. She had several children, and the family treated her well according to their lights. But she outlived the glamour of the East. She was very lonely and always longing for home. And she used to come to the Mission, till she was attacked by typhus and died.

At Yungcheng, which Pereira reached on March 20, he found the Tao-yin to be a Mohammedan aged forty who had been educated in England and who had also sent his son to England. He was one of the handful of really enlightened up-to-date officials, rigorous in suppressing ill and energetic in conducting reforms.

Just south of Yungcheng is the Salt Lake, about 7 miles long by 3 miles wide, from which the Chinese Government derive a large revenue. It is surrounded by a mud wall and trench, with eleven gates; and a guard of 800 men is maintained to prevent smuggling. In normal seasons the part of the Lake producing salt is about 4 miles long by 1 mile wide. On the bed of the Lake about 50 feet from the surface there appears to be a layer of rock salt. In circular pits or wells driven down to this depth the water becomes impregnated with salt. The brine is lifted to the surface by gangs of labourers and is run into evaporating pans and condensed by solar evaporation until salt is formed. It is then sold to salt merchants.

In the old days the Salt Commissioners in China used to make huge profits. But since the administration of the Salt Revenue was entrusted to Sir Richard Dane and an efficient European staff has been organised, the revenue has increased enormously. Salt in China is not a Government monopoly. It belongs to a Guild of Salt Merchants. But the Government puts a tax on what is taken out of the salt enclosures.

Famine refugees in some numbers—mostly from Honan—had found their way to Yungcheng, and those that were fit were put on relief works, such as road-making. Some good macadamised streets were being made in the city. And Mr. Baldwin, the Inspector of Salt, had constructed a steam roller with four corn-grinding millstones. Mr. Baldwin had also started a club on European lines. He was the only European; but there were more than a hundred Chinese members. A tennis court had been made; dinner-parties could be given; there were bedrooms for strangers; and newspapers to date were taken. Yungcheng also possessed a model prison.

Crossing another of the fertile plains with peach trees now in blossom, Pereira reached the range which forms the northern bank of the Huang Ho (the Yellow River). This range he crossed at a height of 3650 feet, and then next day dropped some 1500 feet to the Yellow River, where he encountered a snowstorm which made the roads very heavy and slippery. The river had to be crossed by a ferry. There were six or seven boats, and one of the larger took his caravan of eight mules and three carts, the mules being taken out and the carts man-handled up planks on to the boat. The mules, as is their wont, proved refractory and began kicking about. But luckily none went overboard.

The Province of Honan lay on the other side of the river. The bank rose several feet above the river in a great plateau of loess—a light friable soil which is very dusty in dry weather and cakes into heavy slippery mud in wet weather. After the snow and rain Pereira found the road to Kwanyintang one of the worst he had seen in China. The wretched mules with difficulty dragged the cart through the mud. They often

LOOKING SOUTH UP THE HUANG HO TO MAO TSING TU.

face

floundered in deep pools; whilst the unlucky pedestrian had to wade along the road or climb razor-shaped paths, often on the edge of a big drop, and be constantly meeting strings of laden people. These people were, however, always friendly and ready to lend a hand when difficulties were encountered, or to exchange a word of greeting. Some of them were famine refugees, the father carrying a crying baby and exclaiming, "It is cold," and the mother saying, "Alas! what can I do?"

From these primitive roads Pereira suddenly emerged on to the railway, for Kwanyintang was then the head of the railway, under construction from Chingchow (on the Peking—Hankow line) to Sianfu. He took a three hours' journey to L'o-yang, and from there visited a General who has since come very much to the front in China. This was General Wu Pu Fu. He was then aged forty-eight, and appeared to Pereira to be the most capable General in China. He was keen, energetic, quiet and determined. He was one of the few officials who took an interest in tree-planting, and in his camp had planted hundreds of fir, willow, elm, ash and other trees. His troops were regularly paid seven dollars a month, besides getting two meals a day, though in the old armies the men had often to find their own food. The General himself hailed from Shantung, but the men came from all Provinces, and were well-disciplined, smart-looking and keen on parade. They still used the German drill with the fantastic parade step; and they had a curious crouching double like a cat moving over hot bricks. The German drill was passed on to China by the Japanese, and these

Chinese soldiers took to it readily. On parade they moved like clockwork. The defect was that they totally lacked initiative. They would carry out an attack like a drill movement. But until they learned to use their wits they would have a poor time in fighting a trained army.

The famine was more severe in Honan than in most other Provinces. Pereira saw a beggar gloating over some dirty bones which he would not like to have given to a decent dog in England. And some of the districts were overrun by bands of brigands. It was said that there were fourteen to seventeen of these bands, some four to five hundred strong. But the authorities did nothing to put them down and little to cope with the famine. In one village which put up some resistance several bands combined and killed about three hundred of the inhabitants. In other places a band would capture three or four villages and drive out the inhabitants. Roman Catholic and Protestant missionaries working together did their best to relieve distress; but in the face of the apathy of the officials and the lawlessness around them theirs was an uphill task.

The opinion of one of these missionaries of the character of the Chinese peasant is worth noting. Père Pelerzi had spent seven years in a Chinese village, and he considered that the Chinese peasant led an ideal life, according to his own lights. He knew not what comfort and luxury meant, and so did not miss them. He was accustomed to and satisfied with what little he had, and enjoyed life. There was very little vice among them, and their chief faults were thieving and anger. In reply to Pereira's question whether he thought many of his Christians would go to Heaven, Père Pelerzi said he thought they all would.

Cigarette-smoking seems to be making its way into China as into other parts of Asia; and this and other Provinces are covered with advertisements of a tobacco company. There are sign-scrapers on the roadside, and the towns are plastered with pictorial advertisements.

CHAPTER III

THE HWA SHAN

HAVING made this brief incursion into Honan, Pereira recrossed the Yellow River, returned to Kwanyintang and from there set out for the Province of Shensi and its famous capital, Sian—often spelt Signan—once the capital of China. But on the way he made a short detour to visit the beautiful mountain of pilgrimage—the Hwa Shan, one of the five sacred mountains of China—and for this excursion he received every assistance from the Chinese officials.

On entering Shensi he found practically all the villages were surrounded by a mud wall, thus showing that brigandage was prevalent. The inns, too, were very poor, consisting of two rows of rooms, like cells without windows, each about 8 feet square, on either side of the yard. As a set-off was the goodwill of the Chinese officials: the magistrate called on him late at night and insisted on his taking up his abode in the yamen, and offered to make all arrangement for the trip to the Hwa Shan.

Starting off on a fine April day, Pereira crossed a plain green with wheat and budding trees and sprinkled with the pink of peach blossoms and

Hwa Shan.

face p. 21.

apricot and the white of plums, and reached the Yü-ch'üan-yuan or Jade Spring Temple at the foot of the bleak Ching Ling range. The chief monk here was seventy-one years old. He was very friendly, and produced the usual sweetmeats, and also a Chinese plan, not to scale, however, of the Hwa Shan. On the wall were collections of Chinese cards left by visitors; and Pereira added his, as the old monk said he had none of a foreigner, though several Europeans had been there. This and all the other temples of the Hwa Shan were under Taoist monks, ruled by a superior (Tao-kuan) living at the big Hwayin Miao in the plain. There are two ranks of monks, the Lao-tao or higher monks, and the Tao-tung. The former wear their hair coiled up in a ball on the top and secured by a carved piece of wood, and wear a circular soft cap with a hole in the centre for the coil of hair.

Leaving the Jade Temple, which stands at an approximate height of 2200 feet above sea-level, the path leads up a narrow valley, crossing the very stony bed of a beautifully clear stream a dozen times in the first mile. Afterwards it is sometimes a series of uneven steps, sometimes rocky and sometimes easy. All the way the scenery is magnificent. On the left rises a great mountain with perpendicular walls of rock; whilst on the right the ascent is possible in places. Eight small uninteresting temples are passed. And sometimes footholds are cut in the rock leading up to small shrines in caves. At the end of the valley, due south, rises the Hwa Shan itself. It is connected with a lower ridge on the north-east side, and then runs up into a sharp peak (the Hsi-peng) on the north-west side, below which there is a sharp precipice of some 2000 feet. Down below pine trees can be seen. The hill-sides, when not rocky, are covered with bracken, wild flowers and occasional fruit trees now in blossom; and wild goats, leopards and wolves are to be found.

After climbing for three hours, Pereira reached the half-way temple, Ch'ing-ko-p'ing (altitude 5000 feet), where he stayed the night. It stands at the end of the valley under the perpendicular walls of the lower ridge of the Hwa Shan on the left, the precipices of the Hsi-feng in front and steep but accessible hills on the left. Here he was given a quite comfortable and clean room with a kang to lie on and thick coverlets. In accordance with the usual custom in Chinese temples he was offered a circular box, divided, like the eight Chinese diagrams, into eight outer compartments and one in the centre, containing different kinds of sweetmeat. Cups were then produced and filled with tea. And for dinner he had some really excellent small Irish potatoes with Chinese vermicelli and bread, whilst the remainder of his party had a regular Chinese meal. The potatoes were grown on the mountain, but most of the other provisions had been brought from the plain.

The next day, starting at 7.30, he began the real ascent of the mountain, making for the Pei-feng or northern peak (6280 feet). Close by the temple was a small circular cave hewn out of the solid rock about 20 feet high and 20 feet in diameter, with a circular roof, and filled with the usual hideous idols of the country. A difficult path up rocks a little above it leads to

HWA SHAN.

face p. 23.

one of the numerous little shrines cut into the sides of the walls. Proceeding on his way, Pereira found the climbing up the mountain was often on the side of the rock, with a precipice on one side. The steps were uneven, and in two of the worst places there were 314 and 246 steps respectively. Eventually the top of a long narrow ridge running north and south is reached, and in some places it is barely more than the width of the steps.

The Pei-feng is built on the eastern edge of the precipice. From it there is a fine view to the south along the ridge, studded with three or four small temples and a few blossoming fruit trees in the wider parts. It appears to end at the foot of the huge solid perpendicular rock forming the main mountain; but actually there is a very steep ascent of some 900 steps between precipices; and this is the only accessible approach.

At the top of these steps is the Wu-yün-feng temple; and the ridge here rises again and forms the western end of the mountain, with a small valley on the right and two sharp peaks at the north-east and north-west corners. The top is covered with pine trees, whilst on the four sides are perpendicular walls of rock, that on the west being some 2000 feet above the valley. A comparatively easy ascent from the Wu-yün-feng leads to the Hsi-feng (western peak) temple; and just above it rises the north-west peak (8100 feet), a smooth rock which has to be reached by more difficult steps. From it there is a magnificent view across the Ching Ling (range), some of the adjacent hills being higher than the Hwa Shan, and many rising into needle peaks quite unscaleable.

From the Hai-feng there is a steep descent across a rock by steps, with the big precipice to the right and a smaller drop to the left. The south-west peak (8450 feet) is the highest point of the Hwa Shan. Stand on the top rock and there is another magnificent view, taking in the south precipice. Just below is a small temple (the Yang-t'ien-ssu), and 200 yards away the Nan-feng (south peak temple), 8800 feet. Another steep descent down some very uneven steps leads to the Nan-t'ien-men (south heavenly gate). Here some steps, let into the face of the rock with some hanging chairs, lead down what looks like the face of the precipice to two small shrines, one above the other.

Descending easterly and crossing the valley, an easier climb by steps and chairs over a smooth rock leads to the Tung-feng (east peak), 8110 feet, which stands on the side of a hill at the south-east corner of the mountain. Just below it is a small isolated rock with a little bronze temple, which appears inaccessible from above. Returning to the valley, Pereira reached the fifth and last of the peak temples, the Chung-feng, 7650 feet, built on the side of the hill overlooking the valley; and continuing in a northerly direction down the valley, he again reached the path up which he had come, and returned for the night to the Pei-feng. He calculated that it must be about 5½ miles from the Pei-feng round the top of the mountain and back again. But it might be less. The next day he returned to Hwayinhsien, where he put up in the yamen. The magistrate was most hospitable, and entertained him with feasts. But, like most

HWA SHAN, LOOKING BACK DOWN RIDGE TO PEI-FENG.

face p. 25.

others, this yamen was uncomfortable: the rooms were bare, the floors tiled, the windows of paper and the doors ill-fitting, and even with a charcoal brazier the rooms were cold. The furniture consisted of a few common tables and chairs, whilst the walls were covered with Chinese paper, on which were hung a few scrolls.

CHAPTER IV

SIAN

On his return from his visit to the sacred mountain Pereira set out for Sian. He found all the towns and big villages filled with soldiers. They had not been paid for eight months. At Ling-tung-hsien, about 15 miles east of Sian, he saw some hot sulphurous springs. There were two big pools, one in the open which was patronised by the crowd, and one with four small rooms by it, where, by going early or late, a bather could get a bath in private.

Strings of camels, usually forty or fifty together, and travelling with loads from Kansu to the railway at Kwanyintang, were passed, and wheelbarrows with sails, which are also common in other parts of China, the sail being a piece of cloth, about 4 feet square, sewn on to two pieces of bamboo, fixed on to the front of the wheelbarrow and supported there by strings tied on to the handles.

An interesting feature on the way was a stone bridge at Pa-ch'iao. It dates back to the T'ang dynasty, some 1200 years, and is built of some eighty to a hundred low stone pieces.

Sian is one of the four capitals of China, the

others being Peking (the north), Nanking (the south), L'oyang (the east). It is now again officially called by its ancient name of Ch'angan, though the people still keep to Sian. (Other ways of describing it are Signan and Hsi-an-fu.) Twenty years previously there was a walled Manchu city on the east side; but the Manchus were massacred after the republic was declared, and their city was pulled down. There is now a fine "mali", some 30 or 40 yards wide, from the east gate to the Bell Tower, and on either side are long two-storied buildings with Chinese roofs. The Bell Tower, in the centre of the city, was used in former days for fire-alarms. It is now supposed to ring the hours, though it seldom does. The drum tower had a drum, which was beaten in case of attacks.

From Mr. F. E. S. Newman (a great-nephew of the Cardinal and a high authority on things Chinese) Pereira learnt that Sian, which was built 500 B.C., was a city of some 30 miles in circumference at the time of the Han dynasty, and had a population of about 4,000,000. Later it was destroyed; but it rose again to prominence under the T'angs. At present the population is officially estimated at 110,000, and is probably over a quarter of a million at most, including suburbs, though a missionary put it at a million.

Near Sian are the tombs of the T'ang dynasty, A.D. 618 to 907. In the old days these tombs extended for from 5 to 10 li underground by different passages. To prevent the evil spirits following the Imperial carcases, wives and servants were buried alive with the corpse, and the tunnel was filled in at the end and a mound erected over the entrance. Buried at a depth of from 20 to 30 feet, some 5 to 10 li ($1\frac{1}{2}$ to 3 miles) from the mound, it is difficult now to find the actual resting-place with its treasures. Once, indeed, an Imperial tomb with skeletons of those buried alive standing, sitting and lying down, and also valuable bronzes, were discovered; but after the officials had secured some of these bronzes, they ordered the place to be filled in, and no further digging was allowed in the vicinity.

Shensi, at the time of Pereira's visit, was divided into two factions. The northern party was represented by the military governor at Sian, but only about thirty districts out of a hundred and ten recognised him and paid taxes. The southern was under a Hanlin scholar, with headquarters at San-yuan, only 27 miles north of Sian. He was in league with Kuo-chien, the leader of the official bandits, as opposed to the ordinary soldiers, who were sometimes worse than the bandits, as they got no pay and took wood, fuel, etc., from carts passing through the city.

The governor at Sian, Chen by name, was a determined man, who stood no nonsense from the students. On one occasion they bothered him with a petition whilst he was having a feast. He sent word to them to go to the magistrate's yamen, and when they got there soldiers surrounded them and bambooed the leaders.

Some nine or ten years previously Chen played a mean but thoroughly Chinese trick upon Kuo-chien. He advised Kuo to make a sudden attack on Shensi Province. Kuo agreed, and started off with a thousand bandits. Meanwhile Chen had warned the Shensi governor of the invasion, and Kuo's troops were cut to pieces. Kuo and Chen afterwards associated ; but later on Kuo tried to murder Chen ; and since then there has been war to the death between them.

In Sian, Pereira passed four mountain guns and a battalion of infantry marching eastward. The men were of good physique, but looked sullen and listless, and there was not a smile among them. They had not been paid for months, and in that state might very well mutiny and go over to the other side. They had no transport, and the mules or carts were commandeered whenever they could be got.

The civil governor gave Pereira a feast at the club, which was a good two-storied building with bedrooms in which honoured guests could be put up. There was a billiard room and bowling alley, and a nice garden. But the club had twice to be closed down owing to members failing to pay their bills.

Torture was still allowed, and four soldiers were crucified on the city wall, an extra nail being driven in at the throat, though not at a vital spot. They lingered for two days, though probably they lost consciousness after six hours.

Opium was again coming into Shensi and was grown along the Wei River. When the Chinese heard Pereira was coming they thought he would be investigating the opium conditions, and orders were issued to remove all advertisements for the sale of opium.

The Nestorian tablet for which Sian is famous

was erected in A.D. 787 in honour of the bishop, Izadbuzid of Walk. It is the earliest monument of Christianity in China, and dates back to the second year of Hsüan Chung of the T'ang dynasty. It is an oblong black piece of stone, shining like polished marble, 6 to 7 feet high and 3½ feet wide. It stands on a tortoise, and is surmounted by a top piece 3 feet high, on which are carved two intertwined dragons. The monument is said to have been dug up early in 1625 near Chow Chih. Pereira was the first European after the Boxer Rising to visit it. It then stood in the open outside the west gate. Later a foreigner had the stone copied, and tried to carry off the original. But his plans were prevented, and for greater safety and better preservation the tablet has been removed to the old Confucian temple in the city, near the south wall. This building is now known as the Peilin or "Forest of Tablets", and contains 424 tablets, mostly of the T'ang dynasty, but some are of the Sung dynasty.

One hundred and twenty-two tablets of the T'ang period (A.D. 618 to 907) are inscribed with the five classics, both sides of each stone being used. The tablets are chiefly taken up with writing, but some have poor pictures. One is of the Goddess of Mercy (Kuan-yin) of the T'ang period. Another is of the first Manchu emperor. Others represent the outlines of the Hwa Shan and Tai-pai Shan, the two sacred mountains of the Province.

A seven-storied pagoda, the Ta-yen Ta, of the T'ang period stands about 2 miles to the south of the city. One hundred and forty-seven steps lead up to the sixth story, from whence there is a good view.

In the north-west corner of the city there is a rock called Tai-fei-shih (concubine stone), 15 feet high. It is supposed to have the prints of the hand and feet of Yang (a concubine of one of the T'ang emperors) on the back. As visitors for ages have put their hands into the cavity marked by the Emperor, the imprint is very clear. The supposed footprints are much bigger.

Mr. Su Kuei-san, the great art collector of Sian, showed Pereira some of his treasures. He was a Mohammedan, sixty-five years of age. By an unprecedented stroke of luck he had acquired five vases of the Emperor Ts'ai Shih-ching, A.D. 954 to 959, in whose reign there were five great official potteries, which were broken up at his death. The first, the Ts'ai pottery, is represented by a short bowl with a wonderful glaze, which to the collector is the most valuable. The second, the Wu pottery, is represented by a yellow vase with rude representation of a phœnix and dragon. The third, the Kuan, is a taller bowl than the Ts'ai, and also has a wonderful glaze. The fourth, the Ko, is a white glazed vase of the finest workmanship. On it three sheep and an old shepherd stand out; and there are rocks and a most wonderfully delicate representation of wistaria and a vine. The fifth, of the Ting pottery, is an amphora with handle.

Some of these vases had only been recently dug up, and luckily none had been damaged. They had been secured by Mr. Newman at ridiculously small cost for Mr. Su, who till then had no representative of any of these potteries in his collection.

The museum had some sculptures and bronzes, and four of the T'ang horses, brought to Sian from their tombs 30 miles away. They stand 5 feet high. The horses are in bas-relief, three galloping and one walking, with saddles, reins and stirrups. They are wonderfully true to nature.

Behind the museum are some pleasant gardens, with lilac and other trees in blossom, and a plan of Shensi Province, with a small tree for each city and rocks to represent the mountains.

On April 18 Pereira left Sian. During his travels through Shensi the soldiers at the gates of the cities and town he had passed had been very annoying, haughtily ordering him to stop and showing him no respect. But he had made representations, through Mr. Newman, to the Chief of the Staff. The consequence was that when he left Sian the guard at the gate turned out, and he passed through as a distinguished guest instead of being shouted at to stop.

His party consisted of three chairs with eight bearers (hired for $88 for the thirteen stages to Han-chung), six mules ($132) and an escort of three fort soldiers. The mules had been obtained with great difficulty through Mr. Newman's help, as all mules were being commandeered by the military authorities. The chairs were of the diminutive mountain type. Pereira's was carried by three bearers—though four is the dignified official number—and they had an easy time, as he walked most of the way. His two boys each had a chair with two bearers.

CHAPTER V

THE CHING LING (MOUNTAINS)

Pereira now entered upon one of the most enjoyable parts of his journey, and we wish he could have lived to describe it more adequately. It was now the full spring of the year and he was leaving the plains to cross the beautiful range of mountains which divides the basin of the Yellow River from the basin of the Yangtse. This range is known as the Ching Ling or Sin-ling.

The first stage out of Sian took him to the foot of the mountains. And as he was off the regular mule track and away from the haunts of soldiers, he found none of the usual filth at the inn, and the doors had not been removed by the soldiers for firewood. A mile south of Nantou Kioh the path leaves the plain and ascends a steep narrow valley to the Tu-ti Ling (5220 feet), a rise of 2430 feet. On the way he passed quantities of wild flowers, including white and violet lilies, pansies and honeysuckle. The climb was a hard one for the mules carrying heavy loads. The traffic over the pass is mostly carried on by coolies bearing long bamboo baskets on their backs with a pole on which to rest the load. On descending from the pass there were beautiful views across ranges of hills towards a big range to the south.

Descending to the Feng-yü Ho (wind and rain stream) he had then for 18 miles to ascend a very rocky valley, in which in bad places uneven steps had been laid. The stream was twice crossed by three double chairs. The scenery was grand. The hills were covered with undergrowth and rose high on either hand. One or two temples were perched on the summits. The Feng-yü is a small mountain torrent. The path lies generally on the western side and gradually rises to the Ch'i Ling, which is the main range of the Ching Ling. There is a small temple on the summit. The mules had some difficulty in making the steep ascent, but luckily the weather was fine and the going was good, and only one mule dropped a load into the water.

On the southern side there were some pine trees on the hill-sides. Bears, tigers, wolves and wild boar are found in these hills. The villages consisted of only a few hovels; and the inns had generally one room for meals and cooking and a gloomy den for living in. Forage for the mules was almost unobtainable. At Sha-kou-k'ou Pereira had to put up in a shop and occupy a room overlooking the counter. The shop people rose at 3.30 A.M. From here by a good path he descended the valley of the Hsun-ho, a tributary of the Han River, to Tung-kiang-ko, a town of one thousand families. Fearing to be taken by the soldiers for coolie work, most of the males had fled. This was a great country for pheasants.

Leaving Tung-kiang-ko, Pereira passed some

picturesque roofed bridges, such as are common in Szechwan and South China, but which as far as he could recollect did not exist in North China. The path now again ascends steeply, rising to 7150 feet at the Chi-kung Liang.

At Sünyangpa, 90 miles from Sian, he again found soldiers with little discipline. They awoke him early by trying to get into his house, probably with the idea of looting his baggage. But his escort mounted guard and he was left in peace. This house was a regular gambling den. In the evening the soldiers came to play, whilst at midnight his boys were caught gambling with his chair-bearers.

Gambling and opium-smoking are the two chief curses of the Chinese. When the Government a dozen years before set to work to suppress opium, it for once did a good action without getting much credit for it. But since the introduction of the Republic, opium and morphia pills have again made their appearance, and opium-smoking seems to be constantly on the increase.

Leaving Sünyangpa the path again ascends narrow valleys for 9½ miles to P'ingho-liang, the highest point on this route (8690 feet). Several coffins were passed on the way. They were made of heavy wood and carried by eight men who seemed to sing the whole way. On the top was the usual cock, whose duty it is to let the spirit of the departed know by his crowing where the coffin is, in case he might leave the body and not know where to find it again.

Pereira's escort consisted at this time of one old and two young soldiers. And he remarks that these Chinese soldiers, when away from their comrades and alone with the foreigner, are always docile and anxious to help.

At Ningia the magistrate came to meet him outside the city and prepared an official house with a nice clean room for him. He sent him a lot of ducks, chickens, etc., as a present. But Pereira told him he made a rule not to accept presents and that he had expressly asked the foreign bureau at Sian to send a letter to all magistrates on his route, telling them not to offer him any gifts. Unfortunately these requests were always ignored, as the officials would regard the request as a delicate way of asking for presents.

The scenery, especially after the P'ingho-liang, was very fine and was like the hilly parts of Szechwan. The valleys were green with rice and wheat. Trees covered the hills and on their sides was a profusion of wild flowers, lilac, yellow and white. Added to them were the pink and white blossoms of the fruit trees. April 27 was a glorious day and Pereira walked the whole 24½ miles from Liang-ho to Kin-shui-ho (the Gold Water River). After crossing a river by a ferry he had a steep climb of 1880 feet up the Shan-tzu P'o and a further climb along the top of ridges for another 390 feet. From there he had splendid views all round, over range after range with deep valleys between. Some of the hills were gently sloping and partly cultivated or covered with trees. All along the path was the sweet smell of flowers. And coolies swarmed up and down the slopes, which from a distance looked like a gigantic ant-heap. After a sharp descent of nearly 1500 feet, two more climbs up and down spurs, Kin-shui-ho was reached. And here he found the deputy of the Yang Hsien magistrate waiting for him.

The Han River was reached on the following day. It flows through a small fertile, well-cultivated plain. Pereira now had new peas and cherries for the first time. But the fruit in China suffers greatly from the Chinese preferring quantity to quality and from their picking it before it is ripe for fear of its being stolen.

Han-chung Fu was reached on April 30. It is 243 miles from Sian, and of this distance Pereira walked 221¾ miles, that is 17 miles a day. As he approached, the city officials and soldiers dashed about reporting his progress. Eventually, hot and dusty, he arrived in the eastern suburb, but much to his disgust was there detained that he might be given an official welcome. The friendly officials insisted upon putting him up in a küng-kuan with a nice garden. But he held out stoutly against being given any feasts or presents. He afterwards heard, however, that the people had been forced to pay 300 cash for entertaining him, and this must have gone into the pocket of underlings, while Pereira would be credited with receiving it as a bribe to report favourably on the opium growing. And in spite of Government orders much opium was grown about here, the officials not only cultivating it themselves, but compelling the people to grow it for their own profit. In the previous year, when they grew too much, there was a slump in the opium market, causing heavy loss to many people.

A number of the officials are themselves opium smokers.

There was an Italian bishop and a fine cathedral at Han-chung. The only British were Mr. Easton, who had been there forty years, and his wife. He belonged to the China Inland Mission.

More evidence of the lawless state of the country was afforded by the request of the officials that Pereira should proceed by the small southern road instead of by the big western road. They declared that the Red Lantern Society held part of the latter. This society held other parts as well. They were remnants of the old Boxers and proclaimed themselves invulnerable. They wore red sashes and carried long swords.

And it was not only the brigands who caused trouble to Pereira. Through the soldiers commandeering mules he could get no mules. The soldiers give the muleteers enough money to buy food each day. But often when they have done with the mules they keep them and give the muleteers nothing for them. The soldiers also took things without paying for them, or would only pay what they liked, and if the shopkeeper objected they would give him a blow or threaten him with a knife. They also cut down the trees without paying for them.

CHAPTER VI

HAN-CHUNG TO CHENGTU

In spite of difficulties due to soldiers and brigands, Pereira was able to leave Han-chung on May 4, taking with him eight chair-bearers and fourteen coolies. A bevy of lesser officials came to see him off. And as the main road by Kwang-yüan-hsien was occupied by undisciplined soldiers without any leader, he took a small road. At 1¼ mile from the south gate of the city he crossed the Han River by a ferry. It is navigable the whole way from here to Hankow.

On the far side he ascended the Leng-shui Ho, which comes out of a hole in the mountains. A temple is built picturesquely over its exit and a cascade comes down to join it close by. Here he entered the region of palm trees, and the scenery was very beautiful. The foot-hills of the Pa Shan (the parallel range to the Ching Ling) were dotted over with houses. And as the main range was reached, the hill-sides were steep and covered with scrub, while torrents roared below.

The border between Szechwan and Shensi was crossed 35 miles south of Han-chung Fu. In places here the hills were quite white with wild strawberries. But a robber band of three hundred men was near at hand, and two delegates from a village had to be sent to tell them that Pereira was travelling under an escort and that they were not to molest him on the morrow. But there are honest men as well as robbers in China, for Pereira had left his watch in the inn and the innkeeper walked 12 miles the next day to return it to him.

A little tea and several fields of poppy were seen growing near Pei-pa, 16 miles from the border.

After leaving Pei-pa there was a steep climb of 3100 feet and a drop of 2300 to Shapa, where again there were poppies growing. The scenery was beautiful—high sloping hills, crowned by perpendicular rocks covered with trees. The hill-sides were partly covered with trees and partly under crops. A golden pheasant was seen. After climbing the big hill and covering 20 miles the coolies were very tired—as they might well be.

Since leaving Han-chung Pereira had had an escort of one officer and ten men and these now returned. They were Chihli and Shantung men and were a well-set-up, smart lot, and very well behaved. He could not wish for better men. It only showed what Chinese soldiers can be when properly taken in hand.

The country ahead being apparently free from robbers, he took no local militia as escort from Kuei-min-kuan on May 9. Heavy rain now fell and the glorious scenery was spoilt by the weather. The path was over rocks and often became the channel for miniature mountain torrents. At times the whole country was hidden by mists.

The evening turned out fine, and from the inn, perched high up on the hill-side, he had splendid views across the deep valley below over range after range to the south. Some of the hills were cultivated even high up, whilst many were covered with trees or undergrowth.

The coolies had a bad time, and at the end of the hard march, having no change of clothing, had to sit round a fire to get their clothes dry. Pereira remarks that during his travels in China he had employed some thousands of coolies, but that practically never had he the slightest trouble with them. Patient, quiet and cheerful, they plod along the most atrocious paths, carrying baggage up and down steep mountains, under a tropical sun or in a deluge of rain, dressed in rags and without any change of clothing—and all for a miserable pittance. He could not understand the mentality of some foreigners who are inclined to knock them about.

On May 11 he reached Nan-kiang-hsien, 95¼ miles from Han-chung Fu. The people were slow and stupid and said they could not understand the Chinese of his Tientsin boys. But they were harmless and did not come round in crowds to stare at him as they did in Eastern China. Here he obtained a boat for his baggage and in it went down the Nan-kiang River to Pachow. The scenery was picturesque as the river wound its way among well-wooded hills. At Pachow he found Mr. Parsons of the China Inland Mission, two ladies and a French priest.

After leaving Pachow the country was very fertile. The hill-sides were terraced and all the valley was under cultivation. The scattered farm-houses added to the picturesque effect. The path, like most of the paths along the main routes in Szechwan, was fairly well paved. The mosquitoes, especially in the neighbourhood of paddy fields, now became very troublesome.

Pao-ning Fu (4120 feet) was reached on May 19. Pereira walked the whole 87½ miles from Pachow, and what with making a survey of the road and looking after his coolies he had had a strenuous time. Pao-ning Fu (now called Lang-chung-hsien) had declined under the Republic. It had now about 20,000 inhabitants, mostly in the large eastern suburb, where the Church of England have two large compounds with a fine cathedral.

From here he hired coolies for the whole journey of eight days to Chengtu at about two shillings each a day. Several villages on the road had most of the houses destroyed, probably as the result of military pillage. And the inns were in a ruinous state, with no paper on the windows. All was very different from the life and bustle of the old times.

Another brigand-infested area was reached on May 25, and the magistrate of Tungchwan Sze was very anxious for Pereira to go by the northern road to Chengtu. But the next magistrate after all advised him to go by the main road, as he said the brigands were not likely to attack a foreigner. He sent an escort of four men with Pereira, but sent them unarmed as he said the brigands wanted rifles and would probably attack the escort if they had any. So Pereira had to rely on his revolver. The region he now entered used indeed to be a great brigand centre, but there had been some severe fights with the brigands and Pereira was not molested. And he now descended on to the Chengtu plain.

This state of things so close to Chengtu showed what a state of chaos China had fallen into. Another sign was the prevalence of gambling. In Shensi and Szechwan the inns were filled with gamblers, soldiers and civilians, who play a game like dominoes most of the day and night, and with their shouting and noise making sleep very difficult.

The Chengtu plain is about 90 miles in length and about 40 miles wide at its widest. Its area is 2400 square miles and its population 1,920,000. It is from 1600 feet to 1800 feet above sea-level. It begins about 30 miles east of Chengtu and is one of the most fertile parts of China. It is watered by a wonderful system of canals, mostly crossed by solid stone bridges. The people seemed much quieter and less offensive than the people of Shensi. And the soldier had none of that tendency to be offensive to the foreigner which Pereira had noticed in Shensi.

On his arrival at Chengtu, Mr. Hewlett, the Consul-General, came out to meet him and warned him that the Chinese officials had prepared an official welcome for him in the northern suburb. So at the end of the long trek from Peking, whilst he was still muddy and dirty, he had to go through the ordeal of getting out of his chair and being received by a Chinese General and a representative of the local Foreign Office, whilst the band played the Chinese National Anthem, after which he was given a miniature feast of wine, brandy and biscuits.

And so the first great stage of his journey was accomplished. He had covered 1818¾ miles (436¼ by train and 1382½ by road). Of this distance he had walked 1116½ miles. The journey occupied 103 days from Tientsin, and he spent £188 on the way, exclusive of the stores he had laid in for the journey. The actual transport (train, chairs, coolies, cart, mules, boat) cost £126.

Chengtu is one of the pleasantest cities in China, with clean, fairly well-paved streets, covered arcades and good shops. It is reputed to have 422,516 inhabitants. Pereira stayed here in a charming Chinese house (now the British Consulate) with a nice garden, and was welcomed at a series of entertainments. First, on June 3, was a great celebration of the King's birthday at the British Consulate. This, he says, was very well done by Mr. Hewlett. Flags were flown and an official reception was held from 11 to 11.30. In the afternoon were sports for children, of which there were seventy (English and Canadian) over four years of age. Then there was a patriotic march with the flag as well as songs and recitations to keep up the love of country. All was very effective, and if everybody took the same trouble all over the world as Mr. Hewlett and Mr. Brace (working for the Y.M.C.A.) took, we would not, he thought, be having so much trouble at home.

Then he had a round of Chinese feasts which, in accordance with Chinese etiquette, he was expected to attend. At these big official feasts countless heart-burnings in regard to the correct seating of the guests are caused to those who care and who never seem to rise to as high a place as they would wish; whilst those who do not care where they sit and would prefer a lowly seat next a friend are placed in exalted posts and sit next the same people whom they are always meeting. A vast amount of wine is drunk, and the only way of getting out of having to drink more than one wants is to drink tea and absolutely decline to drink against one's own desires. The Chinese have but vague ideas about time, and somctimes the foreigners are equally vague. So often a guest arrives punctually and has to wait for an hour or more for a late comer. According to Chinese etiquette the lowest in rank should arrive first and the biggest official last. Sometimes the latter sits busily engaged in his yamen waiting to know if all the guests have arrived before he starts. The wearisome functions last for three or four hours.

Brigandage was still rife in the neighbourhood, and on account of it many country people came into the towns. The brigands were so strong, indeed, that they besieged Hang-chow-hsien for twelve hours, and though a force was sent against them from Chengtu the General in command of it thought the brigands were too strong and he returned without attacking them. It was computed that there were 250,000 brigands in the Province of Szechwan alone, and of these 38,000 were armed with modern rifles. This brigand force is regularly organised and its chiefs speak of it as the brigand army—" fei-chün ".

Writing of the Chinese character Pereira says

there is a strain of childishness in the Chinese which comes out even in their wrath. If they have a grievance against a foreigner they will often write him an anonymous letter in which the (usually imaginary) offence is magnified out of all proportion, and the culprit is informed that the wrath of heaven will fall upon him, whilst the powers of justice will first punish him in this world; if he goes by train he will be smashed up; if by boat he will meet with a watery grave. In the same way the young student spirit comes out in the Peking papers published in English. They ignore the present state of China with its rampant corruption and its brigandage. And, posing as the representatives of a state endowed with all the virtues, they censure the foreigner for his cupidity and double-dealing.

Chinese boys are, Pereira says, a curious product of humanity. Like all Chinese they are born schemers. If he caught his boy out in some offence the boy would try to point out that he—Pereira—was in the wrong, for which the blame really rested with Pereira. If he was late it would be Pereira's watch which was wrong. However, on the road, when difficulties had to be overcome, he always rose to the occasion. He was an autocrat among the coolies and an excellent organiser.

The Chinese, with the oldest civilisation in the world and plenty of intelligence and capacity for hard work, ought to have gone ahead of all other nations. But for some inexplicable reason they have dropped behind the nations of Europe and run to seed. This is partly on account of their absurd systems of education. Time is wasted on learning some of their characters, of which there are 40,000.

The West of China University, which is situated in the south of the city, is run by a united body of Canadian, American and British missionaries. At present there are about four hundred Chinese pupils—all from Szechwan. Attached to the University is an excellent Canadian school for the children of missionaries.

A fine two-storied hospital for men and women has been established by Canadian Methodists. It is surrounded by a good compound with wooden houses and gardens. There is also an excellent French hospital attached to the Roman Catholic Cathedral.

Pereira records how fond the Chinese are of using high-flown language for the names of their cities, villages and shops. Everything is "heavenly", "perfect peace", "great calm", "golden", "bright". The usual epithet is beautiful, but generally the object is mean, squalid and dirty.

After a long spell of daily rain it became fine on June 15 and the thermometer rose to 91°—as it usually does in Chengtu four or five times in the year.

CHAPTER VII

TO MOUNT OMEI

PEREIRA now had an interlude from his main plan. He turned off south from Chengtu, on June 20, with the object of shooting and of climbing Mount Omei, another of the sacred mountains of China.

On first leaving Chengtu the fertile plain was covered with paddy fields which extended everywhere. The whole plain was watered by countless rivers, canals and irrigation channels; and with trees and bamboos was a beautiful sight. Large flocks of duck are reared in the paddy fields, and it is a common sight to see a man driving some thirty to forty ducks from one field to another.

The inns, tea-houses and restaurants on the big roads are among the best in China; and in some inns mosquito curtains are provided. It rained every night so that the roads were always muddy. And after leaving Kiungchow on June 23, he left the big main road and travelled by difficult small roads towards the mountain, passing over undulating ground and low hills. Rice and maize were the chief crops; and there were plenty of trees, mostly firs, and bamboos.

The head muleteer showed signs of insubordination when Pereira's boy pressed him to feed the mules properly. So Pereira took him by the collar and threatened him, which reduced him to a chastened frame of mind.

The Min River was crossed by a ferry on June 26. Beyond it for five awful miles Pereira's party passed along a small, muddy, slippery path beside the paddy fields. He himself fell once. His chair-bearers fell two or three times. And one mule with the boys' things fell into a paddy field, and all their clothes were soaked with mud and water.

Soldiers were often passed. Now in the hot weather they took off their jackets, tucked up their trousers to the knees and wore their forage caps with a green oilskin covering. They had, in addition, their bandoliers, worn over their naked bodies, a rifle and umbrella. Excepting coolies no one travels lighter.

Leaving the paddy fields for low hills the going improved, and a stiff climb of 700 feet brought the party to the summit of a hill. Here, weary and hot after trudging 18 miles, Pereira rested and cooled himself under a tree, and admired the view over the low country he had been crossing, which looked like a big plain covered with trees and paddy fields.

The route continued over low hills, and on June 28 he was warned of the presence of two hundred brigands on ahead. They would be afraid, he was told, to attack a foreigner, but they would probably seize the rifles of the escort on the escort's return. The escort, therefore, decided to leave their rifles behind.

E

The travelling was rough for the next few days, but from the hills there were beautiful panoramas for miles round over low-lying well-wooded country.

Tzeliutsing was reached on June 30. It is an unofficial town of 200,000 inhabitants and is situated on the Wei-yüan River, on which there are hundreds of salt locks. The country round consists of treeless hills, and everywhere the heapsteads of the salt-mines stand out like miniature Eiffel Towers. These heapsteads consist of four or more legs, each leg being made up of poles lashed and clamped together. The legs are then tied together near the top. The salt-mines were discovered about the beginning of the Han dynasty, some 200 B.C. The salt wells belong to the salt merchants, and they pay duty to the Government on every picul (130 lb.) of salt sent out. Salt is, with the Customs, the chief source of revenue to the Government. In Szechwan, which had declared its independence of the Central Government, the revenue had been taken by the local government of Chunking on the Yangtse. There are 4500 salt wells in Tzeliutsing, of which about 60 per cent are working.

Pereira went over one of the big salt works. The shafts were sunk to a depth of over 3000 feet and it was a chance whether anything would be found. The sinking of a shaft takes three years' hard work. A hole about 6 inches in diameter is bored down, the head of the well being encased in sandstone for a depth of a few feet. If successful, salt brine or gas is found at the bottom. The gas is used for boiling the salt.

A cable, made partly of steel and bamboo rope or of bamboo rope, has a bamboo tube, about 180 feet long, attached to the end. The cable is uncoiled and wound up, either by machinery, as in the bigger mines, or by relays of buffaloes, as in the smaller mines. When the bamboo tube reaches the bottom the pressure opens a valve and fills the tube with brine and water and closes the valve when the tube is full. It takes two or three minutes to lower the tube by machinery and three or four minutes to pull it up again. When up, a man pulls it across over a bucket, presses on the valve with a hook, and releases the salt water which pours out into a big bucket. From this it runs along bamboo tubing to the boiling office, which may be 4 or 5 miles away. In the office the salt is boiled in salt-pans either by coal (which is quicker) or by gas found on the spot (which is cheaper). The salt comes out yellow, but it is then washed with water containing some chemicals and it comes out a beautiful white. If it is to be used in the crystal state it is then packed in bags of about 350 lb. and sent off by barge. If it is required in cakes it has to be boiled several times, and is mixed with ashes to give it a darker colour.

Kungching, a few miles farther on, is another important centre for salt.

On July 4 at San-ch'ing-chen two English lady missionaries bound for Mount Omei lunched at Pereira's inn—the first time in all his travels that he had ever met a strange party in an inn.

Two days later he reached Omei-hsien on the foot-hills of Mount Omei, which was hidden in clouds. He passed rhododendrons in bloom. On July 7 he ascended the slopes, passing some fine banyan trees. Crowds of beggars and numbers of pilgrims coming down the mountain were met—also many women on foot, some quite old and with small feet, trudging down with the aid of a stick. As he ascended higher there were splendid views up narrow valleys with well-wooded sides and a raging torrent coursing down them. Rain unfortunately came on and spoilt much of the enjoyment.

The monks (hou-sheng) of the lower class, fourteen in all, welcomed him at the Wan-nien-ssu monastery with great cordiality, and gave him some fine, big, clean rooms. And up there it was quite cool. In the afternoon he visited the famous bronze elephant, said by Baber to be the oldest cast bronze figure of any great size in the world. It stands about 12 feet high and is gilded over. Very well modelled, its thick legs stand on four bronze lotuses. It is surrounded by a wooden cage like in a zoo. It supports on its back a huge lotus on which sits a fine Buddha with a crown of glory.

The temple, which Baber says is, after the Great Wall, the oldest Chinese building in existence, has a square base. But by an ingenious arrangement of triangles, segments of circles and projections, it supports a dome. In a neighbouring chamber an old monk showed Pereira one of the four teeth of Buddha. It was a piece of ivory, evidently the molar of some mammoth.

On July 8 he ascended Mount Omei, 10,940 feet. There was a continual stream of pilgrims up and down the sacred mountain, and the Prior of the temple at the top told him several thousands came up daily during the season, though Pereira himself puts the number at not more than two thousand. The women were about as numerous as the men, and with their cramped feet must have suffered much. But some of the richer are carried up on a wooden frame on a man's back. The path is paved practically the whole way, in a series of steps of uneven height. But the climb, though long and tedious, is not dangerous, like the ascent of the Hwa Shan. There are no precipices. The mountain is covered with trees and shrubs, and there are plenty of wild flowers near the top.

Starting at 7 A.M. from Wan-nien-ssu, Pereira reached the top at 5 P.M. The distance was 15½ miles. Unluckily, before he had gone far, a mist settled down on the mountain and remained till he returned on the 10th. In addition, it poured with rain for six hours of the journey up, and for nearly the whole time that he was at the top. On the way he passed some twenty temples with a few shanties for refreshments opposite to them. These temples were not of much interest. In one there were two mummies of Buddhist saints, but the faces had been gilded over and the bodies hidden by clothes. They looked like idols. Outside most of the temples is a queer-looking idol with a painted mud tiger in a shrine like a cage. The pilgrims in passing push incense into his face and this gives an unintentional humorous look of whiskers. In one temple the monk was chanting prayers and banging a gong. But when he saw

Pereira he stopped his devotions and several times called out to him to come and have a cup of tea.

At the summit he stayed in the same temple that he had occupied in 1910. The guest room had been rebuilt and he was given an excellent room with clean plank walls, three panes of glass in the window, two clean bedsteads, a table with drawers and a large charcoal brazier. There were thirty lamas. The sub-Prior was a very nice man who had been to Mandalay. When Pereira gave him his card and he saw that he was a General, he sprang to attention and saluted to show that he knew the right thing to do.

In the Ching-ting temple, which is situated on the highest point, is a fine bronze screen presented by the Emperor K'ang-hsi. Behind the temple is the famous suicide's cliff, believed to be the greatest known precipice in the world. But on account of clouds Pereira could not see more than 50 yards down.

The magnificent panorama extending to the west over countless ranges Pereira did get a view of in 1910; but on this occasion everything was denied him. And he missed the sunrise, the famous Buddha's glory, which apparently is a kind of rainbow reflected down the precipice from the sun behind, whilst figures standing on the brim are magnified into gigantic shadows with their heads touching the rainbow. On a clear evening countless lights twinkle far away in the plain below.

The descent to Omei-hsien, 26 miles, Pereira easily accomplished in under twelve hours. From there he made his way up the Ya River to Yachow, which he reached on the 12th, passing Ki-akiang-hsien, the centre of the wax industry, where he saw some of the trees (pai-la-shu) from which the wax is obtained; they were only about 10 feet high, and the season (August) when they bear wax had not yet arrived. Yachow he found to be a fairly clean city surrounded by high hills. The day he was there was really fine, which was a relief after the month of rain he had experienced. And he spent the evening with Mr. and Mrs. Smith of the American Baptist Mission, who had a charming bungalow on a hill outside the city with pretty views down the Ya valley.

Kiungchow he reached again on July 17, after passing through undulating country by a very bad and slippery road. This was the same place, 56 miles from Chengtu, which he had passed on his outward journey to Mount Omei.

CHAPTER VIII

A SHOOTING EXPEDITION

PEREIRA now prepared for a shooting expedition in the mountains of Western Szechwan, a wild, mountainous country covered with dense scrub and bamboo, except on the higher slopes, and uninhabited except for a few visiting wood-cutters and Chinese farmers. The shooting grounds were at altitudes of between 7000 and 13,000 feet. The game comprises boar, bear, roe, leopard, giant pandar, pandar cat, serow, wild dogs, and (on the highest ground) takin and blue sheep. What he particularly wanted to get was a giant pandar or pandar bear, as no European had ever shot one. But shooting in this region was not easy, as the jungle was thick and the local hunters were not keen and knew little of the habits of the game or where to find them. And for a man like Pereira with a weak spine the physical exertion of climbing very steep slopes and forcing a way through dense bush was great.

Although warned by the magistrate that the region was infested by brigands, Pereira left Kiungchow on July 19. As he could get no mules or chairs he engaged thirteen carriers, and he and his boys walked. Leaving the Lan-ho the path wound up the picturesque valley of the Ta-ho between low wooded hills. Farther on the going became very rough, and owing to heavy rain all streams were swollen. Pereira therefore exchanged his heavy boots for the sandals of the country. Often he had to cross a mad, raging torrent. The path was narrow and steep, leading up and down hill-sides, sometimes over uneven rocks, sometimes over rough shingle in a river-bed. Leeches, too, were an additional discomfort.

Having established himself in the valley of the T'ung-ch'ang Ho, a fierce mountain torrent, Pereira set out on July 30 on a five days' trip to try and get a giant pandar. He limited his transport to four coolies. His baggage consisted of the outer fly of his tent to serve as a *tente d'abri*, a waterproof sheet, a Gladstone bag, wash-basin, rifle, camera, water-bottle and some food. And he was accompanied by his cook and two or three hunters who, as well as the coolies, bore various weapons ranging from a Mauser rifle to flint-locks, and what resembled a cross between a carbine and a pistol flint-lock. He travelled south-west up the Tung-tzuchi valley between high hills. Houses and cultivation were soon left behind, and the hill-sides were covered with trees and undergrowth while the valley bed was covered with shrub and wild flowers.

He halted at an elevation of 7480 feet, at the foot of a hill over which he intended to shoot. The small mountain torrent roared below. His fellows found some rough accommodation in a rickety mountaineer's hut, whilst with logs and stones he fitted up his outer fly, protecting part of one of the open ends with a piece of oilcloth and lying on a waterproof sheet. And in this flimsy shelter and by means of an elaborate system of trenching he was able to withstand a heavy thunderstorm which burst on them in the evening.

The next day he climbed the Ta-pan-au (8640 feet) to the N.N.E. in a vain search for pandar. Though not very steep, after the first mile the going was tedious. He had to force his way through bamboo scrub from 2 to 4 feet high. The hill-side was dense with trees whose branches were often too high to step over and too low to get under. Creepers would catch him round the leg. Branches which looked substantial would give way. Also the ground was very slippery. In such a country there was hardly a chance even of seeing a pandar. And for the small hunting dogs to drive one to him, even if they found one, could not be expected. A pandar might easily pass within 10 yards without being seen. Naturally, therefore, Pereira's search was fruitless.

On another hill which he climbed on August 1 his search was equally vain. It also was covered with bamboo scrub and trees. And his hunters were not keen on their job and knew nothing of the pandar's way or his likely haunts. And as he had not come across a single track or sign of an animal, Pereira returned to Chung-tsui-shang.

On August 6 he set off westward, and after a very stiff climb crossed the Weng-ting Ta Pass (10,170 feet), from which he had grand views down the valley he had been ascending. Then he had a long descent for over 4 miles, constantly crossing a dashing hill torrent. At the end of the march he put up with Father Liu-P'ei, a Chinese Catholic priest, in a charming mission house situated on the hill-side, 600 feet above the valley and with a court inside filled with beautiful flowers. Here Pereira was laid up for fifty-three days with a blistered foot, due to his walking in sandals. And his stay was not rendered any the pleasanter by the weather, for it rained nearly every day in September.

At last he set out after pandar once more on September 28. He took with him his two boys, three hunters and seven coolies and a man with a kind of chair on which he could be carried over rivers. The country was so bad he still could not wear boots, but used some local sandals which he found very comfortable. He proceeded nearly due north up the valley of the Teng-ch'ih-kou. There were a few Chinese hovels scattered over the valley, each with its patch of maize cabbages or buckwheat. But Pereira wondered how their inhabitants could endure the severe winter, as the huts were ill-built of planks and brushwood and had many openings to the weather.

After going 11 miles up the valley Pereira halted for the night and put up his bed under an overhanging rock by the stream, whilst the rest of the party spent the night under other rocks. The next day he left the main valley and ascended a smaller tributary valley on the west and pitched a tent about a mile up it. He then for some days climbed about the neighbouring hills, often in drenching rain, and frequently along a slippery track on the face of a precipice. Taking with him a blanket and provisions he would sleep under some rock at night. And he would search all the day for game. But with the exception of the fleeting hindquarters of some deer and the tracks of takin he saw nothing. His only compensation was the beauty of the scenery. There were rocky gorges and beautiful cascades and trees with foliage of every shade of green, red and yellow. He doubted whether there was any country in the world where hunting was more difficult and arduous. The Chinese are not naturally good hunters. They are restless and fidgety when waiting for game. And their statements are unreliable. After countless investigations Pereira came to the conclusion that the best time for pandar is from November to March. Then the snow drives them down from the inaccessible mountain-tops to the lower slopes where they can find food. Pereira's hunter had assisted in killing two or three pandars in five years. Another old hunter told him that they usually hunted them in parties of six or seven. Pandar skins are not as valuable as skins of the takin and serow and so they are less sought after. These hunters say that they call in May and their young are born in July; that they sleep in tree hollows, the male feeding on the bamboo stalks and the female on bamboo leaves. After a takin has been killed the pandars come and feed on the remains.

After nine days' vain search for game Pereira returned to his headquarters at Teng-ch'ih-kou. And on October 11 he started off south-west down the valley on a second hunting trip. But shortly he turned off westward up a side valley thinly inhabited by Chinese, who in their fight for existence are always spreading out north and west, wherever the ground can be cultivated, and slowly pressing back the natives. The path rises and falls along the hill-side. The stream in this valley was bigger than the Teng-ch'ih-kou stream, and either this or one farther south near Mu-p'ing is the chief branch of the headquarters of the Ya River, that mad mountain torrent which everywhere runs in wild rapids from its upper reaches till it joins the T'ung River to the west of Kiating-fu. Pereira was surprised to find a banana tree at 6000 feet, and he also saw lacquer trees, which the Chinese were busily tapping. He spent the night in a hovel of wooden planks with a roof of bamboo rafters held down by stones on the top; and he seems to have attracted the attentions of the Chinese to more than the usual extent. They watched him consume some eggs and vegetables with as great a thrill as an English crowd would watch a close Derby finish.

On October 12 he climbed 2700 feet to a height of 9180 feet to a shelter on the upper slopes of the Hsü-chia-shan. Round the Chinese hovel the trees had been cleared to a considerable extent. But on the heights the forest was dense. And from his camp he had a beautiful view across the valley to the high tree-covered hills to the north. The following day the dogs put up a serow, but drove him away so that Pereira never even had a glimpse of him. Some wood-cutters said they had seen a pander hereabouts a month previously. But still no game appeared, and on October 17 Pereira returned to Teng-ch'ih-kou determined to try new hunting grounds and new hunters.

His third hunting trip he made on October 20, this time seeking takin. He started northward up the Tsao-shan and pitched his tent that night, just before heavy rain came on, at a height of 9400 feet. Continuing his climb the next day by a very rough uneven trail, through woods and deep undergrowth and along a razor-shaped ridge, he reached a ledge at 12,230 feet where he spent the night. And now at last he had the first signs of pandar—some droppings. And he sent his hunters out to track it.

Starting in thick mist and rain on the following day, he had an awful descent down an exceptionally steep and rocky hill affording very little foothold. He then had to wade through dense soaking bamboo. But after 4 miles of this very rough going he reached a shanty, and beyond it met with two grass-cutters who stated that six days before, whilst they were at work, a pandar had entered the shanty and eaten their food. Hope revived in Pereira. He was evidently in the place for hunting, and before the end of the day he came across traces of pandar, takin and serow. But the Chinese hunters disappeared and all Pereira was able to shoot—and it was with the first shot he fired with his rifle that year—was a hill cat (shan-mao), a beautiful little animal with black legs and belly, dark brown back, a long bushy tail, and a white mark on the face. He is known as the small pandar. He measured 50¾ inches from the tip of the nose to the end of the tail. The tail was 22 inches long, the legs

8½ inches. He was 22¼ inches round the belly and 5 inches from ear to ear. The face was brown on top and white underneath and there was a blackish stripe from each eye. The ears were black on top and white underneath. The skin is regarded as of more value than the skin of the pandar. The animal is uncommon, and Pereira's hunters, though they had seen some, had never shot one.

After this it came on to snow hard. He feared being snow-bound in this uninhabited region, and was about to return to his headquarters, when the hunters returned to say they had cornered a serow high up in the cliffs a long way off, and they wanted leave to shoot it as they said Pereira could never get to the place. Cold and miserable, he was at first inclined to agree, but eventually decided to go on the off-chance of getting a shot. After 2 miles of very rough going he reached the spot, and the serow was pointed out to him high up among the cliffs. He could hardly see it except now and then when it came from behind a rock to look over a precipice. It was only while standing that he could see it, and he had to fire at 800 yards range, one man behind him and another supporting his arm. But he managed to shoot her and she fell over the precipice. She was 80 inches long, 46 inches round the body, and the length of horns was 8½ inches. The serow is the only representative of its family. The Americans call it the goat antelope. And it looks something between a goat and a deer. The Chinese call it ai-lu or shan-lu, that is, precipice donkey or hill donkey.

The return journey to headquarters at Teng-ch'ih-kou, over a mountain 12,000 feet high, was very trying, as he had to wade through deep snow in socks and sandals. In consequence, he had four toes of his right foot partially frost-bitten. And as this precluded all further possibility of hunting he decided to return to Chengtu. Leaving Teng-ch'ih-kou on November 7, carried on the back of a coolie, he descended the valley by a fairly good path. All the way he passed small Chinese villages and hovels with crops. At 23 miles he reached Mu-p'ing, a small Chinese walled town. The native prince (with a few prehistoric Mantzu men as a guard) lived in a yamen surrounded with a wall on a hill-side just north of the town.

Ten miles beyond Mu-p'ing the hills are lower and open out into a picturesque little valley covered with small Chinese villages, paddy fields and trees. His escort here consisted of six Mantzu soldiers belonging to the semi-Mongol-Tibetan tribes who entered Tibet from Mongolia. With the exception of a few soldiers and passing natives these were the only Mantzu he came across in the whole of his hunting trip. They were dressed in old-fashioned Chinese uniforms and retained their pigtails.

Leaving the main Ya-ho valley on November 9 he crossed the divide separating it from the Ta-ho branch, and on the far side passed through a very deep gorge with precipitous cliffs. And the following day he crossed the divide between the Ya and the Min Rivers and gradually descended to Kao-hsin-ch'ang. Beyond this he passed down a fertile valley full of farms and reached Kao-chia-chang, which he had left on July 20. From there he followed his old route and on November 14 reached Chengtu and saw the first white man for four months. His dogged efforts to shoot a pandar had not been successful, as he got so little assistance from Chinese hunters. He had, however, obtained some small reward for his exertions in the rare and beautiful " small pandar ".

CHAPTER IX

TO TA-CHIEN-LU

PEREIRA spent a month at Chengtu and whilst there studied the causes of the student troubles in China. The first cause, he records, is the bad treatment of Chinese by some foreigners. Then he finds that foreign-educated students are educated up to a certain standard and afterwards discover that there is a lack of suitable employment for them. The teachers are over-familiar and imbue students with ideas of equality. Definite Christian teaching is replaced by science and comparative religion. Students under foreigners are called "foreign tripe" by their compatriots, and to show that they are not foreigners turn against their benefactors. Students also strongly resent having to repay the money lent them to enable them to study.

Having recorded these conclusions and also had his boy taught the way to make omelettes, scrambled eggs, ginger bread, ginger biscuits, muffins and other luxuries, Pereira left Chengtu on December 15 for Ta-chien-lu, 294 miles distant, an important town on the Tibetan border from whence one road leads to Lhasa.

The Chengtu plain was mostly covered with

paddy fields full of water. But much of it was green with winter crops just coming on. The weather was quite mild and sunny. South of Kiungchow the plain is left and the road rises gradually over undulating country. Near Ya-chow-fu he crossed the river by a neat bridge of bamboo and planks on bamboo rafts. On entering the city he followed behind a procession of soldiers who were conducting two brigands to execution. The whole city with smiling faces had turned out to see them. Beyond Ya-chow the road was fairly good leading along valleys, and the inns were remarkably clean. But as he approached Tsing-ki-hsien there was first a steep rise of 7000 feet over a badly cobbled road which was crowded with laden coolies, and then a descent of nearly 4000 feet—the height of the pass being 11,130 feet above sea-level. This pass was across the divide between the Ya and the T'ung Rivers, and from it Pereira had a magnificent view over the Tsing-ki plain far below to the S.S.W. and high ranges to the west overtopped by great snow peaks to the north-west.

Beyond Tsing-ki, a small city of only 260 inhabitants, he followed the main route to Yunnanfu for a short distance and then turned up a valley to Nitow. The hills were bare of trees, and though the altitude was 6000 feet there was no snow on them and the sun was bright and warm in the middle of the day, though cold came on after sundown. Both his boy and his cook had taken to wearing spectacles—from vanity, Pereira thought. They posed as his secretaries or Chinese writers and considered that the spectacles gave them the air of students.

There was a gradual rise terminating in a very steep ascent up a defile over a bad stony road to Shang-fei-yüeh Ling (11,000 feet). On the top of this pass there was a little snow and the air was frosty. From it he got a fine view over narrow valleys below. The descent was very steep, and the wonder was that the mules got down without a fall. The total rise was 4740 feet and the descent 2260 feet. The next day—December 24—he reached the T'ung Ho valley after a further steep descent and followed it up to Luting-kiao, 5900 feet. The hills cut up by deep narrow valleys rose to a height of 4000 or 5000 feet, but were almost bare of trees as the Chinese had cut them down. The path wound pleasantly along the hill-sides 300 or 400 feet above the river, which was of a deep blue-green colour flecked by patches of foam in the rapids. By the side of the river was a narrow belt of flat land taken up by farms and small paddy fields green with the spring crop.

Christmas Day he spent in solitary state at Waszekow in the Lu Ho valley, and the next day ascending a narrow, rocky winding valley with the Lu Ho, a dashing mountain torrent, on the right, he reached Ta-chien-lu.

Ta-chien-lu is the capital of the special area of western Szechwan. This area used to extend to Chamdo on the west, to Ya-chow-fu on the east, and nominally to Somo and Damba on the north, Taowu and Kantze on north-west. It lies in a hollow between high bleak hills. And from it radiate three deep gullies—one to the east, the Lu Ho valley by which Pereira had come, one to the north to Tanpa, and one to the S.S.W. from which three roads diverge, one leading to Tauwu, one to Batang and one to Tien-wan. The population is floating and may be put at about 14,000, most of them Chinese. But there are also a good many Tibetans and many Lamas of the red sect.

The Europeans at the time of Pereira's visit consisted of Mr. Louis King, the acting British Consul, a French bishop who is head of the Tibetan Mission which has priests scattered about along the Tibetan border, Mr. and Mrs. Sorrenson of the China Inland Mission, and two members of the American Seventh Day Adventists who keep the Sabbath on a Saturday and thereby disconcert Chinese students of Christianity.

December 27 Pereira spent in making calls. And he had now his first opportunity of coming in touch with Tibetan life. He visited the big Lamasery outside the town on the Cheto road. The outer court was the scene of an annual festival which lasts three days. The officials and those of the better class sit in the balcony above whilst the crowd form a circle below. In the centre is a high pole, at the foot of which is laid a dummy devil. The monks come out arrayed in flowing garments of many colours with five skulls embroidered in front at the bottom. They wear big circular-brimmed hats with high crowns surmounted by a peacock's feather. First the living Buddha comes forward with a small bell in the left hand and sometimes a small knife in the right. He then exorcises the devil. After that two huge trumpets, nine or ten feet long, are blown, and he either takes part in the dance, circling in front of the devil, or retires to a seat under a gaudily embroidered white tent. The monks dance round the circle in a fantastic way, constantly whirling round and kicking up their legs, and holding in one hand a small bowl filled with grain and oil, which they scatter on the ground. On some occasions the monks come out wearing huge masks representing faces with a broad grin or animals or birds and perform for several hours. The object of the dance is to drive out the devil and ensure peace for the coming year. On the third day the dummy devil is seized and driven out.

The Chinese Commissioner, General Ch'en Hsia Ling, Pereira found to be a stern man but fond of sport, and he presented his English visitor with the horns of a blue sheep he had just shot. He rules by severity and the officials are all terrified of him.

Ta-chien-lu had for centuries been the capital of the kings of Chala. Latterly they had been under Chinese supervision. Up to the time of the Republic the present king had ruled jointly with his brother. But his people rose when the Republic was started. The king escaped by flight but his brother was executed by the Chinese. Later on, however, the king was allowed to return and exercise a nominal rule over his people till, just before Pereira's arrival, it was discovered that he was in league with brigands, and he was arrested and put in prison.

Many different tribesmen are found in Ta-chien-lu and they vary much among themselves. They appear to be a mixture of Tibetan, Turk, Mongol and Chinese with the aboriginal race.

The chief traffic was in tea, done up in long narrow bundles, each weighing about eighteen catties. A man carries about eight, one above the other, lengthwise, on his back.

A lawless band of Tibetan brigands occupied the country south of Litang and west of the Ya-lung River. These brigands General Ch'en could easily disperse, but if he did he would run out of ammunition and he would then be attacked by his enemy the general at Chengtu. The brigands therefore defy him.

The hills round Ta-chien-lu are said to abound in bears, roc, wapiti, serow, blue sheep, pheasants, leopard, wolves, and fox. They are bare of trees and there is none of the thick undergrowth Pereira had met with on his shooting expedition at Teng-ch'ih-kou. But he could not now spare the time necessary to find the game.

On January 7 he left Ta-chien-lu and struck up northward as it was impossible to enter Tibet directly. He had to dismiss his boy, as he discovered that he was using visiting-cards describing himself as an official travelling on official business, and evidently meant to pose as one having authority. By this means he might pretend he was travelling to inspect opium, and get bribes from officials and opium dens.

Some notes on the Chinese Pereira now recorded. The Catholic Church, he says, seems to manage natives better than others. Native priests are ordained, but a watchful eye is kept on them.

The native priest is an excellent man, but he is a child in modern ways and requires supervision and direction. When he can take the place of the foreign priest and run the Mission on his own, then will be the time when the Chinese have got up-to-date. And then the foreigner living in the interior will be able to welcome the abolition of extra-territoriality and be able to resign himself with confidence to Chinese jurisdiction.

Foreigners who talk of Chinese being educated do not realise that this is far from being the case. The foreigner who lives at Peking, Shanghai or the seaports lives in a foreign environment. He rarely if ever travels in the interior and knows little about the conditions there. He is either sincere in admiring the Chinese for their many good qualities and, carried away by his enthusiasm, does not realise how little true progress in modern ideas has been made in the interior, or else he is in the pay of the Chinese, and carried away by their kindness to him sees things in too roseate a hue—and, indeed, it may be for his own personal interest to advocate Chinese views.

In military matters the Chinese have only been able to educate themselves up to the point of making an outward show; but beyond this they are unable to go. The Japanese, on the other hand, threw themselves whole-heartedly into the work. When they decided that they must go in for modern ideas the most capable men led the way, and, sinking their pride, they started like children under the best European instructors until they could manage their own affairs. But the Chinese cannot master their old pride and work out their salvation in the same way. When they are on the threshold they think they have mastered everything, discard their teachers and run a show partly on their old lines and partly with what they have learnt. The result is that they fall between two stools and are worse off in many respects than if they had kept to their old customs.

CHAPTER X

TO LAN-CHOW

PEREIRA had now to make a big detour before he could enter Tibet. The direct route would have been through Batang to Chamdo. But this for some reason, of which there is no record, was not available. Perhaps the passes on the way were not practicable in the depth of winter. Perhaps robber bands prevented his passage. Whatever the cause, the result was that Pereira had to make a detour of hundreds of miles, and he did not actually reach Chamdo till July 28.

The General and Magistrate came nearly three miles out of the city to say good-bye as he left Ta-chien-lu on January 7, making first north and then east to Kwan-hsien, a town lying only a short distance north-west of Chengtu which he had first reached so many months ago. Pereira now had his first experience of travelling by ula, the Tibetan corvée system. The inhabitants are bound to supply animals for transport when duly requisitioned by the official. Pereira employed twelve oxen yak, two ponies for himself and servant and two for his escort. These animals only cost half a rupee a day, and he gave the men the same amount as " wine money ". The animals did not carry as much as a Chinese mule. On the other hand, the latter cost three times as much. The two Chinese soldiers who formed the escort acted as interpreters with the Tibetans.

Chungku was reached on the following day. The country was now only sparsely inhabited, though several hundreds of pack animals—yak oxen and ponies—were passed on the way. Besides the Tibetan inhabitants there were many half-bred Chinese. The Tibetans themselves seemed friendly enough and beamed all over their faces whenever Pereira nodded to them. At each house was tied up a fierce black mastiff. Beyond Chungku Pereira passed through a thinly wooded district with stunted evergreens and scrub, and on January 9 camped in a wood at 12,000 feet with a high snow range on the west. In the valley there were only patches of snow, and only the smaller streams were frozen. Again next day not a house was seen, and a party of Tibetans stuck to Pereira all day as a protection from brigands. After a steep climb up a bare rocky hill-side he reached the summit of Ta-pao-shan, 15,300 feet, on the far side of which was a very slippery descent for a mile over frozen snow. Then the path lay down a deep valley and he camped at a height of 12,600 feet.

On January 11 he continued down the valley and passed through fir trees to a hamlet of three houses, Kuei-yün, the first habitation for 29 miles, and 8 miles farther on reached Mao-nui, 10,350 feet, an interesting little village of thirty families, partly Tibetan and partly Chinese. It consisted of two-storied buildings and contained a Tibetan temple and curious high square Tibetan towers. On the corners at the top of the houses were white stones, perhaps the same as the sacred white stones worshipped by the aborigines farther north near Li-fan T'ung.

Changing his transport to carriers, both men and women, he travelled the next day to Tung-ku, 8780 feet. The going was very rocky and stony and the stream flowed through a deep, narrow gorge in a succession of cascades. Tung-ku was a mixed village of Chinese and Tibetans. The Tibetan storied buildings with towers, some in the village and some perched high on the hill-side, give it a picturesque appearance. The Tibetans Pereira found to be quite friendly. They came out to meet him, and went down on their knees bowing low; and an interested but quiet crowd watched him writing in his room.

Continuing down the Tung-ku valley, which was mostly stony and deep cut, he passed more small villages and houses, and reached Tanpa, 7450 feet and 107 miles from Ta-chien-lu, on January 13 and put up in a small Chinese inn. It is a Hsien city of 150 Chinese families—a straggling little town shut in on all sides by bare mountains. The Tibetans live on the hills outside. There are over three hundred Catholics in and near Tanpa. They were under the charge of Père Hsiung Te-lung, whom Pereira believed to be the only Tibetan priest (Catholic) in the world. He had been a priest for over thirty years and was a nice old man of sixty-six. He had a very bad opinion of Lamas.

Leaving Tanpa on January 15 Pereira followed

PALACE OF THE TU-SSU OF THE OOJE TIBETANS AT KUAN-CHAI.

face p. 77.

down the Ta-tu-ho (or Ta-chiu-ho) for $1\frac{3}{4}$ miles and then crossed to the left bank by a fine suspension bridge of planks laid on thick strands of rope with similar strands as a support on the sides. He then followed up a deep valley with small Tibetan and Chinese villages—the Chinese low down and the Tibetans high up, and these latter villages having high four-sided towers, narrowing towards the top, which in the old days were used for defence. The only form of boat used on the rivers in these parts was a coracle made of skins and sewn together. These are circular in shape with a framework of wood or bamboo.

La-ma-ssu, 8050 feet, was a village of nine families, and opposite it, on the right bank of the river Hsiao-chin, was a large Buddhist lamasery. Though in the shade or early and late Pereira felt frozen with the cold, at noon in the sun he was roasted. Next day, January 16, he reached Meng-kung, a district city which really consists of three separate villages of which the centre one is quite small, though it contains the yamen and the French Catholic Mission at the head of which was Père Charrier. The village on the west has about three hundred Chinese families, and the business town on the east has about the same number, of whom about two hundred are Mohammedans from the Kansu Province.

Père Charrier, like other priests of the mission to Tibet, had led a perilous life. When the Tibetan tribes were in insurrection he had some exciting experiences. In May 1917 these tribes came down and occupied Tanpa and he had to escape at the last moment to Ta-chien-lu, after removing his Christians to a place of safety. Several priests of Batang have been massacred. And one at Tao-fu was imprisoned by the Tibetans for sixteen days with his arms and legs chained together. Also his beard was pulled out.

From Meng-kung he might have taken a more direct route by Fu-pien and the Hung-ch'iao Pass, 16,280 feet, and struck the Min River at Hsin-pau-kuan on the road to Choni, an important town about 100 miles south of Lan-chow, but he only heard of this route after he had made all his preparations to go by Kwan-hsien. So he left Meng-kung on January 19 for that town. The country was now fairly well inhabited. At Kuan-chai, a village of fifty-five families, mostly Chinese, there lived the Tu-ssu of the Tibetan tribe, the Ooje. His palace was a curious square building with a high tower in the centre and buildings resembling temples on the south-east corners. The courtyard was small and interesting. It looked very old and had some fine wood carving. The architecture was like old Saxon. Pereira climbed up uneven stairs to a reception-room where the Tu-ssu, dressed like a Chinese, received him. But as he could not speak Chinese, Pereira soon took his leave.

The next day he reached Jih-lung-kuan, 11,050 feet, and here on the following day he had to leave the valley of the Hsiao-chin and ascend a tributary to the south in order to cross the Pa-lang (generally written Balan on maps), the range dividing the Ta-tu and Min Rivers. A stiff climb brought him to a solitary inn which bore

COOLIES CARRYING BALES OF COTTON.

face p. 79.

the cheerful name of "The Grave of Ten Thousand Men". It was situated on a cold draughty spot at an elevation of 14,800 feet. From here the valley opens out facing the snow hills. After a mile the actual ascent of the pass begins. It was not very steep but was slippery owing to frozen snow and ice. The summit is 15,600 feet above sea-level and is 18¾ miles from Jih-lung-kuan. A fair amount of traffic was passed on the way. The descent was very steep and rocky for the first 3 miles, but the cold winds were left behind and the sun was hot for the hill-sides faced south.

Pereira put up for the night at a solitary hovel called an inn situated in the wilderness at an elevation of 12,850 feet. The accommodation was poor, but his relief was great for he had now crossed the second of the great passes he had dreaded for his frost-bitten foot.

No Tibetans were seen on the east side of the Pass. The descent was continued the next day to Hsin-tien-tzu, 9000 feet. Even at midday the ink froze, and in the evening it was very cold. In the inn was a wretched man lying in rags in an icy room far from a fire and groaning with pain from some internal complaint. No one took any interest in him. And Pereira marvelled at the way in which hundreds of coolies will carry loads year after year over these mountains in the depth of winter and for a mere pittance. They are clothed in rags, and if they get ill no one cares for them.

The descent of the Teng-ts'un Ho valley was continued on the 23rd for 18 miles to an elevation of 7050 feet. Then the ascent towards another range, the Niu-t'ou Shan, was begun. The path lay up a narrow, winding, rather steep valley, the small stream of which had constantly to be crossed by logs. Pereira halted for the night in a miserable inn at 9200 feet. There was one long draughty room with doors opening out, and he was frozen with cold even though he was not far from the fire in the centre of the room.

He reached the summit of the pass, 10,410 feet, after 2 miles of steep climb over very slippery snow on the following day. Then he had a very steep descent again over slippery frozen snow for 5 miles. So far the weather had been the coldest he had met. The morning had been gloomy and misty and bitterly cold. The warm sunshine of the high plains of Tibet had been left behind. And the Niu-t'ou Shan, though 5000 feet lower, was much more difficult to cross than the Pa-lang-Shan. But in the afternoon the weather turned much milder and Pereira finished his march at Ts'ao-p'u-p'ing at an altitude of only 5310 feet, the lowest he had been at for a long time.

The next day was again gloomy, with a succession of ascents and descents. He would ascend to mist, frost and snow and descend to damp and chills. He passed through several big Chinese villages and the valley was fertile. He saw a wretched thief stripped to the waist, with his arms suspended at right angles and fastened to a beam, whilst two lictors marched behind. This, remarks Pereira, is another form of punishment which Europeans might have to endure if placed under Chinese law.

Kwan-hsien, 2550 feet, was reached on January

26. It is 168 miles from Meng-kung, 217 from Tanpa, and 325 from Ta-chien-lu. It is a dirty little city containing from ten to twelve thousand inhabitants. It is situated on the Min River and lies on the north-west edge of the Chengtu plain. It has a very poor climate, with constant rain, gloom and damp. Here Pereira stayed for three days with Mr. J. M. Edgar of the China Inland Mission, a frequent traveller between Chengtu and Batang. From him Pereira gathered that the Ch'ang originally occupied Tibet. About A.D. 400 they set up a dynasty which took the title of T'upa. This degenerated into T'u-fan or T'u-bo. The present-day Tibetans call themselves Bö. Lha-sa (spelt with one *s*) means the place of a god. There are three special types of Tibetans: (1) the beak-nosed, who are allied to the black Lolu; (2) the lighter Circassian type; (3) the Mongol type. Tibet was a land to which the conquered and oppressed fled, and intermarriage among these produced the present hybrid race.

Pereira, on leaving Kwan-hsien on January 29, took a general northerly direction for some time, making for Lanchow-fu, and at first following up the valley of the Min River. He had a rough climb over the Nian-tzu-ling, 5000 feet, on January 30, and then descended again amid wild mountain scenery, into the valley through which darted the impetuous Min River over a rocky course, but comparatively small at this time of year. He passed a few large convoys of ponies carrying skins. Wen-chwan-hsien, 4220 feet, is a diminutive walled city with hardly twenty houses. A rope-bridge here crosses the Min River. The weather was dull and cloudy, and a little snow fell at night.

Continuing up the valley of the Min by a good road he passed Hein-pau-kuan (also called Wei-kiu or Wei-chou), a walled town with 415 families, where there is another rope-bridge over the Min, and on the other side a road leading westerly to Lifan-Ling. Beyond this cultivation increased and the hills were more sloping. At Wen-cheng, which he reached on February 1, he had the luxury of a new inn, though the luxury was tempered by the draughts from many gaps in the planks.

Mow-chow (now Mow-hsien), 5800 feet, was reached on the following day. It is a dirty walled town containing 750 families. On February 3 he crossed a small fertile plain for 24 miles, and then the valley of the Min again closed in and the road lay between high, bare, rugged mountains. Often the scenery was wild and grand, and at one place there was a small tunnel through the rock and a little shrine above, with memorial inscriptions to the benefactors who had made the tunnel. At 10 miles from Kou-k'ou-chai the valley of the Min divides, the Min being formed of two branches, one named Sung-pan and the other Hei-shui. The Sung-pan is not much more than a small mountain torrent. And it was this branch that Pereira ascended, reaching Ta-tien on February 4. Occasionally on the left bank were houses with the peculiar high towers. There is great doubt as to the origin of these towers. Mr. Edgar thought they had some religious significance. But others said they were for defence and pointed out that the rear wall was slightly higher than the three other sides, and seemed designed to protect the defenders in the back. To Pereira they did not appear to be meant for defence, for they are too narrow and steep and are built promiscuously, sometimes on the top of a hill, sometimes on the sides, and sometimes in the valley bottom, and sometimes one in front of the other. For this reason Pereira was inclined to adopt Mr. Edgar's explanation, and he thinks that, like Chinese pagodas, they were intended to act as feng-shui and draw beneficent spirits to the house.

The country to the west of the Min at this point is occupied by the Hei-shui tribe, who are divided into Shang and Ssia, that is, upper and lower tribes. So far no white man had penetrated the country. Just opposite Tateng is a village in which lives the chief of the 'Shu tribe of Tibetans.

Continuing up the valley of the Sung-pan River, Pereira passed sometimes through narrow gorges and sometimes over sloping cultivated land. At about 50 miles north of Mow-chow he heard that the giant pandar were plentiful high up in the hills, one day's march to the east, and he thought this was probably true as he passed the bamboo which they eat. But now he could not spare the time to hunt them and had to proceed on his way toward Lan-chow-fu.

The villages were now generally walled, for the Tibetans had invaded the district in 1912, captured Sung-pan, and destroyed most of the villages southward towards Mow-chow. Many of the ruined houses were still to be seen, but many new houses were being built all along the road.

Snow fell during the night of February 6, but it nearly all melted by noon, except at the tops of the highest hills, and the day was sunny though the wind was cold.

One of Pereira's muleteers slipped and fell, but as he writhed on the ground rubbing his ankle the only consolation he received from the other muleteers was a roar of laughter. The sight of pain gives the Chinese infinite amusement.

Before reaching Sung-pan, 9750 feet, on February 8, he for the first time passed several Tibetans. Sung-pan itself Pereira found to be an interesting city with a good many wild-looking Tibetans walking about the main streets. It is 113 miles from Mowchow and 212¾ miles from Kwan-hsien. It lies on low ground on the eastern side, but on the west a wall runs up to a height of 600 feet. A sloping ledge about 300 feet high holds a few houses and the Ch'eng-huang temple—a poor building, but affording a good view over the town. The main north and south street contained all the shops and was always crowded. But the few side streets were very dead.

The magistrate sent Pereira a present of a "pai-mu-chi", a large bird of the bustard family, and a hunk of beef. The bird was dried and coal black, and after giving the runner who brought it a dollar, Pereira handed the delicacy to his boys. The magistrate also sent a guard, and two sentries mounted over his door much enhanced his dignity.

Continuing northward up the valley he left Sung-pan on February 11. The going was good all day. The lower hills were partly cultivated and partly bare. At 11 miles the valley opens out to a small plain. At 14 miles he reached Changla, a quiet little walled town on a hill 200 feet high. The villages passed on the way were partly Chinese and partly Tibetan. The latter were always surrounded with poles carrying flags.

The feast of lanterns was celebrated that evening. The main street was lighted up with red and white lanterns, and the procession of the dragon commenced. It was formed of three dragons followed by two lions, yaks, etc., and at each house it went round the courtyard. After this a long pole with crackers at the end was lighted and the dragon danced beneath. Men stripped to the waist took it in turns to hold the head and dance wildly round amid the sparks. Sometimes a short torch of crackers was fired straight into the naked body of the dancer, and it was a wonder the men escaped without having their eyes put out. Meanwhile the body was whirled wildly round and round, the tail being separate and carried by a single man.

The following day Pereira made a long march of 25¾ miles to Ta-shih-t'ou. Some Tibetan villages with cultivation by them were met at first. The going was good and the country open and grassy. At 4 miles the river divided, one branch coming in from the north. Pereira followed up the branch coming from the north-east. At Ka-mi-ssu there was a Tibetan temple with a long oblong enclosed course, on the west side of which was a covered portico with revolving prayer wheels all the length, and a party of Tibetans were moving along chanting and turning the wheels. From this place to Ta-shih-t'ou, 16½ miles, there was not a house. And even at this latter place there was only a wretched draughty hovel with one public room, which Pereira shared with his boys and escort. The way to this hovel lay up the right bank of the stream. The valley widened to a mile, with high rocky hills on either side, and gradually the grass gave way to low scrub, whilst the hill-sides were covered with fir trees. A broad, good road led gradually up to the Kung-kang Ling, 11,970 feet, the pass over the divide between the Min and Kialing Rivers. Snow and ice gradually increased towards the summit. The descent to the hovel at Ta-shih-t'ou was steep and lay through a fir forest covered with snow. On the east side of the valley were rugged hills rising to a height of 17,000 feet and running north-west to south-east.

The descent was continued on February 13. For the first 6 miles the road ran through a fir forest down a deep valley between huge rocky ranges from 3000 to 5000 feet above the road. Farther on other trees were mixed with the firs. After 14 miles the trees became fewer and three or four hovels were passed. The morning was bright, but deep down in the valley the air was very cold. T'a-tsang, a village of thirteen families and containing a very clean inn, was the first village from Ka-mi-ssu, a distance of 41 miles. The drop from the summit of the pass to T'a-tsang is 3590 feet. From here there is a small road leading direct to Cho-ni up the valley Pai-shui Ho, but in the winter it is snow-bound and is not generally used till April or May. Pereira, therefore, descended the Pai-shui-ho, here an insignificant mountain stream. The valley lies between hills of a height of from 600 to 1200 feet. A high range stands some miles to the north, running from east to west, and occasional glimpses are had of a high rocky range to the south. Only three villages of over ten houses and a few scattered houses were passed on February 14. The inhabitants were mostly Tibetans of the Shu tribe. Pheasants appear to be plentiful.

Nan-p'ing was reached on February 15. It is a town of 345 families situated at an elevation of 5850 feet. The weather was beautifully warm, and Pereira saw a lizard and several butterflies. The inhabitants had seen few or no Europeans, so he had a continuous stream of visitors passing his door and making holes in the paper windows so as to have a view of him. After considerable trouble he found a Mohammedan who could talk Tibetan and knew the short direct route to Choni, and he left Nan-p'ing on February 18.

He first had to retrace his steps up the Pai-shui-ho for 18 miles, and then on the following day ascend the valley of the Hei-shui-ho, which flows down from the northward. The stony path led up the left bank through gorges and narrow valleys bounded by rocky hills up to 1000 feet. A few Chinese villages were passed, and as probably no foreigner had ever been along this route before, the villagers turned out in numbers to see him. A few miles from T'sao-pa he left the Hei-shui-ho and ascended the narrow valley of the T'a-shê-kou. Continuing the ascent on February 20 he pitched his camp at a height of 10,370 feet. The valley was narrow and winding and entirely uninhabited. The stream was small and was crossed many times by log bridges. The hills rose to a height of from 1000 to 1500 feet above the valley and a few trees grew on their sides. On the upper part of the valley snow lay on the ground.

The Yang-pu Shan, 12,800 feet, was reached on February 21 after a steep climb. It is 20¾ miles from Ts'ao-pa, and forms the boundary between Kansu and Szechwan and the divide between the Pai-shui and Pai-lung rivers. From it a good view as far as the Min Shan to the north-west was obtained. Some of the hills near were covered with fir woods. The Min Shan was covered with snow, but generally the snow lay thickest in the valleys. The descent on the northern side was steep for 3 miles. The path lay partly through a fir wood, and in places was covered with ice and very slippery. After the first 3 miles it was easy, leading down the valley of a small stream to Yang-pu-chai, the first habitation since leaving Ts'ao-pa, 30½ miles. This village consisted of 55 families of the Shu tribe of Tibetans. Pereira put up in a temple and allowed the people, who had never seen a white man before, to look at him through the door.

Snow fell during the night and it was very cold at the start next morning as the altitude was still considerable, namely 10,400 feet, and the going at first was slow owing to the ice on the surface. But the day was clear and in the sun it was quite hot.

The going was good all the next day, February 22. The hill-sides were covered with grass and scrub. At Pai-ku-ssu is a temple with 150 Tibetan monks. It is situated on the highest ground on the western side. The mud walls of the houses are painted with broad vertical red and white stripes. At 12½ miles Pereira reached Ra-chih-ssu, where there is a temple with 100 monks. It is situated at an altitude of 8410 feet. Here was stationed a solitary Chinese from Choni. He is director (ch'ih-hui) under the Prince of Choni, of the district which extends from the Yang-pu Shan to the T'ai-li-ho. He had been there a year and was feeling very lonely, and he put Pereira up in a nice clean room. The lamas in the temple belong to the yellow sect, and their rooms were clean and comfortable. The Tibetan women in the village wear shorts and overcoats. They dress their hair in a pigtail and oil it well. Their head-dress is a fur cap like an astrakan cap.

Pereira continued for 10 miles down the Tu-erh-kou valley on February 23. The ranges on either side rose about 2000 feet above the valley and were covered with fir and scrub and in places with cultivation. At 10 miles the path led up a stiff rise of some 1600 feet to Ku-ya, 9210 feet, a village of 30 Tibetan families, where Pereira again lodged in a clean but chilly temple. Everywhere round the hills were cut by deep valleys. The general trend of the ranges, which are about 10,000 or 11,000 feet above sea-level, is from west to east, or W.N.W. to E.S.E.

Chien-tsang, 27½ miles distant, was reached on February 24. First there was a steep climb of

4 miles to the top of the K'uya Shan, 10,700 feet, and then a very steep descent to Shui-pi'-kou, which consisted of seven wretched Tibetan hovels situated on the Pai-shui Chiang, which farther east is called the Pai-ling Chiang. It is a swift river sunken between steep banks over 100 feet in height. Shui-pi-kou, 7050 feet, is the limit of the territory of the Prince of Choni. Ta-ku-ssu, the next village, is under the magistrate of Minchow. The Tibetans between Yang-pi-chai and Shui-pi-kou are Hsia (lower) T'ich-po. Their hovels are wretched buildings of wattle and planks, and are very dirty and uncomfortable. Leaving the Pai-shui Chiang the road ascends the Ta-la Ho valley to Chien-tsiang, 6600 feet, where another Chinese is stationed as representative of the Minchow magistrate.

Pereira halted here for a day, and on February 26 marched to Ta-la, 22 miles. The road lay up the valley of the Ta-la Ho and mostly through gorges. For the first time Pereira met about a dozen Chinese either on the road or in villages. Ta-la is a village of about 25 families, and three Tibetan villages were passed on the way.

After a steep climb of 4 miles, on the following day, the Ta-la Shan, 11,700 feet, in the Min Shan range was reached. It was the last pass on the journey from Chengtu to Choni. And here Pereira left the basin of the Yangtse-kiang and was now in the basin of the Yellow River once more. There was snow on the top of the pass, and a bitter wind blew from the north. On the far side was a steep descent of nearly 1800 feet for 1½ mile, and then an easy descent for the rest of the march to Chan-cha-lu, 26 miles down the valley of the Shang-ch'uan Ho. The hills were bare and rose to only from 300 to 500 feet above the valley. At Chan-chu-la 58 out of the 60 families were Mohammedan.

Descending the Shang-ch'uan valley the road improved, and two-wheeled carts drawn by one bullock were seen. The hills were only 300 or 400 feet in height and covered with grass. At 11¼ miles Minchow, 8400 feet, a town of 575 families, was reached on February 28. There were shops here and a poor inn, but the inn-keeper gave Pereira his own comfortable and clean room. Ascending the Ta'o Ho by the left bank on the following day Pereira reached Shih-ch'i at 27¼ miles. For the first 7 miles the valley was as much as 2 miles wide, and it was fertile and contained many villages of the mud huts such as are found in the North. But near Shih-ch'i it narrowed to a width of only 200 yards. Pereira passed a lady missionary going to new Tao-chow and a missionary coming from old Tao-chow.

Choni, 8880 feet, was reached on March 2, after a march of 17 miles, still up the left bank of the T'ao Ho. Some Chinese villages were passed, and others partly Chinese and partly Tibetan. Choni has 320 families, of whom about half are Chinese and half are Tibetan, but of these latter only about one-fifth are pure Tibetan. The Prince of Choni, a man of thirty, was very friendly to foreigners. He had been on very good terms with the previous Governor of the

Province, but the then governor was of the opposite faction and the Prince was not so sure of his position. He was under the new T'ao-chow city magistrate, who had fined him 30,000 taels. Pereira presented him with an electric torch of an ingenious pattern : if a handle was worked it would always give light. According to the Prince the Chinese place the Tibetans in two categories. In the first are the Shu Fan, the "experienced" Tibetans, who living directly under and near the Chinese are supposed to have learnt something of Chinese civilisation. In the second are the Sheng Fan, the wilder tribes who live behind. The name of the tribe of Tibetans who inhabit the country between Yang-pu Shan and Shui-pi-kou just passed through by Pereira is Hsia (lower) T'ieh-po. They are under the Prince of Choni, who also rules the Shang (upper) T'ieh-po farther to the north-west.

From Chengtu to Choni, Pereira estimated the cost at $1287 and spent $1244. The average cost per day was $15.95. During the whole journey from Chengtu to Choni he met only four Europeans—all missionaries. At Choni he stayed with Mr. and Mrs. Hansen of the Christian and Missionary Alliance (American).

Leaving Choni on March 7, Pereira arrived that day at T'ao-chow, New City, 11 miles distant. The Prince insisted on coming to see him off outside the city and upon entertaining him in very comfortable "kung-kuan" in T'ao-chow. He also sent five mounted men under an officer as escort. It was a wretched, cold, dull, windy day. The snow was half thawed and the road very muddy. There was a gradual rise of some 900 feet over the Ma-ch'ang-Kou Shan, 9910 feet, then a descent and afterwards a rise to 10,000 feet over the Nan-men Shan. Three or four big villages inhabited chiefly by Chinese were passed. The country all round was hilly, the ridge rising some 500 feet above the valleys. T'ao-chow, 9520 feet, was a dead-alive town of 600 families.

March 8 was a bitterly cold and very gloomy day, with a few inches of snow on the ground. The road lay up and down over bleak bare hills. One village was passed and there was then a steep climb to the Shih-t'ou-kou Shan, 10,700 feet. After this there was a descent to 9800 feet, and then another climb to Pai-sung-kou Shan and another descent to Pan-ch'ise. Then the road passed down a narrow valley which joined the broader Yang-sa-kou and crossed by a good covered bridge to Yang-sa, a town of 55 families situated at an elevation of 8500 feet. A good many pheasants were seen on the march.

From here the road lay down the fairly fertile Yang-sa valley for 6 miles, and then turned to the left by a narrow valley to Kan-kou, a village of 80 families, at 10 miles. Then there was a rather steep climb to the Lien-hua Shan, 10,150 feet, at 14 miles and a gradual descent along the hill-side and a final very steep, muddy, slippery descent to Shan-shen-miao, 8170 feet, a village of 17 families which was reached on March 9. Though the sun was out the weather was bitterly cold, and there was 3 or 4 inches of snow on the pass.

From here Pereira made a long march of 31¾ miles to Hung-tao-yü-kou on March 10. For the first mile and a half the descent was through snow and frozen mud to the valley. The going was then good and free of snow. After 5 miles the T'ao Ho was reached and the road ascended the valley for 4 miles. Then the road leaves the river and ascends some small valleys with a few small villages set amid low bare hills. The road was exceedingly muddy and snow lay on the ground. At 16 miles the Chin-ku-ch'eng Shan, 7880 feet, was crossed and then the Kuei-hsiao P'o, 8300 feet. The road then lay down the valley to Hung-tao-yü-kou, a village of 17 families, and containing one wretched inn. The discomforts were increased by donkeys being made to share the common room. The atmosphere was appalling, and the braying chorus made up in power what it lacked in music.

Ti-tao, a town of about 17,000 inhabitants, was reached on March 11. It is 97 miles from Choni and lies at an elevation of 6800 feet. The valley of the T'ao River through which the road runs is 3 or 4 miles wide and is bounded by low hills bare of trees. Several small villages are scattered about it. Ti-tao is a go-ahead place. It is very anti-Mohammedan, and since the Mohammedan rebellions no Mohammedan has been allowed to settle on the right bank of the T'ao Ho. Kansu is a very conservative Province and wisely backward in modern education. There are not the same student troubles as in other provinces and Lan-chow is the only place in which students are prominent. Kansu still gets its officials from outside provinces, and they carry on in the same old way of squeeze and oppression.

Pereira stayed here with Mr. and Mrs. Mosely and Mr. Christie of the Christian and Missionary Alliance.

On March 13 he proceeded again down the broad valley of the T'ao Ho. The soil was loess and fertile and there were plenty of villages. It is a great tobacco-growing country, most of the tobacco being sent to Szechwan. The important market towns of Hsin-tien-pu at 12¾ miles and Hsin-tien-chen at 20½ miles were passed, the former having a population of 350 families and the latter of 100 families. And at 24 miles was T'ao-sha-hsien, a new "city" of forty houses, with a mud wall which had only recently been built. Sha-leng, a town of 97 families, was reached at 25¾ miles. The weather was fine and mild.

Next day the road first lay down the valley of the T'ao River and turned to the right and ascended through loess cuttings on to a bleak, bare hilly country with practically no trees. A few villages were seen. Then there was a rather steep climb to the top of the Kuan-shan-ling, 8110 feet, followed by a descent to A-Kan-chen, 6650 feet, a town of 300 families. The weather was again fine and mild.

Lan-chow was at last reached on March 15.

CHAPTER XI

LAN-CHOW TO TANGAR

LAN-CHOW, now officially called Kao-lan-hsien, is a city of some 300,000 inhabitants and is 5300 feet above sea-level. It has a dry climate—except during the rainy season in July and August. And even in March Pereira experienced beautiful warm summer weather. The city has an inner wall, and on the west, south and east sides an outer mud wall enclosing an inner suburb. Beyond this is a more scattered outer suburb. The Huang Ho (Yellow River) flows past the north wall. An iron bridge built by a German firm in 1908 spans the river north-west of the city.

Several Europeans live in Lan-chow, and Pereira was entertained by Mons. Geerts, the Salt Commissioner, and his sister, and lived in luxury and comfort through their overwhelming kindness and hospitality. Père Esser, of the Belgian-Dutch Mission Étrangères, and the members of the China Inland Mission also showed Pereira the greatest hospitality. Mons. Geerts was formerly director of some copper and gold mines near Sining. If he had been allowed to manage them they would have been profitable, but as usual a horde of Chinese officials, whose sole business was to squeeze as much money as possible out of the venture was tacked on, and the result was that they swallowed up all the profit and the mine had to be closed down.

By the Chinese officials also Pereira was hospitably entertained in Lan-chow. The Postal Commissioner, Mr. Chan-bu-to, he describes as belonging to the very small number of really honest Chinese officials. The Military Governor, Lu Hung-tao, he found to be a nice easygoing official of the old school who did not trouble much about political affairs. He was handicapped by having no money, as his predecessor had cleared the Kansu bank and got away with all the money in 1921. The Civil Governor, Pen-lung-Kao, a Chihli man, was much more energetic. The Peking Government, wishing to appoint him to the post but fearing that if they sent him at once as Civil Governor the local people would refuse to accept him, sent him first as Opium Inspector. The plan worked well, as he waited till he was firmly fixed in office and then declared himself Civil Governor.

Jen-chien, the Taoyin-Hsui, was reported to be absolutely honest and a poor man in consequence. When he was asked by his superiors what reforms he advised he boldly replied that all Provincial Treasurers should be foreigners—a bold suggestion for a Chinese official to make. The police magistrate was a fat little man of not much enterprise. The police force of the city numbered three hundred and were a slovenly, useless lot of men. The Military Governor gave Pereira and other European guests an excellent and not too long dinner. Behind his yamen was one of the largest and pleasantest gardens Pereira had seen in China. It contained some fine old elms besides other trees; and there were picturesque little summer-houses and a private path up to the North Wall, from which there is a fine view over the city.

The arsenal was situated in a mud-walled enclosure in the north-west corner of the western suburb. It is a very poor place where about three hundred workmen are employed—principally in making two-cent pieces. They also repair rifles and mountain guns and manufacture bugles.

As to the corruption among officials, Pereira says it had never been so bad before. Under the Manchus officials had not the same opportunity, whilst at least some of the money that went to the Court returned to the people. Now the officials hold on to it. But the love of money among the Chinese is extraordinary, for when they get it they do not know how to make themselves really comfortable, and unless they are in the security of the foreign concession there is always the risk of their being forced to disgorge. Everywhere in China are sinecure posts in which officials accumulate money and then bolt to Peking, Tientsin or Shanghai with their ill-gotten gains.

The people of Kansu struck Pereira as being taller than the Szechwan men. At Chengtu his Tientsin boys towered over the natives of that place, whereas in Lan-chow they were not noticeable.

The poppy is again being extensively cultivated in Kansu. Under the Empress Dowager and

Yuan-shih-kai it was banned; and these two rulers of China deserve credit for the work they did in suppressing it. But under the corrupt officials of the Republic it has not only been allowed but sometimes its growth has been forced upon the people, so that the officials might make money by putting a tax upon it. When an investigating foreign Consul comes to make inquiries the officials, having pocketed their "squeeze" tax, order the poppies to be pulled up and then declare that poppy-growing is still forbidden. In only a few provinces of China is it now forbidden.

One very sad sight Pereira saw at Lan-chow. This was General Annenkoff's Russian refugees. Two years before, he had retreated from Siberia to Urumchi with six hundred men and a flock of refugees fleeing from the Bolshevists. The Chinese Governor had induced him to disarm and hand over his money—about three million roubles in gold. Whilst he himself was temporarily detained as a hostage his troops and refugees gradually filtered through to Peking. They arrived at Lan-chow practically destitute and herded together in two or three wretched inns. A miserable dole (in paper money), just enough to enable them to sustain life, is grudgingly dealt out to them. But their hardships in this part of their journey were much lightened by the kindness and generosity of Mons. Geerts. They could not afford to eat meat and lived on dry bread and tea. Officers sold their horses and women their rings and jewels. Pereira visited these Russians in their wretched inns and was astonished to find what fatalists they were under such heart-rending circumstances. They seemed to be quite cheerful and to have no thought of the black future before them when they would reach Peking or Shanghai and join the ever-increasing crowd of Russian refugees dependent entirely on foreign charity. And in spite of their distress they wanted to give Mons. Geerts a feast in acknowledgement of the kindness they had received.

Several thousands of Russians were still scattered over Mongolia and Chinese Turkestan; and Pereira reflected how impossible it would have seemed ten years ago that a great Empire like Russia should be dragged down so low and give such an exhibition of impotence and misery.

Pereira stayed at Lan-chow nineteen days and on April 3 left for Sining. There exists a shorter mule track by which that town may be reached in seven days. But he was tired of mules, and using carts travelled by the longer route. After crossing the iron bridge over the Yellow River he followed up the fertile valley of that river for 11 miles. At this time of year it was as bare and desolate as the rest of the country. Except for some fruit orchards there was not a tree to be seen, and the hills which rose to 200 or 300 feet above the plain were quite bare. Even villages were few. At 11 miles the road leads up a narrow desolate valley and is very sandy. At 24 miles is Hsiao-lao-ch'ih, a town of 70 families. A number of Mohammedans were passed on this march, and Pereira notes how strange it was in a country where prayer is little used to see two Mohammedans get out of their cart, take off their shoes, and bow themselves down in prayer.

The same bare, treeless, desolate-looking country was passed through on the following day on the way to Hung-ch'eng-pu, 26⅓ miles. The only exceptions were two fertile valleys each about 4 miles long. The road was very sandy and dusty and was constantly rising and dipping, 6580 feet was the highest point reached, and Hung-ch'eng-p'u lay at 6270 feet. It contains 820 families and is situated in the fertile valley of the P'ing-fan River. Next day Pereira followed up the valley, which was fertile all the way and covered with many villages, to P'ing-fan-hsien, 24¼ miles. This is a prosperous city of 1250 families at an elevation of 6910 feet.

The divide between the P'ing-fan and Ta-t'ung Rivers was crossed on the following day by the Hsiang-lu-shan, 8460 feet, and the road descended among downs and sandy hills to Shuang-niu-kou, 7470 feet, a hamlet of ten hovels and a poor inn, 23¾ miles from P'ing-fan-hsien.

Continuing to descend on April 7, Pereira struck the Ta-t'ung Ho valley at 12 miles and found it fertile and dotted with villages and a few trees. The intervening country in this region is generally barren and treeless and holding only an occasional village. But the valleys themselves are fertile and well inhabited. The road led down the Ta-t'ung Ho and at 15 miles Pereira crossed the river by a rope ferry. The river was here 50 yards wide and 20 feet deep. Chinese were here washing for gold, and a few miles to the south were the gold and copper mines which Mons. Geerts used to work till Chinese corruption necessitated closing them down.

Next day there was a rather steep ascent for 3 miles to the top of the Ping-kou Shan, 7840 feet, the divide between the Ta-t'ung and Sining Rivers, from which there was a fine view to the south-west over a low range to a high snowy range beyond. The descent at first was good but later very bad with steep places. The fertile valley of the Sining River was reached at 11½ miles. The soil was loess and it was about 1 mile wide, lying between bare, treeless sandy hills. It contained many villages and some trees. At 12 miles was Lao-ya-ch'eng, 6270 feet, standing on rising ground and containing 55 families. At 19¼ miles was Kao-miao-tzu, 140 houses; and at 30 miles Nien-pai-hsien. This latter is a small city of about 2000 inhabitants, situated at an elevation of 6270 feet. Pereira had pushed on so as to be there on Palm Sunday, as it contained a Roman Catholic Mission station. This Mission was presided over by Monseigneur Otto, who after fifty years in Kansu was moving with the Belgian-Dutch missionaries to Mongolia to make room for German priests. Monseigneur Otto on account of age had resigned his vicariate and was acting as a simple missionary.

After Mass on Palm Sunday, April 9, Pereira breakfasted with Monseigneur Otto and Père Costanoble, and then left for P'ing-chung-yi, 19½ miles. After half-a-mile he crossed the Sining Ho by a rope ferry. The river was here

40 yards wide and 5 feet deep. Slight snow had fallen in the early morning, but it soon melted in the valley making the road very heavy going. The road lay all the day up the fertile valley of the Sining Ho. It was about 1 mile wide with hills on either side 200 to 400 feet in height. Several villages were passed.

Giant pandar, according to Père Costanoble, are to be found in the hills north of Sining-fu, but as there are no bamboos in that part Pereira was surprised to hear this : he had thought that they were not found north of Sungpan. Père Costanoble also said that tigers were to be found there.

Some aborigines, whom the Chinese call " Tu-jen ", that is " men of the soil ", live in the hills to the south-west of Nien-pai-hsien and in the hills north-east of Sining-fu. Père Schram says they are of Mongol origin. Driven out of Liau-t'ung in Manchuria during the Chin dynasty they moved slowly westward across the Ordus, taking seventy-one years to reach Kansu. Here they flourished for several hundred years though they had to fight with the Tibetans. But under the T'ang dynasty they were finally subdued by the Chinese and have now diminished to a mere remnant.

Sining - fu, 200¼ miles from Lan-chow, was reached on April 10. It is 24¾ miles from P'ing-chung-yi, and the road lay all day up the Sining Ho valley, which is from 1 mile to 1½ mile wide, lying between sandy hills from 500 to 600 feet in height. The valley is mostly fertile, but belts of land are impregnated with alkaline and uncultivated. The villages are small. A few Mongols and Tibetans were met with. Passing through the suburbs and the eastern gate Pereira arrived at the house of Père Schram of the Belgian Mission.

The city of Sining has a population of about 40,000, and Pereira computed its elevation at 7140 feet, though various other travellers have put it between 6978 feet and 7500 feet. The district of Sining was not brought under Chinese rule till about 1720 or 1730. Since then all the troubles in Kansu have been caused by religious antipathies. The rivalry between old and new sects of Mohammedans has been seized on by the Chinese for their own ends, but this has had the opposite effect of uniting the Mohammedans against them. At the time of Pereira's visit the new sect, of which Ma Ch'i was the leader, was in the ascendant. After the rebellion of the Mohammedans in 1895, when they attacked and failed to take Sining, the east suburb where they lived was totally destroyed. It was rebuilt entirely by Ma Ch'i, beginning in 1918, and by 1922 was once more a busy centre with a fine new mosque.

Ma Ch'i was originally a small military officer. He was pushed on by Ma Fu-hsiang, and when strong enough to act on his own quarrelled with the then head of the Kansu Mohammedans, who favoured the old sect while Ma Ch'i favoured the new sect. The difference between the two was that the old put their faith in the Koran whilst the new thought that book was not of much value and put their faith in later traditions. But of this new sect itself there are several varieties, a small one at T'aochow admitting a mixture of Christianity and Buddhism. The influence of Ma An

Liang began to decline about 1915 and in 1920 he died, partly from chagrin at the growing influence of Ma Ch'i.

The Mohammedans of Kansu are believed to have come from Samarkand about the 8th century A.D. They gradually adopted Chinese customs though retaining their old religion. About a hundred years later the Salars also came from Samarkand and settled round Sun-hwa on the Yellow River to the west of Lan-chow. Being more remote they retained most of their Turkish customs.

Ma Ch'i had a certain number of regular troops but depended chiefly on his raw levies. Each village when called on had to provide a couple of men, and the village had to pay their families for a substitute to work in the fields and also provide the soldier with a horse if he was a cavalry soldier and a rifle and two hundred rounds. These levies were quite untrained but were of good fighting material.

Pereira gives an interesting account of Ma Ch'i's methods in fighting the Goloks, a Tibetan tribe who had hitherto never been conquered. Ma Ch'i sent Mohammedan and Chinese traders among them to act as spies. When the time was ripe for attack he called out his levies, of whom 20 per cent were buglers. But he did not attempt to attack the Tibetans: he simply made his buglers blow, while with some old Krupp guns he fired at the rocks; and the noise of the bugles and the guns and shock of the shells on the rocks so terrified the Goloks that they fled. Ma Ch'i then pursued them and slew them in large numbers.

The average for a family in Sining is five. For instance, five years previously 995 families consisted of 10,083 persons. Now 2009 families have 9971 persons. Though it is generally stated that the children of Chinese-Tibetan marriages become Tibetan, Père Schram said it depended on place and influence whether the children became Chinese or Tibetan. In villages where Chinese predominated or possibly where the chief ruler was Chinese they usually become Chinese, and vice versa.

The " Gurong ", an important Buddhist Abbot of the red sect, lives between Kweite and Sunhwa on the Yellow River in Kansu. In or about 1919 he went to Lhasa to try and arrange certain matters with the Dalai Lama. Ma Ch'i did not approve of this and sent two Chinese ahead to Lhasa to report. He also sent a third man to Lhasa to spy on the Gurong. The Gurong could not get an interview with the Dalai Lama, and on making inquiries discovered he was hindered by the spy. So he invited the spy to dine with him and then had him tied up by the fingers till he confessed. After the spy had confessed the Gurong murdered him. When the Dalai Lama heard of this he fined the Gurong. And the two Chinese also hearing of it returned ahead of the Gurong to Sining-fu and told Ma Ch'i, who took away his arms from the Gurong when he arrived at Jyekundo and fined him when he arrived at Sining. The Gurong then retired to his monastery.

Pereira found Père Schram to be a most energetic man. When he first came to Sining the only Catholic was his boy. In five years he had made nearly 10,000 converts of whom about

1500 had been baptized. The converts were all Chinese except a few Mongols, and none of them were Mohammedans. No Tibetans had been converted, but he had not had much opportunity of going among them. Père Schram had twenty-nine schools, which, as Pereira remarks, was more than enough for one man.

Catholic communities were established by Père Lefebre the Jesuit in the 17th century—though there may have been earlier ones. Missionaries disguised as petty merchants used to visit them from Sian-fu in Shensi. The Christians were mostly people exiled to Kansu for their faith. These communities continued to flourish, chiefly near Liang-chow-fu and Kanchow-fu. And when the present Belgian-Dutch Mission was established about 1871 they found about four hundred of these old Christians.

On April 17 Pereira left Sining for Tangar, his real starting-point for the journey to Lhasa, and reached it on the following day. The day was beautiful and the road lay up the fertile valley of the Sining Ho, which is over 2 miles wide and lies between sandy treeless hills from 500 to 700 feet high and covered with scanty grass. The cart road was fairly good in fine weather, except in parts where it is sunken and flooded with water from the irrigated fields. The Sining River is crossed by a bridge or forded by carts at Cha-ma-Lung. Beyond this the road is stony and leads up a defile with the Sining River on the left. But on approaching Sining the country is more open. There are rolling downs and away to the south a high range partly covered with snow.

Tangar, 8640 feet, is the headquarters of a district with a population of about 50,000 inhabitants. The town itself has some 4000 or 5000 inhabitants. The Magistrate, Ch'en Tsê-fan, was an old Honanese who had not been in his native province for forty years but had spent his service on the Siberian frontier and here.

CHAPTER XII

THE START FOR TIBET

PREPARATIONS for the journey to Lhasa had now to be made, and a most anxious time followed. The physical difficulties Pereira did not doubt he could overcome, though his general health was not good, his frost-bitten foot was still giving him trouble, and ahead were more than a thousand miles of mountainous country where he would generally be at an elevation of about fifteen thousand feet and seldom less than twelve thousand. But these physical obstacles would not stop him. What really caused him anxiety was the possible attitude of the Tibetans or Chinese. The Chinese might prevent him entering Tibet at all; and the Tibetans at the frontier might prevent his going to Lhasa. And his hopes of success were sadly shaken by the arrival in Tangar on April 26 of the Danish traveller, Sorensen, who had just made an attempt to penetrate Tibet but had been stopped at Nagchuka, while the final blow came when he heard from the Legation in Peking that the Government of India refused to ask the Tibetan Government for a pass for him. Prospects were about as black as they well could be. However, he set about his preparations with his usual thoroughness and never gave up hope of success.

Jye-kundo was his first objective, and his future plans he would have to settle there: he might go from there either to Nagchuka or to Chamdo, and so on to Lhasa. And if both these ways of entering Tibet were barred he might have to make for Tachien-lu. But even that line of retreat might be forbidden, as it was to Sorensen, and he might after all have to retrace his steps to Tangar, a dreary prospect when pressed for food and money and perhaps ill. These points would have to be decided after his arrival at Jye-kundo. To get there he started buying mules and ponies, though as soon as he had bought them he found it would have been best to hire animals. By May 3 he had bought eight ponies and fifteen mules. The latter cost 406 taels and the ponies (exclusive of one he had before) 180 taels.

Presents for the Tibetans he also bought—five pieces of yellow silk, enough to make a short coat, for 28 taels, seventy-two feet of red cloth for 14 taels, and six blue katas or scarves for presentation on visits, and small presents, such as coral beads and children's cheap toys.

His luggage, including his private boxes, store boxes and presents, only came to 1600 catties, which was only 110 catties a mule, about thirty catties under the usual load. He also hired five mules and two donkeys to carry beans as forage to Ta-ho-pa, 126 miles.

Arthur B. Sorensen, a Dane in the employ of the North Eastern Telegraph Company, arrived at Tangar on April 26. He had tried to reach

PERREIRA'S CARAVAN MARCHING DOWN THE MAIN STREET OF TANGAR.

face p. 111.

Lhasa but had been stopped at Nagchuka. He had then gone eastward 378 miles to Jye-kundo hoping to reach Ta-chien-lu, but had again been stopped, so had made his way north to Tangar. He came to several meals with Pereira and kindly gave him information about the distances, altitudes and stages between Nagchuka and Tangar, and many notes for Pereira's guidance. He had travelled much in unexplored tracks on the way to Kuei-te on the Yellow River and on his journey to Nagchuka; and he struck Pereira as a plucky man.

Having made his final preparations for his plunge into Tibet, Pereira sent back to England instructions for the despatch of mails to him. His brother was to chance sending letters by India to Lhasa. He was asked " to put *Racing Up-to-Date* in each enclosure, and a summary of important events, deaths, marriages or news of special import of any of his friends; cuttings about important racing events, such as the four days of Epsom, the Two Thousand, City and Suburban, etc., but nothing about weather or minor details ".

" I think I shall get to Jye-kundo," he added, " but beyond it is all doubt. . . . Money is also a difficulty, as I shall want more than I had calculated. . . . I might reach Lhasa without money. My caravan might be looted on the way. My mules might fail. There are so many unforeseen chances. . . . Still I hope for success."

In this rather doubtful frame of mind, hoping for the best but almost expecting the worst, Pereira left Tangar on May 11. His caravan consisted of his boy, six followers, including a Tibetan and Mongol interpreter, four soldiers, eight horses and fifteen mules besides the five mules and ten donkeys.

After crossing the Hsuang-shui Ho, the north branch of the Sining River, the road ascends the narrow but fertile valley of the Sining Ho. Treeless hills from 500 to 700 feet in height bounded the valley on either side, though in the valley itself there were trees for the first 3 or 4 miles and a few small Chinese villages. The first stage was only 12 miles and Pereira pitched his tents at San-kun.

Shara-kuto, the last Chinese town, 22½ miles from Tangar, was reached on the following day. It consists of some fifty houses surrounded by a mud wall. Leaving this town and the Sining River valley the road ascends a grassy valley with some recently started cultivation to a pass, 10,780 feet, over the Jih-yüeh Shan range, 27 miles from Tangar. This is the boundary between the Kansu and Ch'ing-hai Provinces. It is also the real boundary between China and Tibet, though the present frontier is the Tang-la Range, running east and west, the divide between the Salween and Mekong rivers.

Typical Tibetan grass land, valleys and hills all grass, and not a tree nor a house to be seen, was the character of the country on the far side; and Pereira encamped on May 12 1½ mile from the pass at a height of 10,770 feet. It was generally warm in the daytime, though the winds were rather strong, and it was cold in the mornings. Away to the south could be seen

FIRST CAMP IN TIBET.

face p. 113.

about a hundred animals grazing. Next day Pereira marched for 24 miles across the great grass country, crossing the two low ranges running north and south, and then another great grass plain, bounded by the Ko-Ko Nor range on the north, and with a small lake, Wa-yen-nor, about half way. Huge flocks of sheep, goats, yak cattle and horses were grazing on the plain; and sixteen or seventeen black Tibetan tents could be seen in the distance. There were two mud buildings at the end of the lake and a small mud-walled Chinese camp by the road. All these buildings were uninhabited, but were evidently intended for the control of the salt. A small stream, the Tou-t'a Ho, running north into the Ko-Ko Nor, was crossed in the morning, and Pereira camped on the banks of the Dum-ka-tsao stream which flowed south to the Yellow River. Higher up was a small Chinese village with patches of cultivation, while in the plain beyond were several more small Chinese villages. Into places like this, where they can live in houses and cultivate, the Chinese will come. But the pastoral work is done by Mongols and Tibetans, living in tents among their flocks and subsisting chiefly on mutton, tomaba made from a coarse barley, and—usually rancid—butter.

Up to the previous year the route had been little used as the Goloks had raided it for centuries. But since their defeat they have retired to the east, and General Ma Ch'i has garrisons at Ch'a-pu-ch'a and Ta-ho-pa and has opened the country.

On May 14 Pereira left the small stream and

after passing through low sandy hills and crossing another small cultivated valley in which were three or four small Chinese villages and beyond this some low hills, he reached the fertile irrigated Ch'a-pu-ch'a plain, which is some 3 miles wide and stretches 6 miles to the north and 12 miles to the south to the Yellow River. Ch'a-pu-ch'a has some 85 families of whom 25 are Chinese and the rest Tibetan. The houses were of mud with mud walls round the enclosures. There was a Chinese camp with 200 men about 4 miles to the south.

Gung Nor, the "Egg Lake", 17½ miles, was reached on May 15. After descending the Ch'a-pu-ch'a valley for 4 miles Pereira struck south of west for 10 miles across a great grass plain, where he saw several herds of cattle and some horses but only one solitary Tibetan. On the plain were also several gazelle, some hares, red-legged partridges and many lizards, while on the lake were some wild duck. On the banks of the lake there was a big flock of sheep under the care of a Tibetan woman. But Pereira was surprised at the absence of Tibetan tents: he saw only one. The Tibetan sheep he bought were very tough and appeared to him to have been trained for a Marathon race! The weather was fine and warm, but there was a strong south-west wind blowing, filling the tent with sand.

Leaving the Gung Nor on May 16 he passed over a great plain stretching away for 10 or 12 miles to a high range of hills to the south This plain was mostly covered with scrub and small streams running south flowed across it.

Big flocks of sheep and some cattle were grazing on it and there were some Tibetan tents. He also saw many Brahminy ducks and sixteen geese. Some stray horses walked up to within 20 yards of them. The western part of the plain was very sandy, and on May 17 the party crossed a dreary valley of sand and scrub for 8 miles, when they came to another huge grass plain stretching north to the same range as had been crossed on the previous day. Fine grazing country with many Tibetan flocks and tents was crossed on May 18, and in places the ground was honeycombed by countless rats (possibly a small species of marmot). He also saw a few gazelle, but they were very wild. In the daytime it was warm enough after the first hour for him to shed his coat and gloves.

Ta-ho-pa was reached on May 19. Pereira had taken a day longer than Sorensen, but he had travelled by a longer route where water was more plentiful. Here there was a fort with about 70 infantry under Ma Ch'i's orders; though beyond placing these garrisons he had done nothing to develop the country. Pereira made the distance from Tangar 150 miles. In the valley of the Ta-ho there were some trees—the first he had seen since leaving the Sining Ho valley. He was delayed here by a snowstorm. He had also to await the arrival of an escort, for it was unsafe to go beyond this unescorted on account of the Golok raiders.

Some 30 or 40 mounted soldiers with 50 or 60 mules having arrived, Pereira set out again on May 24 and climbed the small Cha-su-ra

Pass, 12,820 feet. The descent was rather steep among grass hills to the broad valley of the Ta-ch'i, a branch of the Ta Ho. On the west was the Za-Lung range. At 15 miles he forded the stony bed of the Ta-ch'i, here 2 feet deep, and 5 miles farther on left this valley and ascended the narrower Cha-su-ra, camping at an elevation of 12,300 feet.

Snow fell that night and on May 25 Pereira had a disagreeable climb through mud and snow to the top of the Ch'i Cha-su-ra, 14,607 feet. He descended to the great Lung-ch'i plain, where the pasturage was very poor, and camped at 13,987 feet. The day was cloudy and cold. A strong west wind was blowing with occasional sleet, and he was in great anxiety about his mules. Light as their loads were he now found they ought to have been lighter still. They ought not to have been heavier than 100 catties or even less.

The Chü-ri or Chi-da Pass, 14,507 feet, was crossed on May 26. The ascent was easy and the descent lay through gloomy valleys between snow-covered hills for 6 miles to the Lüan-ch'üan plain, which was mostly sandy with poor pasturage. Here Pereira encamped by a stream as his mules were done. He had meant to make only a short march, but he came across no suitable pasturage and had to march 19 miles. Consequently one mule collapsed and died in the night. Another mule only just crawled in.

From this plain Pereira saw what is of extraordinary geographical interest—the great mountain Amné Machin. Rumour had said that it was higher than Mount Everest, and certainly it must be a giant. Pereira says: "It towers above everything else in its snow-clad grandeur and must be well over 25,000 feet high as I was at an altitude of 13,000 feet. It looked 30 miles away but was very likely 70 miles off to the south-east." By the Chinese the mountain is called Ma-chi Hsieh-Shan.

The next day two more mules collapsed as there had been practically nothing for them to feed on. And on May 28 the party crossed Tung-ri Pass, 13,867 feet, and a little farther on had a beautiful view of the Tung-ri-tso Nor, or lake of a thousand hills. Lying between hills and of a beautiful blue, the lake reminded Pereira of Italy. The Mongol name for it is Tosu Nor. The descent from the pass was easy and the party made their way among low hills, across a gravelly valley and through grass hills to the broad Ch'ang-shih-t'ou valley. Here there was good pasturage, and he halted by an encampment of Yü-shu Tibetan merchants of the Gaba tribe, who were the first inhabitants he had met since leaving Ta-ko-pa. These Tibetans were as usual very quiet and very curious about Pereira and his tent. They had with them about six hundred yaks and were preparing to move.

Thunderstorms and a heavy downpour of rain made it cold for this time of year, and the thermometer fell to 38°; and the following morning a bitter north-west wind sprang up and the rain turned to sleet. Pereira, after crossing the Ch'ang shih-t'ou valley, passed through a gap in the Ch'ang-shih-t'ou Shan, a range which ran south-east and apparently joined the great Amné Machin mountain—or Anyè Machin, as it is called by the Tibetans. He encamped in a plain with good pasturage by the Bu-lou stream, but the strong wind and sleet made it cold in his tent. He was also finding difficulty in breathing at this height, 14,000 feet. Four or five miles was as much as he cared to walk, and uphill he preferred even less.

The Tibetan merchants with their yaks and also a Mohammedan merchant were marching along with Pereira. They had left their wives behind and were travelling for five or six months in the year. They numbered about twenty-five and were now on their way back to Jye-kundo. The Mohammedan merchant somewhat tried Pereira by sitting for hours in his tent. Conversation for these lengthy periods was impossible so Pereira would play "Patience" and let the merchant look on.

The Bu-lou Pass, 14,300 feet, was crossed on May 31. The descent was easy and he encamped by a stream flowing between grassy hills about 500 feet high. This day he lost his third mule, but was able to hire four yaks to take surplus boxes of stores. A party of Tibetan merchants travelling from Tangar to Jye-kundo passed him this day. They expected to make the journey in sixteen days.

On June 1 he crossed a great plain with very little grass and passed some small lakes or ponds of a beautifully blue colour, and with duck swimming on them. He then ascended a narrow bare valley to the East Ma-la-yi Pass, 14,580 feet, and by an easy descent reached Ma-la-yi-kou, a big open valley or small plain with a stream and fair pasturage. At the start a bitter north-east wind had been blowing, but when the sun came out in the early afternoon it was quite hot.

The Yellow River plain was reached the next day after crossing the West Ma-la-yi Pass, 14,490 feet. The Huang Ho, or Yellow River, so mighty and so dangerous in its lower course, was here a small river, 30 yards wide and from 2 to 2½ feet deep, flowing over a gravelly bed. No bridge was here necessary, and Pereira records with justifiable pride that not many other Europeans could say they had forded the Yellow River. He also records that this is perhaps the only big river in China that keeps its name throughout its course. Other big rivers change their names, and small rivers generally have different names at each village on their banks. Possibly the Han River might also keep its name, but Pereira had not seen so much of it as he had of the Huang Ho. Of course the Tibetans have a different name for it. They call it Ma Chu, mother of rivers. Pereira made it 286¾ miles from Tangar.

On the Yellow River the uninhabited region stretching back to Ta-ho-pa is left behind and the country is now inhabited by nomadic Tibetans, and Pereira saw several camps of Yü-rung-wa Tibetans with their flocks of sheep and yaks. Leaving the plain he ascended a bare ridge and encamped by the Tsa-shung-chu, a river flowing from a beautiful lake 3 miles long and 3 miles wide and of a deep blue colour. The pasturage was poor but there were three Tibetan encampments round the lake. Here he stayed for a day.

On June 4 he made a short march by a small shallow lake with Tibetan encampments round it and halted for another day at a good grazing ground to give his mules a chance of feeding on better pasturage. On June 6 he reached a big plain, mostly boggy and broken ground but with good pasturage, where there were several encampments of Yü-rung-wa Tibetans. Most of their tents were black but some were white.

On June 7 he marched to Ta-yeh-ma-t'an, or Big Wild Horse Plain, a great plain stretching away to the west and south. The ground was very broken and looked as if countless men had started making shallow military pits and after digging out several spadefuls had stopped. All the Tibetans were moving in the same direction as Pereira and looked like a Biblical scene from Exodus.

The meteoric changes in the weather at this time were specially remarkable. Like the strong winds they were characteristic of Tibet. On this day, after east wind and rain, the afternoon turned out beautiful. Then the wind suddenly shifted to the north and blew like a hurricane and rain fell. Another fine spell followed and then a hurricane and rain again. Finally there was a fine and peaceful night.

The great plain was crossed the next day for 6 miles and Pereira then ascended the Yeh-niu-kou, or Wild Ox valley, fording the Dug River, 1 foot deep, four times. This river he followed up on June 9 and camped at 14,802 feet. He was

Loading the caravan at Chuh-chich Monastery.

face p. 121.

now on the range marked as Baian Kara or Baian-tu-kou on our maps, though nobody knew those names. It is the watershed between the Yangtze and the Huang Ho. He camped at an elevation of 14,802 feet, and on June 10 made a short march of only 8½ miles up a grassy valley and over the Ch'a-la Ping Pass, 14,892 feet. Then he had a nasty descent through heavy, sticky red clay and up another grassy valley lying between low hills.

His mules were again causing trouble and he hired six yaks from Tibetans to go with him to the Yangtze. After starting in mist and sleet on June 11 it turned milder and he marched 11 miles to the Sa-yung, 14,792 feet, after crossing the Ch'a-la-p'ing plateau, 15,012 feet, the highest point he had so far reached. A broken range about 5 miles S.S.E. running roughly E.S.E. is called Mu-mo-di-ya and is apparently a branch of the range marked on the maps as Baian Kara. Some of the hills were covered with snow and about 1000 feet above the valley.

Following up the broad Sa-yung valley for 11 miles on June 12 he halted at the foot of Ch'a-la-ya-k'ou Pass at 15,269 feet and reflected that there were very few people in the world except Tibetans who had encamped at that height at the age of fifty-seven. "Of all the countries I have visited," he writes, "Tibet is the most detestable—one visit is enough." He now found no difficulty in breathing even at this elevation, though a climb of even 200 feet would make him pant, and none of the other people or animals appeared to be affected by the height.

But what seemed to distress him were the rain and snow and the broken marshy ground, and the paucity of inhabitants and lack of anything to be bought.

The Ch'a la Shan, the divide between the Yangtze and Huang Ho, he crossed the next day at an elevation of 15,489 feet. Hills on either side rose some 400 to 600 feet higher and were covered with snow. This main range runs N.N.E. to S.E., and its branches are likewise covered with snow and must be about 16,000 feet high.

The headwaters of another great river, the Ya-lung, which flows down to Szechwan, lay on the far side of the Pass. It was the only great river of China he had not yet crossed, and is here known as the Ch'a Ho. He reached it after a very boggy descent from the pass, and having waded across it followed down the broad, grassy, boggy Hsia-ma-t'an valley and gradually leaving the snowy hills entered a fine rolling grass country where he camped, having marched 11 miles.

Following down this same valley on June 14 he camped by a pond after a march of 17 miles. The going was good for the first 6 miles, then marshy and broken. On the way he saw a herd of about a hundred wild asses. Snow lay on the ground as he started and a cold wind was blowing, but the snow soon melted, the day became mild, and in the afternoon he basked in the sun. There was a fine view to the south-east of a range 20 to 30 miles away, apparently of black rock and partly covered with snow.

Again, on June 15, he followed down the same

GROUP OF TIBETAN MERCHANTS—THE YÜ-SHU TRIBE.

face p. 123.

broad marshy valley for 12 miles. Then he left the Ch'a Ho (Ya-lung) valley and crossed a 200 - feet saddle into a small side valley, but on the following day came back into the Ch'a Ho valley, or Dza Chu as the Tibetans call it. The river was here 100 yards wide and 3 feet deep at the ford and flowing in three or four channels. The main range, the Yo-Lam-Sung-na, is farther south and apparently runs W.N.W. to E.S.E., diverting the Ya-lung easterly. About 5 miles on either side are two ranges running roughly north and apparently forming branches to the Yo-Lam-Sung-na. Pereira camped by the small Ba Chu stream near where it joins the Ya-lung. There was good grazing, and he was again among nomads for there were several encampments of Yü-shu Tibetans of the Gaba tribe.

Continuing down the valley of the Ya-lung for another 20 miles, on June 17 he reached the Chu-chieh Monastery which Sorensen called the Drip-yu. It is situated about half-a-mile west of the river and is enclosed by an uncemented stone wall with the square temple in the centre and in front of it the monastery green, a filthy place, some 60 yards square, on which Pereira camped; much relieved, however, to reach an inhabited place again. The monastery contained a hundred lamas of the red sect, who lived in small single- or two-storied mud buildings. Outside the walls were a few Tibetan encampments. Excepting the barracks at Ta-ho-pa and the village of Ch'a-pu-ch'a, this was the first building Pereira had seen since entering Tibet.

From here onward he again used " ula ", that

is, hired transport, and said he would never again use mules in Tibet. The poor animals are not suited to it. Well fed for several months before and with light loads they could manage it. But even in the mild season his poor mules felt the cold, and as they had been poorly fed when he bought them they were never properly fit.

The Ka-na Monastery was reached on the 18th at 16¼ miles. The way led down the broad Ya-lung valley, which opens out to a plain called Jamba about 5 miles wide. Two miles from the Monastery the Ya-lung bends away E.N.E., and the road leads over a low hill into the narrow Retchin valley. The monastery contains two hundred lamas of the red sect.

The next day's march of 19¼ miles led first over the La-m'e ridge, 14,050 feet, then down and up narrow valleys with small Tibetan camps, and at 9 miles up an easy ascent to the Ja-rong Pass, 14,060 feet, over the divide between the Ya-lung and Yangtze Rivers. From this the way lay down a narrow valley between hills from 12,000 to 15,000 feet in height. This was the steepest country he had been travelling through for a long time. The western hills were rocky and the path often stony or leading over broken or marshy ground.

The first cuckoo was heard on the march and Pereira saw the first marmot since leaving Ko-Ko Nor—also four wild pigeons. In the valley were many five-petalled buttercups and some small red and blue daisies. Also he came across scrub a few inches high and small bushes 2 or 8 feet high—the first he had seen since leaving Ta-

Hsiu Monastery.

face p. 125.

ho-pa. It was quite a summer's day for these parts.

He lodged that night in a room of the Hsiu Monastery. It contains about eighty lamas and is pleasantly situated at the confluence of two streams which flow into the Yangtze and facing grass hills. In front is a level patch of grass about half a mile wide. Here Pereira halted for a couple of days waiting for the yaks with his baggage. Of four mules which he had left with the Tibetans two had died and two had been sold for twenty-two taels for the two. At the monastery he bought some quite good butter and rice. He was also brought a dish of "chiao-ma", banana hemp, small long brown roots with bulbous ends. It tasted like sweet potato but much better. This was the first vegetable he had seen since Tangar.

Very steep paths, barely 1 foot wide, led up the rocky hill-side, past coarse vegetation, to the narrow uneven tiers of terraces on which are built the monks' houses, small mud buildings painted slate-grey in the centre, with narrower bands of red and white on the sides and above. The roofs were flat. The temples are of mud painted with red above a broad tier of brushwood into which are let bronze designs of various patterns, some circular, some like bells and some representing stags. On the edge of the flat roof are curious large bronze ornaments apparently representing bells and other ornaments. There were a few patches of barley cultivation. And at the foot of the hill is a Tibetan village of about twenty houses.

Pereira tried to pay the owner of the room he had occupied, but he would not accept payment. Pereira therefore gave him five squares of red cloth as a present. His baggage having arrived on June 21 on yaks and with it nine hundred taels intact, he resumed his journey on the 22nd, following down the Hsiu-we Chu valley for 12 miles and passing two monasteries, a few Tibetan farms and one small Tibetan village with some patches of barley cultivation. He then reached the Yangtze, or Di Chu, here called the T'ung-t'ien Ho by the Chinese, and followed it up for 1½ mile to the ferry.

The Yangtze river is here 80 yards wide and very deep, with a strong current and small rapids. The party had to cross it in seven skin coracles, each paddled over by one or two Tibetans. These vessels are very light, and the current sweeps them down till the paddlers can make the final effort and get through. The eight horses and six mules had to swim across, most of them with the head held by a rope from a coracle. Luckily it was a really hot summer's day and the water not too cold, and all got over safely.

The hills about here were from 700 to 1000 feet high. One hill to the south-east rose about 1500 feet above the valley and had some snow on it.

Jye-kundo was reached at last on June 28. The way led down the right bank of the Yangtze for 5 miles. A Tibetan village of eight houses and a little cultivation was passed and also a willow, a fir and two or three other trees, the first Pereira had seen since Ta-ho-pa. He then

CROSSING THE T'UNG-T'IEN HO (YANGTZE) IN CORACLES.

face p. 127

followed up the Pa Chu, 20 or 30 yards wide, with a strong current and clear water. The valley was from 2 to 400 yards wide and the hills from 700 to 1000 feet high. In this valley were about a dozen small Tibetan villages, mostly of from six to eight houses, and small fields of barley. And Pereira saw a snake eighteen inches long, a marmot and three or four bittern. At 18 miles he passed Shin-tai, a village of forty houses, where there was a large square wall of stones which looked like a ruined temple. And at 22½ miles he reached Jye-kundo, 11,820 feet, a poor city of mud houses built on the hill-side, the camp and the yamen being about half a mile off in the valley of the Pa Chu.

From Tangar to Jye-kundo was 518¾ miles, and Pereira had accomplished the journey in thirty-six stages exclusive of eight days' halt. But his horses and mules were thoroughly exhausted on arrival.

CHAPTER XIII

JYE-KUNDO TO CHAMDO

JYE-KUNDO or Chieh-ku in Chinese is officially called Yü-shu-hsien, pronounced locally Yü-fu. Yü-shu, meaning "jade tree", is evidently taken from a Tibetan name. The Tibetans in these parts are of the Gaba tribe and appear to be a very mixed race, unlike the Mongols or the fine types of Aryan and Lolo at Ta-chien-lu. They are short, about 5 feet 6 inches in height, with almond eyes, sunken cheeks, long unkempt hair, snub, hooked or aquiline noses, long moustaches at the end but no hair under the nose and hairless lips. They dress usually in long cloth coats with trousers tucked into long cloth boots, the upper part usually red or red and blue; and wear no head covering.

The Monastery of Jye-kundo stands on the saddle of a 200-feet spur, about half a mile to the north end of the city. Three hundred lamas and "huo-sheng" of the red sect live here and are presided over by an abbot (khem-po), who is sent from the Sakya Monastery south-west of Shigatse in Tibet and changed every two or three years. All houses in Sakya monasteries, as at Hsiu-Gomba, are painted in slate colour, with red and white band borders on sides and top. The exceptions are the abbot's house, the temple and some houses of the higher monks, which are painted red. The owner of the land, somewhat corresponding to a "Father procurator", is called the Pum-po. He also lives in a red-painted house.

To this house Pereira was invited by the Pum-po. At the door and in the entrance chamber were suspended skins of a horse, yak, sheep, dog, etc., stuffed with straw. From here Pereira ascended some steep wooden ladder steps to a small room where he was regaled with dried persimmons and uninviting tea with rancid butter in it. The Pum-po was anxious to know whether China and Tibet would now fight, as the prophecy had been that there would be peace for three years, and that period was now up. He said that both Jye-ku and Jye-kundo were used as names for the town and they were both Tibetan words, the latter being derived from the former and "du" meaning "assemblage". So the longer word meant the assemblage of the people who formed the town after the erection of the monastery. The Chinese name, "Yü-shu", he said, came from the Tibetan words "Yül-shül", meaning "country formed". When the twenty-five tribes of Gaba amalgamated they gave the district this name.

The annual festival took place during Pereira's stay at Jye-kundo. The lamas collected in the courtyard of the temple, seating themselves round the abbot who sat by the portico facing and in the centre of the monks. These monks recited prayers and rang small bells and then adjourned to the temple, where they were each given a big bowl of tsamba, the higher lamas sitting on raised stools being given in addition special delicacies such as pyramids of rancid butter. To this ceremony the common people were not admitted, but Pereira and Madame Nèel, a French lady on a visit to Jye-kundo for the purpose of studying Tibetan Buddhism, had received a special invitation to be present.

Two monks with long ropes walked about belabouring the shoulders of any lama caught talking. And for some minutes the noise of the whacking dominated over all other sounds. When all the monks had gone out the two Europeans as a great privilege were admitted to see the decorations. There were some circular things impossible to describe which looked like linoleum camp baths with sides six inches high. Around them on the sides were numerous brass bowls of various sizes, some filled with evil-smelling wax and looking like huge night-lights, some with grain, and some with rancid butter painted brown to resemble a tree with coloured butter flowers.

In the courtyard was a crowd of Tibetans, chiefly beggars, who were given the remains of the feast after the ceremony. There were many types among them, but the principal type more resembled a Red Indian than the puffy-cheeked Mongol.

Bronze ornaments decorated the top of the temple. The centre one looked like a long bell placed on a coronet. The side ones, also looking like long bells, are, according to Madame Nèel, symbols of victory. Gold ornaments are only allowed on temples and houses of kings. The houses of lesser people, like the Pum-po, are adorned with erections made of black yak rope, tied round and round with broad strips of white linen.

Higher up than the monastery was the red two-storied verandahed house of the abbot. And higher still is a small white-washed house with a high wall where lamas retire to meditate in solitude—some for a few months, some for life.

The horrid smell of rancid butter and the dirty narrow streets on the hill-side make the place very unsavoury. In the more open parts there was a coarse vegetation which the Tibetans call "deer grass".

Madame Nèel was an elderly Parisian lady, the wife of the Chief of the Railways in Tunis. She had been five years in China and Tibet and had been collecting Tibetan books. Two or three of these years she had spent in the Kumbum monastery, and she had adopted as her son a young lama of the red sect who was a minor "living Buddha" from South Tibet. She used to dress in a long red robe.

She could talk English fluently, and from her long and intimate acquaintance with Tibetan life she was able to give Pereira much valuable information. She said P'eu-yul was the right name for Tibet. It means the country of the Peu people. The tribes round Jye-kundo are called Gaba. Khamba means people of Kham, which is farther east, but includes these twenty-five Gaba tribes. These Tibetans hate the Tibetans of Lhasa and would much prefer to be under Chinese rule. In Tibet the red sect, the original Buddhists, are stronger than the yellow sect, the reformers. They are chiefly found in Kham and outer Tibet, while the reforming yellow sect are found in inner Tibet. There is also a black sect, called Pun, who have kept up some of the superstitions of the old pagan religion, worshipping, for instance, the snake and a white stone with the characters for snake on it. The adopted son told Pereira that this Pun sect is scattered about Tibet, and there are some on the Chinese border near Li-fan-ting and Kwan-hsien. While the Buddhists go round the Men-dong—prayer wells—from right to left, the black sect reverse the process.

Madame Nèel said the only really orthodox Buddhists are in Burma and Ceylon. These do not worship images and do not recognise the spiritual authority of the Dalai Lama at Lhasa or the Tashi Lama at Shigatse, who in many ways has more spiritual authority than the Dalai Lama though he has not the latter's temporal power.

The big square pile of stones which Pereira had seen at Shih-tsi on the last stage into Jye-kundo Madame Nèel said is called a " mani ", *i.e.* jewel. It is one of the biggest she had seen. It is supposed that the sacred stone came out of the ground here. People throw stones on it, and after generations the present huge square, perhaps a hundred feet or more of a side, is built up. The outer flat stones have pious ejaculations inscribed on them and are let into the sides, and prayer wheels are put in niches.

According to Madame Nèel the monks are divided into two classes, Lama and Traba, pronounced Taba. Lama means "excellent one ", and the Lama class consists of living Buddhas, re-incarnations, heads of monasteries and learned professors. The Traba class consists of all who wear the monastic habit. The Gelong must be over twenty-one and are vowed to perpetual chastity. They start as boys as "Gegner". Then they become "Getsul". Lastly they become "Gelong".

Together with Madame Nèel and her adopted son Pereira rode out one day—a beautiful hot day—to the Tangar monastery fair. The fair is held in a narrow valley 4¾ miles from Jye-kundo. Here small white or black tents are pitched. Animals, meat, cloth, silk, carpets, brass pots and many lesser articles are offered for sale. The crowd presented every variety of Tibetan physiognomy. There were long-shaped and round-shaped heads, snub and aquiline noses. Most men were rather short, but some were tall. And some had long hair partly hanging down in front of the ears, as was the fashion in the time of Charles II. One man from Kham had a false queue of rope wound round his head to protect him from sword-cuts.

Pereira and Madame Nèel arrived just in time to see the procession of monks descend from the monastery on the hill-side opposite. They were dressed in red robes with an extra yellow or bright scarlet jacket. And all wore rather picturesque narrow hats, almost flat in the centre, but with brims turned up both in front and behind, with red underneath and yellow on top. These head-dresses are peculiar to the Kangyut sect and are only worn at certain functions. A small altar had been erected by the river-side, and on it was a big bowl probably filled with holy water. After a short ceremony, accompanied by beating of gongs and clanging of cymbals, the monks dispersed.

Later the son of the king of the twenty-five Gaba tribes passed the fair on his way to Jyeku monastery. He was escorted by some fifty Tibetans preceded by Chinese soldiers with banners and trumpets.

Jye-kundo, though far from being a fashionable summer resort, was to Pereira infinitely preferable to Tangar. He found interest in strolling by the river outside the town and watching Tibetan life in summer weather. To the south was the Chieh-kou river, generally quite shallow, with two plank bridges across it. It breaks into several channels, between which are flat stretches of very green grass on which were pitched several of the white tents of Tibetan merchants who were squatting inside them with the side walls fastened up. Hundreds of naked boys were running about, some in circles, some in lines, all in the highest spirits. Small groups by the road-side were chatting, turning prayer wheels or spinning cotton. One party of girls were playing with a skipping rope; another small girl had a garland of flowers round her brow like a miniature Ophelia. Around in the valley and on the lower slopes were green fields of young barley.

Prices at Jye-kundo were absurdly high. Tsamba cost four times as much as it cost at Tangar. The Commandant, or Ma P'u-chou, was a Mohammedan, tall and of military bearing and very agreeable. Pereira called on him, and he told

Pereira there were seventy cavalry at Jye-kundo, sixty or seventy at Cheng-tu monastery, three or four stages to the north, and sixty or seventy scattered around in small detachments.

The Hsien yamen is in a mud-walled enclosure at the extreme west end of the town. The magistrate, Liu-Ling-yün, was a Kansu man and very friendly. He told Pereira there were 240 families in Jye-kundo, of whom two hundred were Tibetan and forty Chinese.

On July 10 Pereira set out again on his journey, making now for Chamdo. He took with him his boy, his interpreter and two mounted men. He had four riding ponies, besides a pack pony and one mule which he had not sold. But for transport he now relied upon " ula " yaks and engaged twenty-three. He crossed the Jye-kundo valley, here a grass plain 1¼ mile wide, and after fording the west branch of Ba Chu left the Jye-kundo valley and ascended a narrow stony valley. After a most tiring climb of 1870 feet he reached the small irregular Ba-tung plateau, 13,798 feet, and passing among some hills reached the Ba Chu again. It was here 12 yards wide and 8 feet deep. The valley was three or four miles wide and covered with pleasant green grass. It was bounded on the north by the high rocky peaks of the Sing-nak-ri-ja, which had some snow on them and form the divide between the Mekong and the Yangtze. The green grass slopes leading up to them formed a pretty contrast with these rugged peaks, and several big Tibetan camps were pitched upon them, for the grazing was excellent. This was, indeed, the pleasantest camp Pereira had found in Tibet; there were many small wildflowers, though still no trees. It was a fine hot day, and he discarded his vest for the first time in Tibet and looked about for a shady spot at the end of the march.

Next day he crossed the Ba Chu valley for three miles, seeing three or four gazelle, a marmot and two hares, besides the usual "ara" rats. Then he reached the hills and followed up the narrow valley of the Rong-do stream, which was 2 feet deep and flowing swiftly. The hills were high and rocky, but there was grass on them, and a little scrub and three small trees, and the valley was thick with small wildflowers. In it were a few small Tibetan camps. At 10¼ miles he started a steep climb over a hill and then over a southerly spur and up a bleak winding valley to the summit of the Shung La Pass, 15,724 feet, on the Yangtze-Mekong divide, and the highest point he had yet reached. The descent from this was very steep and stony, but at 16 miles from Ba Chu the way led down the pleasant Jye Chu valley, which, though stony and marshy in part, had some good grazing and was occupied by some Tibetan camps.

Travelling was now proving much pleasanter. On July 12 he followed down the Jye Chu, which is here joined by the Yeay Chu and forms the Lung Chu. It was a nice grassy valley lying between high rugged peaked hills of fantastic shapes. At 6 miles the La Chu stream from the north was forded, and from there the way was between grass hills with at last some small fir trees and a fair amount of scrub. At 11 miles he reached the Rashi Gomba, which contains a thousand monks and has a temple with a fine small gold roof.

Near here, according to Teichman, the Dutch missionary Rijnhart disappeared in 1898. He started to cross a river by himself to a Tibetan camp, but was never heard of again. He was probably drowned. His wife, who was travelling with him, reached the Rashi monastery and travelled thence *via* Jye-kundo to Ta-chien-lu. She is the author of *With Tibetans in Tent and Temple.*

A little farther on Pereira passed a Chinese caravan from Lhasa. They said they had taken forty-five days. At 17½ miles he left the Lung Chu, which soon joins the Dze Chu, and went northerly for a mile up the latter, which is the eastern branch of the Mekong and is seventy or eighty yards wide with a very strong current. This Pereira had to cross by a coracle ferry. There was only one coracle, and taking the baggage over occupied some time. The six animals swam over safely. The " ula " yaks did not cross. The party camped during a downpour of rain on the opposite bank at Lu-ga-rung, 12,490 feet. He here found that he was following the route Teichman took to Chamdo in 1918.

On July 13 he followed down the Dze Chu valley for 8½ miles and then climbed to the Ja-he-la, 12,770 feet, and farther on to the Sha-ru-la, 13,870 feet. The descent from here was down a grass valley to the camp at Chih-ku-ch'a-mo, 17¾ miles. The people of these parts are of the Rashi tribe under the rule of the Rashi monastery. On arrival one Tibetan, to show his respect, not only extended the palms of his hands but also put out his tongue several times.

The ula transport arrangement worked excellently. He found the yaks waiting for him in the morning, and he gave their owners eight rupees a day and three extra as wine money.

On the way Pereira passed a living Buddha. He was a boy of ten riding with two monks. He wore a broad-brimmed, low-crowned yellow hat, surmounted by what looked like a top.

Göche Gomba, 14 miles, 12,370 feet, was reached on the following day after crossing two low passes. The monastery is under the king (Jyelbo) of Nang-chen and contains thirty lamas. Two miles to the south is a range of rocky hills about 1500 feet high called Göche-doma.

Following up the Ray Chu valley, on July 15, for 4 miles between high rocky hills, there was then a steep climb to the top of the Ka-la-la, 13,360 feet, and 3½ miles farther on the Kearzung La, from which there is a fine view to the west over countless ranges on the west side of the Mekong. The descent at first was very steep and rocky, and then very slippery down a grass slope. At 15 miles there was a steep stony descent for a mile through a small pine wood to the Ku Chu, a swift stream, 2 feet deep. Afterwards the going was easy down the valley. The hill-side was partly red sandstone. Pereira camped that night at Kanda, 11,900 feet, a hamlet of thirteen hovels, close to the Dze Chu or Mekong.

The Mekong is here from a quarter to three-quarters of a mile wide, and with a fairly strong current and many sandbanks covered with beech.

The hills on either side are about 600 feet high and covered with grass. In the valley are several small villages with mud or stone houses and fields of still green barley round them.

This valley Pereira followed down on July 16 and at 10½ miles reached Gurde Druka, 11,630 feet, where there was a coracle ferry over the Mekong. There was only one coracle and the animals had to swim, being stoned to make them swim across. The river was here 200 feet wide. The ferry operation occupied two and three-quarter hours. The village consisted of eight houses. Beyond the ferry Pereira passed over a small sandy plain and crossed a small valley to Nay Rawa, 11,720 feet, a village of eight mud houses. These Tibetan villages, like the Chinese, are ruled by a headman, Kanpu, who arranges the "ula".

The route on July 17 lay up the Cham valley for 3½ miles. The going was good, though marshy in places. It led among irregular grass hills devoid of trees or bush. There was grass in the valley and barley fields near the small villages. At 4 miles Pereira forded the Cham Chu, which was only 18 inches deep, and encamped on the left bank, as enough "ula" transport had not been collected. It was a dull cloudy day and a little rain fell in the morning. He was now east of Teichman's route.

Continuing up the Cham Chu valley on the following day he crossed the Cham La, 12,880 feet, at 10¾ miles. It is probably east of the pass marked Rudeb on the maps. The descent was easy, leading down a broad grass slope to Bay-ja, a village of twenty-two families, with three Chinese in charge of salt. Bay-ja lies in rolling grass country, and the salt works are on the opposite side of the Say-shung Chu. Here Pereira rested for a day. He was travelling on a route probably east of Kozloff's, whose route he thought must lie between his own and Teichman's. The Tsedosi of Kozloff is probably Bando—at least the latter is at the confluence of the Ba Chu and Dze Chu.

On July 20 he ascended an open valley for 4 miles and then gradually ascended for another 4 to the Jyu La, 13,180 feet, with a rocky range, 1500 feet high, on the left. This pass, like the Cham La, is on the divide between the Mekong and the Ba Chu. On the far side the way lay down a pleasant grass valley between grass hills from 500 to 800 feet high. There was one village in the valley and some barley fields. There was, too, a wealth of wildflowers, making large patches of blue and yellow. And for the first time in Tibet Pereira saw frogs and grasshoppers.

About 5 miles from the pass the Lung Chu from the west and the Do Chu from the south-east unite and flow north-east into the Mekong. He forded the Do Chu, which was 20 yards wide and 2 feet deep, to Panchang, a hamlet of six houses, and there he encamped as usual on the clean mud roof terrace of a house. The headman came to meet him with palms extended and tongue put out.

The inhabitants said they belonged to the Durung tribe under a T'u-ssu, who is himself under the king of Nang-chen who lives at Ma-shung, three stages to the south-west over the hills. The Hlato tribes are farther to the north.

Rain fell heavily as Pereira started on July 21, but cleared subsequently. He had a stiff climb to the Sera La, 13,810 feet, on the Mekong-Ngom Chu divide, and from there had a fine view over ranges to the north, with one great range partly covered with snow about 30 miles off running south-east. From here he passed down a valley with many wildflowers, and at 14½ miles reached Ganda monastery, the last 2 miles being through fir trees. This monastery is situated among fir trees at an elevation of 12,810 feet and holds one hundred monks. It is under China, the Chino-Tibetan border being a short way to the south. The Nang-chen king is the ruler.

Pereira was now in more wooded country than he had been in for a long time. The hills were covered with fir as he followed down the Ganda Chu on July 22. At 6 miles he forded the river and then had a stiff rough climb over rocks and among the firs in a side valley till at 8 miles he crossed the Si-tsou La, 12,910 feet. The descent, still among firs, was also rough and steep and led to the Tang-kwa valley. At 10 miles Pereira reached Tang-kwa, 12,330 feet.

The Chino-Tibetan frontier was crossed on this march 1½ mile from Ganda monastery and 172 miles from Jye-kundo. The country north of it is under the king of Nang-chen. South of it the people are under Chamdo.

Proceeding down the Tang-kwa valley the next day Pereira reached Su-rü, 11½ miles. Twice he crossed the river by brushwood bridges. The valley was narrow and the hills about 800 feet high and mostly covered with fir. At 6½ miles the Tang-kwa stream is joined by the Ganda stream and forms the Si Chu. At 9½ miles he reached the Ngom Chu, the western branch of the Mekong which unites with the other branch at Chamdo. This Ngom Chu valley he followed down to Su-rü, the hill-sides being rather steep and covered with fir. His boy picked a lot of quite good wild strawberries, and he saw three French partridges. Pereira was told here that if any Tibetan is caught killing an animal, the tendons of his arms and legs are cut.

The night was wet and the next day was dull and drizzly. He continued down the Ngom Chu valley between rather steep hills covered with trees, mostly firs. Where the valley was open there were a few houses and barley cultivation, and there were a good many donkeys of a small type and cattle grazing. At 7½ miles he passed the Monda monastery of fifty monks. He stopped for the night at Benor (the Benortsoma of Teichman). The scenery here was very picturesque.

On July 25 he again followed down the Ngom Chu, and at 7¼ miles crossed it by a fine pile bridge. This was built long ago, it was said, by the monks. For Tibetans it is a wonderful engineering feat considering the fierce current which dashes against the piers. These piers, 15 to 20 feet square, are built of logs with stones, two on the banks and two in the river with blockhouses over them. From the bridge there is a steep climb to the Sagang monastery, and Pereira went on to Jara-kara which is off the road high up on a small

THE SI-WA-LA OF CHAMDO.

face p. 1/3.

plateau. The headman here was a woman. Small wild cherries and, farther on, unripe wild peaches were seen here.

Continuing down the Ngom Chu valley on July 26 the hills were at first covered with grass, but after 9 miles there were again some trees and bushes. A few small villages and some cultivation were passed. At 10½ miles is the Yangda monastery with thirty monks, from which the road descends to the small Yangda Chu and crosses it by a plank bridge. Beyond this the Ti-za La, 10,950 feet, was crossed at 14 miles, and Lamda, 10,760 feet, was reached at 15½ miles. Here Pereira put up in a clean room. He was treated with the greatest respect at every village where he halted, the people coming out to lead his horses, and the headmen bustling about to make things comfortable.

Again, on July 27, he followed down the Ngom Chu valley between grass hills 1000 feet high. Only a few were clothed with trees. By the roadside was some bush, including wild gooseberries. At 10 miles was Nguro-zamba, a village of seven families, where he ought to have crossed the river by a fine pile bridge, but it had been temporarily damaged by the swollen river. He halted for the night at Sagang, 13 miles, and here a small official with a secretary arrived to welcome him on behalf of the Si-wa-la of Chamdo. He brought a scarf and three small plates of sweets and dried fruits.

Chamdo was reached on July 28. The road wound down among the hills along a muddy and often stony path and along rocky hill-sides. At 9½ miles the Ngom Chu was crossed by a pile bridge consisting of three piles in the stream and two on the sides, and a quarter of a mile beyond is the dirty little village of Chamdo, 10,500 feet, situated on a narrow wedge of land at the junction of the Ngom Chu and the Dze Chu. The whole of Chamdo turned out to see Pereira, the women wearing wonderful head-dresses, the men with big ear-rings in the left ear, and small boys grinning and saluting in English fashion.

Chamdo is 258½ miles from Jye-kundo and 793 miles from Tangar.

CHAPTER XIV

CHAMDO TO LHASA (1)

THE crucial point of the whole journey had now been reached. All depended upon whether he could get leave from the Dalai Lama to go to Lhasa. If that were granted all would be well. If it were refused Pereira would have liked to go *via* Batang to Yünnan. But he might be stopped there also and have to retrace his steps over a weary 800 miles to Tangar, and that not in the summer but in the autumn and winter. He had started from Peking in February 1921 and it was now July 1922: it would be a dreary business after the year and a half of effort to have to go back on his tracks just as his goal was in sight.

He called upon the Drepon to discuss the situation. This Tibetan official explained that in the previous year strict orders had come from Lhasa that no one was to be permitted to go there without a passport. Pereira asked him to send a messenger to Lhasa to obtain the necessary permission. The Drepon agreed and suggested that Pereira should also write to Major Bailey, the British Political Agent in Sikkim. The messenger started on July 31, but as he would take at least eleven days to get to Lhasa and eleven days back, and there might be delay at Lhasa itself, Pereira would have to possess his soul in patience for some time and assume, in the face of the Tibetans, that of course the reply would be favourable.

Chamdo is a remote spot in which to have to wait for several weeks, but it is not entirely unknown to Europeans. Three British Consuls, Teichman, Coates and King, had visited it, and perhaps other travellers as well. And dirty as was the town the surroundings were by no means without beauty: the lights and shades on the mountains were often very beautiful; and the weather was warm—sometimes even hot.

The population of Chamdo, when it was under the Chinese, used to be about three hundred families. But in the fighting the village was partly destroyed, and now there were only 180 families. These were nearly all Tibetan, though a few were Chinese with Tibetan wives. The shops were evidently very poor, and a few pounds would have bought up the whole contents.

The monastery is situated on high ground on the narrow peninsula between the two branches of the river. Formerly there were three thousand monks attached to it, but after the Chinese burnt it in the fighting of 1912 there were only four hundred. And from the number which Pereira saw when he visited it he judged there were even fewer. A steep climb of 80 to 100 feet brought him to the higher ground of the monastery. It had been partly restored, but many ruined mud and stone walls still remained. Pereira thought it had not the curious attraction and novelty of most Tibetan temple buildings, and the new edifices of stone covered with mud are mostly low and sombre. In the chief temple there were only about a dozen monks chanting prayers and beating drums with curious hooked sticks. Two rows of square wooden pillars ran across the square hall. They had huge mud heads, apparently of Chinese design, with dresses to represent the bodies tied round the pillars. They appeared to represent Chinese deities and warriors. A small flight of steps led up to the doors of the inner sanctuary. The Pu-sa was hidden under "Katas" (ceremonial scarves), and big black mud devils were arranged down the sides. Pereira climbed to the top of the chief temple up several almost perpendicular flights of stairs, at the top of which was a bear pole, a log with notches cut in it for foothold.

The Chamdo Province is governed by a lama called the Kalon Lama. A lesser lama called the Si-wa-la rules in the interior. The Dalai Lama has a representative here and also a lama, called the Drepon, in charge of the soldiers. The Si-wa-la was a nice old lama aged 69. He lived in a pleasant little country house which from the outside looked rather like a temple. It was surrounded by willow trees and guarded by three mastiffs. He was supported on to the roof to be photographed by Pereira.

The soldiers numbered about sixty. Some had khaki jackets and coloured breeches, and some khaki breeches and coloured jackets. For headgear they wore a sort of felt hat. They looked like a rabble. They only drilled on Sundays, and one Sunday Pereira went out to have a look at them. They were dressed in a variety of uniforms. Most had puttees and brown ammunition boots of very poor quality made in Tibet. They were a slovenly-looking lot and held themselves badly. Several men were 5 feet 9 inches or 5 feet 10 inches in height, but most were shorter. They had Lee-Metford rifles but with the sights missing; and the rifles were dirty, though they did show some signs of having been oiled. The instructor knew his English drill fairly well. He pronounced his words of command clearly though not sharp enough, and did not trouble to correct errors. They did the manual squad drill, extending and closing, and practised snapping, standing, kneeling, sitting and lying down. With a good English instructor, drill for an hour twice a day, care of arms and some shooting practice, they might have been made a smart squad in a month, Pereira thought. But their present practice was to drill only two hours a week.

The bandmaster came from Darjiling and had been ten years with the Tibetans. He spoke a certain amount of English. The band consisted of seven men. They had two bagpipes from England (or perhaps Scotland!), bugles from Shanghai and side drums. The bandmaster assured Pereira that they had a thousand pieces of music and could play "God Save the King". At Pereira's request the Indian sergeant and one man marched up and down playing "Highland Laddie" on the bagpipes. They played it quite well and without any notes on the spur of the moment.

Praying is the chief duty of the soldier in

barracks; and twice when passing the barracks in the evening Pereira heard them chanting vigorously.

The people of the place seemed to be cheery and friendly. Pereira says they were fond of flowers, and put pots of flowers in their balconies. The little children were very jolly, dancing about and full of fun. On a Feast Day in August several picnic parties went out to the open ground across the river, taking with them their kettles and pans and cooking in the open, after which there was dancing. In the kitchen gardens at the extreme end of the peninsula overlooking the river junction there were diminutive plots of cabbages, turnips, onions and tobacco—also some flowers. Excellent wild raspberries were also procurable in plenty.

News of Sorrensen, the Norwegian missionary—not to be confused with Sorensen, the Dane—was brought in by an arrival from Ta-chien-lu. He had attempted to get to Lhasa, but had been turned back and was now just arriving at Ta-chien-lu.

Pereira's luck was better—though at the very last moment there appeared to be a hitch. The messenger returned from Lhasa on September 1. But nothing was communicated to Pereira till the 3rd, and he heard that the messenger had not brought any passport. Pereira believed that the Lhasa authorities had advised the Drepon to try and induce him to give up the journey to Lhasa. For the Drepon suggested that he should return to Jye-kundo. But Pereira indignantly refused to return. Then a second message came from the Drepon to say that if he was determined to go to Lhasa he could not stop him and would provide "ula". Pereira replied that he would go. And on September 3 the Drepon paid him a visit, and besides a welcome present of three tins of salmon brought with him a letter from the Kalon at Lhasa saying that he would be glad to see him at Lhasa. He brought also a belated letter of June from Major Bailey giving the result of the Derby.

"Many obstacles have blocked me", writes Pereira in his diary on September 3, "but I was determined to win through at all fair costs. And at last it looks like coming off. I would rather have died in attempting it than have chucked it up from funk. If the Government of India had said 'No', I would out of duty have chucked it. But I gather from their refusal to help me that they do not mind or will be glad if I get through on my own with the consent of the Tibetans. . . . I shall always remember that Père Schram stood out to help me at Sining-fu. He was as keen as myself for my success. How he will rub his hands if he hears I have got through."

So Pereira set about his final preparations. He enlarged the Indian map of the road from Chamdo to Lhasa, put in a lot of new detail, correcting the names of places and giving all the stages in green. But Huc's places and passes he entered in red because, though he was fairly accurate, he exaggerated the perils! Also he got both Chinese and Tibetan names of the stages.

His following now consisted of his old boy Liu, the half-caste muleteer he took on at Tangar, a

Chinese who spoke Tibetan well whom he took on at Chamdo, and a Tibetan named En Ju whom the Drepon sent with him to Lhasa.

At last, on September 6, in great spirits he started for Lhasa. But he had 670 miles of very up-and-down mountainous country to cross before Lhasa could be reached. And even Lhasa would not be the end of his journeyings. He would still have to cross the Himalaya before India was reached—no mean undertaking for a man of his age and state of health to have to contemplate.

However, on this first day's march he had a real encouragement. He met a messenger bearing a letter to him, with an excellent English translation, from the Tsarong Shapé, the Commander-in-Chief of the Tibetan Army, welcoming him to Lhasa and saying he would give him every assistance. He also said that the telegraph line had been opened to Lhasa.

For the first eight stages he would follow the main road to Nagchuka, and the first day he retraced as far as Lamda the route he had followed on his way to Chamdo. The Ngom Chu was now much sunken. Though still swift it was no longer the mad, swollen, red-coloured river of July, and the side torrents were now quiet streams. He found many wild apricots, small but quite eatable. The sun was still hot enough for him to need a helmet.

At Lamda he left the Ngom Chu and ascended the small La Chu valley. It was well wooded. At 8 miles there was a steeper rise and more trees, mostly spruce, and he saw here a musk deer. Then followed some stiff zigzags, and at

11 miles he reached the top of a spur which he thought must be a pass, but there was still a hard climb beyond to the Nam-tso La, 14,867 feet. The descent was awful over countless stones—one of the worst roads he had ever been on. But at 17 miles he reached a pretty grass valley with many trees. And at 19 miles he reached La-me, commonly called Lagang.

Eleven of these 19 miles he walked, and after writing up his notes he felt quite played out. His back ached and he felt "very ancient". He would rather have done 30 miles on the English level roads. Both at Lamda and La-me there were other villages with both barley and wheat cultivation. He saw many marmots, and on the high ground several ma-chi, white bustard pheasants.

Ascending the Dze Chu valley on September 8 he reached Ngenda, wrongly called Nyulda by Rockhill, 15¾ miles. The going was mostly good and there were only two climbs. The valleys were well wooded, chiefly with fir, but there was some spruce, maple and acacia. Ngenda is a village of eleven families. And westward from here probably no white man had been since Huc and Gabet, seventy-six years before.

The main road to Lhasa goes south-west from Ngenda, but as the bridge over the Salween had been damaged by recent rains Pereira had to leave the main road and strike off north-west, for a few miles following the road to Riwoche up the right bank of the Dze Chu, an affluent of the Mekong. The going was good and the scenery beautiful. The hills were high and fairly wooded with fir.

WA-GE-WA VILLAGE.

face p. 153.

There were several small villages with fields of wheat and barley. Then at 8 miles he left the Dze Chu valley, and the Riwoche road turned more westerly up a beautifully narrow valley between high well-wooded hills. The path, though, was very stony, and at 10 miles there was a very steep climb of 1700 feet to the Wa la Ri, 14,357 feet. On the lower slopes there were trees and bushes with grass and a profusion of flowers. From the top, at 13¼ miles, there was a grand panorama of mountain ranges all round, free of snow and mostly bare. About 10 miles to the south-west was the Li-jou la, the Wa Ho mountain of Huc, a bare high hill. The descent was very steep for 1630 feet to 16¼ miles, when there was easy going to Kama Sumdo, 20¼ miles.

The only building here was a rest-house built a few months before. But nomads dwelling in tents and now living 20 or 30 miles away occupy the country. Pereira's caravan was augmented by four damsels on a pilgrimage to Lhasa, who seized the opportunity of his protection. A monk from Ta-chien-lu also joined him.

On September 10 he continued westerly up the valley of the Om Chu and passed a monastery of fifty monks. Beyond was an uninhabited country with bare hills and occasional enclosures of stone or brushwood for grazing. There was a stiff climb to 8¼ miles to the top of the Mula, 15,667 feet, which is the divide between the Salween and Mekong Rivers. The descent was easy down the bed of a stream to a house at 17 miles. At 18 miles he entered the broader grass valley of the Ta Chu, where there was one house and some tents. Mi-ru tam-da, a single house, was reached at 24¼ miles. He was assured that the Ta Chu flowed into the Salween.

"Tibetan names are most jaw-breaking", says Pereira. "I make the natives keep on repeating the accursed harrowing sounds. The following is my system of pronunciation :

é—like *ay* in *day*.
o—like *ow* in *low*.
u—like *oo* in *room*.
ch—like *ch* in *church*.
t—like *t* in *time*.
ou—like *oe* in *Joe*.
ü—like French *u*.
g, k and j—as in English.
ee—like *ee* in *week*.
gia—like *jya*.

The accent is always on the last syllable, and often on the second if three syllables."

On September 11 he marched 25¼ miles to Jung-erh, commonly called Gar-mé, where he rejoined Rockhill's route to Nagchuka *via* Riwoche. He calls it Merjong. It should be Mi-ru Jung-erh. Mi-ru is the name of the district.

After descending the Ta Chu for 1¾ mile from Kama Sumdo and passing a solitary monastery of ten monks high up on the hill-side, Pereira turned to the left and started a steep climb, then up and down over five hills, the highest, Rab-ché La, at 10 miles, 14,300 feet. Away 3 or 4 miles on the left was the high, ragged, rocky-peaked Sama Réjig, here called Gee La. From the top of the last hill, the Dung-re La, at 15 miles, there was a beautiful view westerly down the Mi-ru valley with two or three monasteries high up on the hill-side, and many small villages in the valley lower down. Most of the hill-sides and valley were cultivated. It was the most fertile valley Pereira had seen, and looked more like China than Tibet. Far away to the W.N.W. was a great snow-clad range running north and south, perhaps 40 miles off, called the Tu-ré La. This was the only thoroughly snow-covered range, except the glorious Amné Machin, which he had yet seen in Tibet. As a welcome change, too, the hills here opened out into broader valleys.

There was a steep descent for 1000 feet to the Mi-ru valley, and the Ta Chu was again reached and crossed by a log bridge. Jung-erh or Gar-mé is a village of twenty-eight families, and there were 230 soldiers on the left bank who surprised Pereira by blowing English bugle calls. He lodged in a comfortable two-storied house reserved for big officials and enjoyed a mug of Tibetan beer for dinner. He had walked 12 miles and was dog-tired. Ten years before he could race up the hills and leave all behind him. Now all was different, and instead of being first in he was usually last, behind even the yaks and the pilgrim ladies with their bundles. [But perhaps when he thus lamented his deficiencies he did not take into account the altitude at which he was marching.]

September 12 was another fine warm day with a cloudless sky, and Pereira marched 21 miles to Sia La. The Mi-ru valley is blocked on the south side by a high rugged range for 11 miles. The valley is choked by lower hills, but there are several villages with fields of wheat and barley. The path keeps to the high ground, and at 16 miles reaches the Bu Chu La, 13,550 feet, from which there is a gradual descent to Sia La. Both on this and the last march Pereira saw numbers of wild gooseberry bushes covered with small sour fruit. At Sia La was a single house—an official rest-house. The wife of an official arrived here. She had a wonderful head-dress and was bound for Shigatse *via* Nagchuka.

Denchin, the Chungbu Denchin of Rockhill, was reached on the following day after an easy march of 13 miles. At 3½ miles he crossed the Sié Chu by a log bridge and then ascended the fertile valley with several small villages—one with a five-storied mud house. At 9½ miles is the junction of the Sié Chu and the Zong Chu, and Pereira followed up the latter, fording it twice. Denchin has ninety-three families and is a very important village, as routes radiate out from it, north to Jye-kundo, west to Nagchuka, and south to Shobando. Pereira put up in a small clean room in a small monastery, the official bringing him a tray of sweets, raisins and Chinese dates.

New arrangements for "ula" transport being necessary Pereira stopped at Denchin for a day. It was a beautiful autumn day and Denchin was a charming spot. From the terrace of his house he had a fine view of the valley and of high red sandstone hills covered with grass and with patches of yellow fields. Between the Zong Chu and the village was a fertile little plain 2 miles long by half a mile broad, yellow with stubble. To the south was the Ri Ma hill, 2000 or 3000 feet high. And in the background were high limestone hills, one with a hole through the rocks.

The Tibetans seemed to be very joyous and always laughing, but also very servile. They would pass Pereira anxiously, but when they saw him nod to them they beamed and put out their tongues. He took a stroll through the village, much to the excitement of the natives, who declared he beat Barnum's freaks all to nothing! The whole village followed him, though not offensively as the Chinese do. Some of the men had queues, and the queues were some long and some short. The women wore several plaits down their backs. The soldiers were in a mixture of khaki and Tibetan garments.

The village was mostly of one-storied mud houses built at the end of a spur about 100 feet high, with the Zok Chu flowing down by the Nagchuka road on the south-west and the Zong Chu coming from the Jye-kundo route on the north-west. In the village is a pile of stones, a few of which have prayers on them, here called a Do-bum.

The official here is called a Ken-jung, and he has the same rank as the Chamdo Drepon. Pereira called on him, and for the sake of dignity rode there, though the distance to his residence was only 50 yards. From the entrance there was a very steep ascent up a ladder to the first floor. Here he was received in a large room and was offered milk and excellent crystallised fruits and sweets. He sat on a chair of state, while the Ken-jung sat on his left on an ottoman arrayed in very fine garments: a long brown robe with a bright yellow jacket, and wearing the official hat surmounted by a long pinkish stone. On his feet were wonderful coloured boots. His three secretaries squatted on divans.

There were fifty soldiers at Denchin. They

were poor at drill but very good with the bugle. Pereira heard the Officers' Call, and looking out saw eighteen soldiers, preceded by buglers playing, escorting a poor lama who had been sentenced to have his right forefinger cut off. Later the soldiers returned preceded by bagpipes playing " The Campbells are coming ".

CHAPTER XV

CHAMDO TO LHASA (2)

Setting out again on September 15 Pereira left the Nagchuka road and the tracks of Rockhill and Bower, and striking south-west took the road to Shobando, never before traversed by a white man. By a Blondin-like performance he crossed a bridge of three logs over the Zok Chu and then followed up the narrow Kwom Chu valley for 8 or 9 miles. After 2½ miles villages and cultivation ceased and the valley became very stony. At 4½ miles there was a steep ascent between rather bare grass hills about 2000 feet high. At 10¼ miles the top of the La-chin La, 14,800 feet, was reached. A steep descent led down to the La-chin Chu valley. Two brushwood bridges and one log bridge had to be crossed, and at 23¾ miles he reached I-ta-shi, a village of six families situated in a narrow valley and surrounded by four or five other small villages and a little cultivation.

Much stone-posing was observable in this valley. It is a favourite devotion of Buddhists. Some of them are remarkable feats of equilibrium. Sometimes one stone, sometimes three or four, would be used; and the most difficult stones seem to be selected. The custom exists in China, but Pereira had never seen so many as here. Piling stones is a Buddhist hobby. The piles Pereira liked best were the small piles on the top of every pass surmounted by small prayer flags. They let him know the top had at last been reached.

Great preparations were being made here for the arrival next day of the new Kalon Lama of Chamdo. He required over one hundred horses, brushwood for fuel, tents, carpets, etc.

Sing-ka was reached on September 16 after a march of 19¾ miles. There was a steep climb for 8 miles to the Do La, 14,360 feet, from which there was a glorious view—everywhere a panorama of hills with one high partially snow-covered range running N.N.W. and probably 30 miles off to the north. Most of the tops of the higher hills were bare, but many of the near hills were covered with bush and fir. The descent was very steep, as it usually seemed to be on the southern side of passes. The path was then very narrow, leading along the hill-side with a steep slope on the right.

A surprise awaited Pereira. When he was 800 feet on the hill-side above the valley, about 7 miles from Sing-ka, he was met by a view of the mighty Salween coming in from the west. The course of this great river, which flows down through Burma, was unknown as high up as this and was incorrectly marked on the maps. Here below him it was winding through a narrow valley between hills 2000 feet above it and with mountains higher still behind.

Far below were small patches of crops, and

here and there villages or a farm surrounded by yellow fields. A very steep rocky descent brought him to Sing-ka, a hamlet of two families on a small level patch 100 feet above the Salween. Pereira made the elevation of this important place 11,090 feet, which would put the Salween at about 500 feet higher than the Mekong at Chamdo.

Speculating on the population of Tibet, Pereira remarks here that the experts who put the population of Tibet at 2,000,000 must err badly. He thinks it must be far more in spite of the country being so sparsely inhabited.

A few Machi snow-white bustard pheasants were seen on the march.

Following down the valley of the Salween on September 17 he reached Ru-a-tung at 19¾ miles. The river was very winding and of a greyish colour. The path kept high up on the hill-sides, rising to 12,290 feet at the Tung-ka La at 9¾ miles. The hills were fairly wooded and covered with bush. There was a gradual descent to the ferry across a small plain with some dozen farms and a monastery of sixty monks. The fields were bordered by low trees or hedges, chiefly of wild roses and gooseberries, giving them an almost English look. As the Kalon Lama was coming, occasional attempts had been made to repair the road and improve the bridges. The spades used were of a most primitive type and more suitable for children to play with than for serious work. Pereira's party crossed the Salween near Ru-a-tung in five coracles. His two ponies swam it, and had now swum the Yangtze, Mekong and Salween.

The river is full of fish, but the Tibetans are not allowed to catch them.

Shobando was reached on September 18 in 19 miles. At 1½ mile the Salween is left, and there was more interminable climbing among scrub and bush, and on the highest slopes firs, amidst which a leopard was seen. There was a descent to the beautiful little Yim-da valley, dotted with occasional fields among the bush and with the clear stream like a blue riband running down the middle. Pereira crossed it by a log bridge at 10¼ miles at 11,300 feet, and then had another climb to the Ba-tou La, 12,100 feet, at 14 miles. Here the mountains slope down steeply on the left to the Dze Chu coming from the E.S.E., with the main Chamdo road along it, while in front is an equally steep descent to the Do Chu. Pereira went rapidly down this last and, joining the Chamdo road near the stream, followed it to Shobando.

He had had to make a long detour for the last fortnight, but he was now again on the main Lhasa road immortalised by Huc; and he had studied it so thoroughly during his stay at Chamdo that it now seemed like an old friend.

Shobando has a population of three hundred families, and there are three hundred monks and about a dozen Chinese. The Kalon Lama was here. Major Bailey had told him about Pereira and he sent many greetings, and his representative brought Pereira a present consisting of stacks of vegetables, red turnips, a kind of lettuce, potatoes, eggs, butter, tsamba, a carcase of a sheep and a huge piece of beef.

Next day Pereira called on the Kalon Lama. He was in a little sanctuary with Buddhas. He appeared to be a good man without vice, and cautioned him not to let his men squeeze. He told Pereira that a foreigner travelling in Tibet had got a bad name owing to the squeezing of his interpreter. Afterwards there was a dance in the courtyard of Pereira's house, four men whirling round and five women beating tambourines fixed on short poles with hooked sticks. Two diminutive girls occasionally joined in, while an old dame directed with a tambourine. Some of the men in single dances whirled round with great impetus.

Pereira himself took great trouble about his interpreters. He warned them that when he got to Lhasa he would ask the officials in English if there had been any misdoings, and if there were he would give the culprit a warm time.

Owing to the Kalon Lama leaving on the 20th there was not enough ula for Pereira and he had to wait another day. Shobando is probably the same as it was five hundred years ago, with its narrow, winding filthy streets, partly paved with big uneven cobbles. The houses were of mud and generally two-storied. The upper part of the little town appeared to be deserted. Beyond it, higher up on the south-east, is the old Chinese crumbling mud wall enclosing an empty space. There are one big and two small temples, and at the north-east end of the town three big chortens in which big Lamas are buried.

On September 21 Pereira marched 24½ miles to Pa-ri-nang, the Barilung of Huc. The first

7 miles were easy going up the Do Chu valley, then there was a rather steep ascent to Uk-dé La, or U-la, 13,200 feet, at 11 miles. Some of the hills were covered with fir, but most had scrub and bush, very beautiful in their autumn tints, the deep red and yellow predominating among the green. There were quantities of berries, too, in these parts. They were chiefly red. A covey of partridges was seen. From the pass there was a steady descent to the Jang-pu Chu, which was crossed at 16 miles by a bridge. It flows N.N.W. and is here 12,250 feet above sea-level. Then there was another very arduous climb to the Ja La, 13,850 feet, at 21 miles, and a steep descent to Pa-ri-nang, 12,250 feet. It consists of nine houses situated in a pleasant little valley.

The weather and the country and the people were evidently all agreeable. But Pereira was even here undergoing considerable hardship. He mentions having his provision boxes damaged on this march and losing half of his last tin of coffee and so being reduced to one tin of cocoa, after which there would be nothing but horrible native tea. Luckily in this mild weather he could drink water for luncheon and dinner. But he would generally be busy in the morning about 5.30; or marching and mapping his route till about five in the evening, and not finish writing up his notes till past nine at night. So even the best day was very tiring.

Lha-tse, 28½ miles, was reached on September 22. It is wrongly called Ga-thang on the Indian map, evidently from the Ga-tung river which flows past it but which is called Sa Chu farther

PEM-BAR.

face p. 165.

east. There were trees and bush for the first 6 miles, then bare hills for another 5, after which trees again. There was a most tedious ascent up the Baré Chu valley, very steep for the last mile and a half to the East Semé-gung La, often called Gung La, at 6 miles. At 8 miles was the West Semé-gung La, 18,800 feet. Then there was a descent along the hill-side to the Gatung Chu, and at 12 miles good going across a grass belt. Then the Gatung is joined by another river and is called the Sa Chu. Here the valley narrows, and at 20 miles the road passes through the beautiful Sa Chu gorge between high fantastic rocky hills covered with bush in gorgeous autumn tints of deep red and gold. Such scenery, Pereira thought, puts the Saxon Schweitz into the shade. The Sa Chu was here 25 yards wide, of a grey colour and deep. It was crossed by a brushwood bridge, and the road then wound round rocky hills to Lha-tse, 12,850 feet, a village of sixteen families, where there is also a small temple with thirty monks. The country was almost uninhabited; on the march only four nomad tents were seen. To the south-east of the Semé-gung La snow had recently fallen and an icy blast came from that direction. Otherwise the weather was fine and warm. The Sa Chu joined by the Jua Chu flows N.N.E. to join the Salween.

A shorter march of only 15 miles took Pereira to Pem-bar, and he was glad to rediscover traces of Huc, which are not on the Indian map, for this is obviously the Pian Pa of Huc. At 2 miles he crossed the Jua Chu by a bridge in a ravine 70 feet deep. It was, like most other bridges, made of brushwood. At 8 miles there was a very stony, steep, steady climb for 1¾ mile to the top of the Pu-dé La, 18,650 feet, from which may be seen a fine panorama down the Dam Chu valley. To the south some of the hills have small glaciers. A fairly easy descent leads to the Dam Chu valley, which is flat and half a mile wide with four farms in it. The Dam Chu is a deep torrent 80 feet wide flowing between rocks. The road, after striking the river, passes through a short and very rocky gorge, and at 12 miles reaches the Pem-bar valley, which is about a mile wide.

Pem-bar has two hundred monks and thirty-five families. Four of these families were Chinese, and they brought Pereira presents of eggs, cabbages and Chinese wine. On the S.S.W. is the peak of the sandy Riu-ma, about 16,000 feet.

On September 24 Pereira marched down the very fertile Mé Chu valley, and at 16¼ miles reached Urjien Tanda. This valley was second only to the Mi-ru valley at Jung-erh. It was undulating, cut by many spurs, and there were only occasional flat stretches. But there were a good many small villages of from four to nine houses surrounded by cultivation. At 18¾ miles was the Roka La, some 500 or 600 feet above the valleys on either side. From it to the right front could be seen the Bar-jung monastery, which has 110 monks and is situated very picturesquely on the top of a spur 800 feet high. A winding descent from the pass leads to the Sa-la Chu, soon to be called the Jung Chu, and the road along it to Urjien Tanda, a dirty little village of thirteen families and a solitary Chinese. It lies in a narrow

Mé Chu Valley.

face p. 167.

valley with high snow hills to the west. The inhabitants gave Pereira a performance of dancing, discordant singing, and acrobatic feats, such as standing on the head and vaulting on to the shoulders.

First signs of changes in the weather were now felt. Owing to rain and snow his start had been delayed. At nine it had stopped sleeting but snow remained on the hill-sides, and it was chilly enough for a coat and gloves. The day's march used generally to end with the pack-horses, the boy and interpreter arriving first, then Pereira himself and his interpreter, and the rollicking old yaks a bad third. He would then find his chair, bed and table ready upon arrival.

The highest pass so far crossed, and what was reckoned the worst on the road, the Shiar-güng La, on the Salween-Tsang Po divide, was crossed on September 25. First there was a steep climb up a bare hill-side to the Dor-jee La, 14,600 feet, at 5 miles. Then the path wound along the hill-side through snow, and finally there was a very steep ascent to the top of the famous Shiar-güng La, 16,528 feet, which was the highest altitude Pereira had ever reached. All the high mountains round were snow-covered, but as snow had fallen two nights before he could not say whether this snow was normal. There was a regular jumble of high mountains in every direction. But towering over the rest was one in shape like the Matterhorn, which must have been well over 18,000 feet in height. A very steep descent through snow for a mile and then a gradual descent led to the Chara Chu valley and over most terrible boulders and rocks, strewn about as if some Titan had broken them up for road mending, to a beautiful gorge covered with bush. The road then crosses the stream, and, much to the consternation of Pereira, there was then still another climb of 700 feet to the little plateau on which stands Nam-jé-garm, where he halted after a march of 20½ miles.

Looking east from below the Dorji-La.

face p. 169.

CHAPTER XVI

CHAMDO TO LHASA

THE basin of the Tsang Po, the Brahmaputra, had now been reached. Pereira sighed with relief at the thought that the worst pass was now behind. He was in country whose waters drained to India. He was in the basin of a river into which the water from Lhasa flowed. He was obviously nearing his goal and was half-way from Chamdo to Lhasa. But he had still a succession of high ridges to cross and winter was drawing near.

Alando was reached on September 26 after a long march of 24 miles. The way led at first down the Chara Chu valley. The river flows into the Tsang Po, but it is only possible to go down the valley in winter when the river is frozen. On the south on this day's march were ranges with snow-covered peaks which must be 16,000 feet high with higher still behind, and one solitary high peak. The lower slopes were covered with fir. The going was good for 10 miles and the path lay about 600 feet above the river. A good many villages surrounded with fields were passed. Then there was an ascent of 600 feet by a not very wide rocky path with an almost precipitous drop to the river. After this the path leads down again to the river, which at 18 miles narrows and winds through a beautiful little wood. This wood Huc describes as a thick fir forest, but Pereira says it was like an English wood with undergrowth and trees of all sorts. Beyond the wood the river is crossed by two rickety log bridges. Alando is a poor village of nine families, on a narrow strip in a narrow winding valley. There had been frost in the night but the day was quite hot.

Of the march next day Huc had spoken in exaggerated terms, and parts indeed were shocking; if it could be called a road it was the worst Pereira had seen in 40,000 or 50,000 miles of travel in the Far East. But there was nothing alarming in it. The scenery was magnificent, the route lying between fir-covered hills 2000 feet high and through delightful woods. Leaving the Sia Chu valley the path turns first northerly and then westerly through the Nok Chu defile. The Nok Chu, a foaming torrent, is crossed twice by log bridges and the path zigzags up and down the mountain-side never more than 400 feet above it and sometimes alongside it. Between 11 and 18 miles there is some very bad going over rocks and boulders which have been falling for centuries and are of all shapes except smooth. At 12¾ miles is A-lan-ga, a hamlet of three houses on a rather more open piece of sloping ground. A mile farther the defile narrows to a gorge. At 19½ miles a more open valley is reached with a sloping grass belt and some trees, and the hills are less precipitous. Beyond this the Ja-bu Chu, a torrent 3 feet deep, is crossed by a log bridge and there is a steep climb of 150 feet to A-la-ja-güng, a poor village of eleven families on a small plateau at the end of a hill dividing the Nok Chu and Ja-bu Chu valley. The length of this march was 22 miles.

Continuing up the valley of the Nok Chu, on September 28 Pereira reached A-la-dor-tu, 18¾ miles. It was well wooded up to 14 miles and then the trees and bush got less and less till at the end of the march there was only scrub on stony hills. The going was fair for 9 miles, then stony and rocky. There was a rather steep climb of 700 feet to Ta-ké La, 15,250 feet, at 7¾ miles. Six miles farther on the I-fü was crossed by a rickety brushwood bridge. The road then ascends the narrow stony Nok Chu valley to A-la-dor-tu, where Pereira camped at an elevation of 15,200 feet beside three nomads' tents. On this march he overtook a caravan of 150 ponies on their way from Batang to Lhasa.

Another difficult pass had to be crossed on September 29. This was the worst stage Pereira had ever been on. The going was appalling. For 4 miles the path still led up the Nok Chu valley between barren stony hills and over many rocks and boulders. Then it turned to the W.N.W. and the ascent became steeper through a veritable sea of boulders, rocks and stones in an open valley. Finally there was a steep ascent of 400 feet to the summit of the Nur-güng La, the Chor kou La of Huc. Pereira had exhausted his spirits of wine so could not use his boiling-point thermometer, but he estimates the altitude as 16,800 or perhaps 17,000 feet. On the top of the ridge and extending some 200 yards down were rocks in profusion, and the difficulty was to get over them. The descent was by a very steep zigzag over the stones or hopping from rock to rock. Pereira was badly jarred and feared for the old spine injury or a possible acute attack of lumbago as he had once experienced at Aldershot. However, though he felt jarred in the small of the back he got through all right, and on arriving at more level ground passed a beautiful serpentine blue lake, the Tso-düng-wu-ngi, 1 mile long, 800 yards wide and very deep. Then there was an easy descent, though the rocks were still awful, to the Yeh Chu, soon called the Sa Chu valley, at 12¾ miles. At last at 16 miles there was good fairly level going over grass to Sa-chu-ka, 18¼ miles, where there were five low stone hovels, beside which Pereira pitched his tent. He made the altitude about 14,800 feet. Huc, the Chinese and the Tibetans all consider the Shiar-güng La to be the worst pass on the road. And it certainly is steeper and has more snow. But Pereira considered the Nur-güng La to be much the worse of the two on account of the rocks and boulders.

A very easy stage followed this effort. The way led down a valley a quarter of a mile wide between barren sloping hills. The Dé Chu was crossed by a fragile log bridge, and Pereira halted at Lhari-go, a poor village of fifty families with a monastery of sixty monks on the spur behind it. He was accommodated in a nice clean room, and halted a day here to rest after his ten strenuous days of travel.

The place is of some importance as several routes radiate from it. And it is the headquarters

ATSA LAKE.

face p. 173.

of a small official, who called on Pereira in his robes of state bringing a present of eggs and vegetables. Pereira returned his call. He sat cross-legged on a divan while Pereira was enthroned on the chair of state. He expressed wonder at Pereira at his age walking up all the hills, and said that he himself always rode, though he was only forty-four. From his account Huc did not exaggerate the terrors of the passes in winter, when the Shiar-güng La is the worst.

The Banda La was crossed on October 2 and Pereira marched 11 miles to Atsa. The way lay up and down barren hills with no inhabitants, and at 7¾ miles there was a steep climb to the top of the Banda Pass, which he made, 16,000 feet in height. Though snow covered the ground the path was clear. There was a rather steep winding descent and a beautiful view of the Atsa Lake lying light blue amidst the white mountains. Atsa is a village of ten families and thirty monks situated in a small valley at an elevation of 13,000 feet. To the south is a range about 17,000 or 18,000 feet in height.

Pereira was not well this day and walked only 2 miles. The climb up the zigzags to the top of the pass made him gasp. And when he rode he shivered badly. His boy had brought two cocks from Chamdo, not for eating, but to call him in the morning as he had no watch.

On October 3 he marched 18½ miles to Guo-lê. It was an easy stage but rocky and stony after the first 5 miles. Except for a few nomads, the country was uninhabited. The Atsa-shung Chu was crossed by such a poor log bridge that the pack animals had to go much farther up to ford it. At 5 miles the path led along the south edge of the Atsa Lake, which was beautifully blue and very deep. It is 3¼ miles long. At 9 miles the road ascends the Pok Chu valley to Guo-lê, a hamlet of stone hovels at 14,450 feet. Pereira was still weak, but feeling better. By a very great effort he walked 10 miles. If he could walk 83 miles before reaching Lhasa, he would complete 3500 miles on foot. He saw two cranes and some mandarin duck—the first of the migration.

The Tro La, 16,050 feet, was crossed on October 4. The way led up the barren stony Pok Chu valley. At 1½ mile there was a steep ascent and then some very steep zigzags and a final easier circular rise, and at 3¼ miles the top of the Tro La was reached. This was the last of the four great passes which had to be crossed on the way to Lhasa and was higher than any on the way from Tangar to Chamdo. Of these four the Nur-güng La is the worst in autumn and the Shiar-güng La is the worst in winter. From the Tro La there was a steep, winding stony descent to the Tro Chu at 7 miles. This river is forded and the road leads down the valley between high barren hills. At 10 miles the valley narrows to a gorge with huge perpendicular rocky mountains on the right and a glimpse of snow mountains through a gap on the left. At 10 miles the going is very rocky and gets worse down to Chomdo, 12¼ miles, a hamlet of three stone hovels in a small strip at a bend in the river.

Cramp in the left leg made the last 8 miles very painful for Pereira. He walked 8 miles, including all except a quarter of a mile of the climb. "The old man has weathered the four great passes, thanks to Providence", he writes, "but he feels very limp." He hoped the downhill would not be very rocky and stony, but Tibet seemed to present every possible difficulty and obstacle. It was cold at the start, but with the sun and a fur coat it was quite pleasant at 5 P.M. He saw four ram chicor (partridges) on the mountain and a vulture and a marmot in the valley.

Following down the Tro Chu all day on October 5 he reached La-ru, 15¾ miles. The valley is generally from 300 to 800 yards wide, between hills rising 1500 to 2000 feet above it and having trees and bush on one slope. The going was mostly fair though in parts rocky and stony. Innumerable small streams were crossed all full of stones, which he says is a peculiarity of Tibet. One monastery prettily situated on a hill and two or three small villages were passed. La-ru has twenty families and its altitude is 12,400 feet, so after a steady descent all day Pereira was at last off the high ground, and sitting in his room in the sun he was quite hot. To his relief he had walked 10 miles without experiencing any cramp.

Some square stone towers, 35 to 40 feet high with narrow slits for windows, were passed on this stage. Pereira was told that these were put up in the old days when the Jungar Mongols, also known as the Eleuths, were powerful in the Ko-Ko Nor region. These Mongols several times invaded Tibet but were finally crushed by the Emperor Chien Lung. He banished part of them to Chinese Turkestan, where a tract of country is still known as Jungaria. Pereira came across a fragment of the race when shooting in the Tian Shan.

Giamda was reached on October 6 at 18¼ miles. The road leads down the same valley, though the name of the river changes to Niem Chu and then to Jya Chu. The valley is mostly from 200 to 400 yards wide, with hills from 1500 to 2000 feet high rising above it. The path is fairly good though often stony and occasionally rocky. Four or five small villages were passed. At 18 miles the Jya Chu is crossed by a precarious temporary bridge, the old bridge having been washed away by the summer floods and a new one not having been built, as bridges in Tibet are built in winter.

Giamda, 11,750 feet, has forty families, of whom seventeen are Chinese. It lies between the Jya Chu and the Siarp Chu, which, uniting below the village, form the Güng-bu Zong Chu. This name is derived from the district of Güng-bu, which extends from Giamda to I-Tsé-la-gong on the Tsang Po. There is a small official here who with the head-man sent Pereira the usual present of eggs—most of them bad.

This was a glorious sunny day and the most enjoyable he had had; and the scenery was lovely. The evergreen mingled with autumn-tinted trees and bushes; and the clear stream was often in rapids and formed small islands which were covered with trees, prominent among which were small fluffy dwarf cedars. There were, too, quantities of blue flowers. Inner Tibet in September and October is in parts a beautiful country.

GIAMDO.

face p. 177.

Everywhere there are high mountains and generally deep valleys. Pereira had seen nothing elsewhere to compare with it in grandeur. Huc saw it in winter. At this time of year, excepting at great heights, it is as mild as England in autumn, with sunshine most days and hardly a drop of rain, and frost at night.

There was a sort of post from Giamda to Lhasa. For a junka a letter can be sent to Lhasa in a day and a half. Pereira sent one to the Commander-in-Chief telling him of his arrival so far.

The two colossal temples mentioned by Huc do not now exist. He also said there were many Pebouns, natives of Bhutan. Now there was only one and a "Kaza", who apparently also came from Bhutan. He was right in saying there is rhubarb in the hills. The women wear a hard cloth circle like a coronet round the head. It is bordered with red stones which look like berries. The houses are of stone, with very thin planks held down by stones for a roof, and it is little wonder the rain comes through.

On October 8 he marched to Tsen-da, 14¼ miles. The road turned westerly up the Siarp Chu valley, which is from 300 to 500 yards wide. The hills are mostly covered with trees and bush; and the path, though very stony, is generally good and leads through a pleasant wood, winding up and down over low spurs. After the usual chilly start the day became gloriously hot. The yellow autumnal tints were unrivalled by anything Pereira had seen, with occasional light green patches to add to the effect and dark green patches higher on the hills. One small monastery with a few fields round and half-a-dozen farms were passed. Tsen-da, 12,500 feet, is a hamlet containing five families. From it there is a route northward to Nagchuka, which is reached in nine stages.

Following up the Kam Chu valley all day on October 9, Pereira reached Siang-ba-tang, 18 miles. The valley was from 200 to 400 yards wide and the hills from 1500 to 2000 feet above it. On this stage many bushes of a deep red colour added to the beauty of the scenery. It was chilly at the start, but later again gloriously fine. At 8 miles the valley is about half a mile wide and flatter, and with a nice grass belt. Three small villages with cultivation were passed. Siang-ba-tang, 13,100 feet, consists of two hovels on a level grass belt, an ideal spot in such weather.

Numari, 10¾ miles, was reached on the following day. The road still led up the Kam Chu valley all the way. Only one house and two tents were passed. At first the road led through a delightful wood with numbers of dwarf cedars. Then trees and bush gradually grew less. At 10½ miles the Kam Chu is crossed by a log bridge to the left bank, and from it there is a rise to Numari, 14,000 feet, a hamlet of eight families.

Pereira had determined to walk 8 miles, leaving only 30 to complete the 3500 miles, but after going about 5 miles he was laid out with a bad touch of sciatica. Luckily he had just got into the sunshine. So after lying in the sun for twenty minutes he was able to ride a mile and then slowly complete the extra 3 miles of walking.

The last pass, the Güng-bu-Ba La, 15,300 feet,

LOOKING WEST TO NGUI-CHOR-KE.

face p. 179.

was crossed on October 11. Returning from Numari to recross the Kam Chu by the bridge, Pereira continued to ascend the Kam Chu valley, here 200 or 300 yards wide between bare hills. The path was mostly stony. At 4 miles the Kam Chu was again crossed by a log bridge, and then there was a winding, easy ascent till at 11½ miles, the summit of the Güng-bu-Ba La was reached. It was by far the easiest pass on the whole road. It is Huc's Loummà Ri. Though the day was sunny, there was a bitter head-wind and some ice on the streams in the pass, though only a little snow on the hills. There was an easy descent from the pass to Chou-me-ra, 21¼ miles, a hamlet of four hovels.

Pereira was able to walk 8¼ miles, and had only one slight touch of sciatica. With his last pass behind him his anxieties were over, and he was in the highest spirits at feeling there was now no more climbing, and all the rest of the way to Lhasa was downhill.

On October 12 there was an easy march of 16¼ miles to Ö-ser-chang. It was bitterly cold at starting and chilly in the wind even after the sun was up. The descent was easy and the hills were at last lower, only 500 to 1000 feet above the valley, and they were mostly covered with grass. Lower down there was some scrub on the lower slopes and some bush again in the valley, but the leaves were off, so it was apparently colder. The stream changes its name three times. A good many side streams had to be forded, and bigger ones were crossed by bridges of logs, brushwood and stones. Ö-ser-chang, 13,900 feet, has eighteen families.

Another easy march of 12½ miles brought Pereira to Rin-chen-ling, in the same valley. The going was fair; though rather stony. The valley was mostly about 400 yards wide, and there was some brush and scrub, but no longer the beautiful autumn tints. Only two solitary houses for the courier service were passed. Three mountain torrents were crossed by brushwood bridges. Rin-chen-ling, 13,150 feet, has twenty-one families, and lies in a rather stony valley on the left bank of the Shung Chu. The rooms in the hovels are poor and draughty, sometimes with a hole in the roof for additional light.

Pereira completed his 3500 miles of walking on October 14 and reached Me-tro-kong-kar, 17¼ miles. There was a great change in the country, the road leading down a broad flat valley at first, three-quarters of a mile wide, and then opening out to 1½ to 2 miles. It was the flattest and most open country he had seen since leaving the country north of Jye-kundo. The hills were only 500 to 800 feet above the valley, and were covered only with grass and low scrub. There were practically no trees except a few round the villages, and dwarf cedar and small evergreens along the banks of rivers. The going was fair but stony. Eight small villages were passed, but none had more than eight houses; and there were other villages on the opposite side of the valley. There were also some big square two-storied, flat-roofed houses of the better class. The last of the barley crop was being gathered in. Me-tro-kong-kar, 12,290 feet, was a village of thirty-seven families, with some good stone and mud houses. The day was chilly and was the first

JOGON (CATHEDRAL), LHASA.

p. 131.

which was only partly sunny. A letter received from the Commander-in-Chief said that a nice house in a park was being prepared for him.

Still marching down the Song-pu Chu valley, here from 2 to 5 miles wide, Pereira reached Zong-do, 16½ miles, on October 15. The river is 40 to 50 yards wide and 2 or 3 feet deep. The country is treeless except round the villages. Eight villages were passed. Zong-do, 11,530 feet, has sixteen families. A good many pilgrims returning on foot to Kanze and Dergé were passed, and several caravans for Chamdo and Yünnan.

De-chen, 13 miles, was reached on October 16, the road still following down the broad valley of the Song-pu Chu. There was a fair amount of cultivation in the valley, but much of it was stony waste. At 1½ mile the Gaden monastery, one of the biggest in Tibet, was just visible on a hill 800 feet high. De-chen has thirty-two families and some good stone houses. On the east side is a rock 200 feet high, with what looked like a ruined fort. There was now daily a chilly wind.

Pereira records of himself: "The old man gets very weary each day and is so stiff that he has to be lifted off his horse on arrival. However, the goal is at last in sight. Only one more stage of 14½ miles to Lhasa. I shall be the only white man living who has been from Peking to Lhasa direct."

Lhasa was reached at last on October 17. The road still lay down the valley of the Song-pu Chu, officially known as the Kyi Chu. There were farms and villages with an occasional monastery dotted about. At 10 miles off the famous Potala came in sight, standing on a small hill, and as

Pereira advanced he got a glimpse of the glitter on its golden roof. The country was still treeless till getting near to Lhasa, when villas and walled enclosures full of willow and other trees were seen. At 10 miles was Drukpa or "the Ferry", with a very stony beach on either side. The river was 80 yards wide and 10 feet deep. As usual, coracles were used for the passage. A small official stationed here brought Pereira some Chinese cakes and small unripe peaches. He then crossed a stony plain stretch 4 miles to the north to barren hills, at the foot of which was the great Sera monastery, a several-storied block of whitewashed buildings. At 14½ miles he entered Lhasa, a rather dirty city with houses of stone, two or three storied, and with the usual quaint Tibetan windows. And here, once more, were shops, pink potatoes, eggs, sugar, etc. It was a treat to him to see a shop again.

He rode straight to the newly established telegraph office and despatched a telegram to his brother, worded, "Lhasa Englishman first." He had to economise words, and what he meant was that he, an Englishman, was the first to reach Lhasa from Peking.

"I entered with my white beard, very tired but happy", he writes, "for the great trek was at last a thing to look back upon. The weary miles of tramping were over.

"Riding through the city I passed the wonderful Potala, one of the wonders of the world—a gigantic block of buildings. I have not yet counted how many stories high, mostly whitewashed, with the centre painted red and surmounted by small

POTALA AT LHASA.

face p. 185.

roofs of gold. It impressed me like the great ruins of Ankhor Wat in Cambodia, St. Peter's, the Mosque Omar and the Taj Mahal—all, of course, in different ways. The Dalai Lama no longer lives there, but resides in a country place near by, and a fine broad modern road has been constructed to it, along which, at about 100 yards intervals, are small columns like milestones, on which incense is burnt when the Dalai Lama passes by."

A very nice villa, surrounded by a park or garden full of trees, had been provided for Pereira by the Tsarong Shapé, the Commander-in-Chief. In it was a big painted room which took up more than half the house. It had six continuous windows on one side and two rows of columns down the centre, and a roof of rafters painted blue. The furniture included a substantial wooden table. Sir Charles Bell, Sir Henry Hayden and other Englishmen had stayed there.

Some news of the outer world, which had been a closed book to him for over six months, he now learned from the telegraph officer, Rosemeier—the troubles in Ireland (the same old story), the utter rout of Greece by Turkey, the death of Lord Northcliffe, etc.

And then he sat down and reflected—reflected as only a man can who has set his whole heart on a great task and has done it.

" After all the worries, anxieties and hardships it seems like a dream that the great trek is really over. I look back on the rather heart-breaking preparations at Tangar when everything seemed against me and only the fiery Père Schram stood behind me with a helping hand. Then the odds were against me with the probability that after trudging to Nagchuka I should be turned back and have to return disappointed across the frozen, wind-swept plains of North Tibet. How glad I am now that in those dreary Tangar days I decided that there should be no consideration of failure, and that barring a direct veto from India I would go through *coûte que coûte*. And now I look back it is wonderful to think how I was protected by Providence. The old weak spot on my spine might not have been able to bear the strain and I might have got a stroke on one of the great passes—or even minor evils like lumbago or sciatica. Or the old game leg might have gone. But luckily he proved game to the end. My feet, too, though tender at times in the frost-bitten spots, have kept sound. In the end everything has fitted in in its right place. But I would not make the return journey for a million pounds."

The distance he had travelled from Peking was 6860¼ miles, of which he had walked 3527¼. He was curiously particular about the ¼ miles, and recording them like this is characteristic of his methodical, accurate habits.

The distance from Chamdo to Lhasa was 670¼ miles. The " ula " transport from Chamdo had cost him 750 tankars plus 358 tankars for wine money, total 1108¼ tankars, or about 102⅛ Tangar taels, which is equivalent to about £20 : 10s. For this he had the use of from twenty to thirty animals a day. So it was a remarkably cheap journey.

His stores at the end of his journey consisted

TSARONG SHAPÉ (COMMANDER-IN-CHIEF).

face p. 185.

of half-a-dozen tins of jam and sardines. For salt he had native stuff looking like glass. His sugar was the coarsest brown sugar, looking like pieces of brown soap. His tea was the coarsest native brick tea; and his milk was yak milk with a pungent taste.

On the day following his arrival in Lhasa he received a cablegram from England in answer to the one he had despatched on arrival—a striking illustration of how much closer Lhasa now is to the outside world.

On this day he also visited the Tsarong Shapé or Commander-in-Chief. He was thirty years of age and had learnt a few words of English. He was dressed in a khaki uniform with a "coat-warm-British". His little son of three or four was also dressed in khaki. The next day he invited Pereira to lunch and afterwards to inspect the troops, and told him he was the first British officer who had inspected them. Four companies, one from each of the four barracks of Lhasa, were paraded. The rifles, khaki and equipment were all of British pattern, and one company wore turbans. Considering everything, and that the words of command were in English, the drill was very good, and much better than Pereira had anticipated. One sergeant who had been in India had a very good word of command.

The Dalai Lama received Pereira on October 24. As Pereira was travelling as a private individual he had not liked to ask for an audience, but finding that the Dalai Lama expected to see him, he was glad to have the opportunity of visiting him. The Dalai Lama received him in his special audience room behind the barracks, having walked there from his charming villa just behind. He was without a hat and was dressed in a picturesque long orange robe with a bright yellow jacket. He was close shaven, but with a small twisted moustache and a minute beard. On Pereira entering he remained seated. Pereira then presented him with a khata (ceremonial scarf) and received a very fine large one in return. After this Pereira took a seat, and quite an interesting conversation followed, for he found the Dalai Lama very intelligent. The Lama himself drank Tibetan tea, but he gave Pereira Indian tea and milk in a little English tea-service.

After this visit Pereira called on the Prime Minister, "Long Chin" by name, in the Potala. He was a nice old man. But his office, consisting of three small rooms, had to be reached by a flight of slippery stone steps and long dark passages.

Pereira also, while at Lhasa, visited the great Sera monastery, which nominally has 5500 monks, though he would have estimated the number as lower. The way to it leads across a sandy plain, and it is situated at the foot of bare stony hills 2½ miles north of the Potala. It is a regular little town from 600 to 800 yards long, with streets of two- or three-storied houses. There are three big temples with gold roofs of the usual small Chinese pattern. On the whole, Pereira was disappointed with the monastery. If there were five thousand monks, it was only a little bigger than the Labrang monastery in Kansu, and for situation and general appearance Labrang is much finer.

The Commander-in-Chief came to say good-bye

SERA MONASTERY LHASA.

on October 26. Pereira had given him a pony and a Jaeger lining for his " coat-warm-British ". In return he gave Pereira two fine bronze Tibetan pots, one for tea and the other for wine; also a bottle of crème-de-menthe and two bottles of ginger.

On October 28 Pereira began his journey to India, taking with him only his Chinese boy-cook and the half-caste Chino-Tibetan interpreter from Tangar. On October 30 he crossed the Tsang Po (Brahmaputra) by ferry. It was the last great river on his journey. He still kept up walking his eight miles a day, but found it tried him, and at night he was very weary. The next day he passed the beautiful blue serpentine Yamdrok Lake, on which there were swarms of quite tame geese and duck; but he thought the scenery spoilt by the bare, treeless hills. The weather was fine, but chilly, and on November 1 it was bitterly cold. On November 3 he crossed the Karo La. The morning was one of the coldest of the entire journey. His hands were in torture, and the sun made no difference. And that night he wrote: "For the last two or three nights I have spent nearly twelve hours in bed to get warm. Each night it requires arduous rubbing to get my frozen right foot warm and to get the sting out of the old frost-bitten patches. How I long for the warmth of India, then never again I trust to travel in ice-bound countries. I long to be able to look back upon Tibet as a reminiscence. How nice it will be in the winter to sit by a blazing fire in a comfortable chair and think of the sufferings I endured there, and of the marvellous way in which Providence protected me from even worse. I think a second such journey would kill me."

Gyantse was reached on November 5. Here he met the first Europeans, except Madame Nèel, since leaving Tangar in May. They were Dr. McGovern and Captain Ellam of a so-called Buddhist Mission. There were, too, Mr. Macdonald, the British Trade Agent, and about seventy Indian soldiers. These last were very smart. "It was a treat", he writes, "to see again a man who *could* present arms, and also to see the Union Jack once more flying in the afternoon breeze. Good old England!"

And he saw here Indian papers up to October 28, and containing the news of his arrival in Lhasa—also the results of the Leger, Cesarewitch and Cambridgeshire, "all won by rank outsiders I had never heard of".

On November 7 he resumed his journey, but now onwards there were dak bungalows with glass windows and real fire-places, doors, a bed, tables, chairs—such luxuries as he had not seen for months. There were even books, and he re-read *The Velvet Glove*. On November 18 he crossed the Himalaya by the Tang La, 15,200 feet, and reached Phari. Everybody had dwelt on the cold of this stage, so he had dreaded it badly, but found it not so cold as the Karo La. Next day he marched down the Chumbi valley, thickly wooded and with delightful smell of pine. On November 16 he crossed his last pass, the Nathu La, 14,700 feet. At last he was out of Tibet and could say he had been right across it.

Street in Lhasa.

face p. 189.

" Thank Heaven! Tibet is a memory of the past, and I can now get warm again, with no more thoughts of frost-bite. It is nice to feel I am in India and on the downward grade at last, with no more climbs ahead."

And that day he received a budget of letters from home, but to his annoyance no *Racing Up-to-Date*, so " I have no news of what happened in the Derby, Ascot, etc.".

Gantok, " a most heavenly place ", was reached on November 17, and here he stayed with Major Bailey, the Political Agent, who had a huge and beautiful garden—a regular Paradise.

He had now completed his journey. From Peking he had travelled 6681½ miles, of which he had walked 3682 miles, or considerably more than half the distance.

CHAPTER XVII

RETURN TO CHINA

MOST men, if they had made a journey of between 6000 and 7000 miles, would return to their native country and take a rest. And most assuredly they would do this if at the end of their journey they were both weary and ill. Not so Pereira. He was dreadfully travel-weary during all the last part of his journey from Peking to India. And when he reached Calcutta he had to go to a nursing home to be treated for thrombosis, or clots of blood in his left leg. Yet, as soon as he was able to move again, he set off for Burma and across the Chinese frontier again to Yünnan. He left Calcutta on January 9, 1923, reached Rangoon on the 12th, Mandalay on the 18th, and Bhamo on the 21st.

From Bhamo he began marching again, leaving there on January 24 for Teng-yüeh, where he arrived on the 31st. Setting out again on February 5, he reached Yünnan-fu on March 2, making the distance 410¾ miles from Teng-yüeh and 549¾ miles from Bhamo. This is a well-known route, and there is no need to describe it in detail. The only noticeable feature in the journey was the amount of brigandage which was being carried on. Pereira was escorted by Chinese soldiers. But the brigands themselves were soldiers who had deserted because they were never paid. But sometimes when one faction drives out the other the soldiers of the first become brigands and the erstwhile brigands become soldiers. The line of distinction between a brigand and a soldier is, in fact, rather difficult to define. With these brigands Pereira had an encounter on February 27 near Lu-feng-Hsien, four days' march from Yünnan. They fired at him as his party was descending a ridge. But fortunately their fire was ineffective, and no harm was done.

Pereira would have wished from Yünnan to travel in Lolo Land, but the country was too disturbed. Père Walta, who had been there, told him they were tall, but not a race of giants. Some were 2 metres in height, but the average height was about 1·85 metres. The Chinese used formerly to have a small garrison and a walled city at Chao-chu in the centre of Lolo Land, but two years previously the Lolos had attacked and massacred the Chinese soldiers, and the country was now too disturbed for any one to visit it, and Père Walta had heard nothing of his converts. The Lolos say of themselves that they came from the direction of Burma. They consider a man who captures another man to be a man: a man who allows himself to be captured they regard as a sheep—as only half a man.

Leaving Yünnan-fu, 6400 feet, 200,000 inhabitants, on March 16, he made northward in the direction of the Yangtze, first following the main road to Kwei-yang across undulating country on the edge of a fertile plain. But on the following day he left this main road and marched to Tung-ch'uan-hsien, which he reached on March 21. The country was mostly undulating and well populated, and there was much poppy cultivation in spite of the interdicts on it. As before, this country also was infested with brigands, and one day he passed an enormous caravan of 1400 animals, with an escort of nearly a hundred soldiers. Rhododendrons, mostly of a deep red colour and in full bloom, he saw near Lai-t'ou-p'o, 7500 feet. And on March 20 he crossed the Chih-ch'ang Ya-k'ou at 9100 feet, the highest point he had reached in Yünnan. From here he had fine views on the left of ranges 10,000 to 18,000 feet in height, all covered with a coating of snow. The descent was very steep and the road bad, and the wind bitterly cold.

Tung-ch'uan-hsien is situated in a very fertile valley at an elevation of 7250 feet and has a population of over five thousand families. His next objective was Chao-t'ung Hsien, which he reached on March 27. Halting for a day, he left Tung-ch'uan-hsien on March 28, he himself, as usual, travelling in a chair or walking, while his baggage was carried on mules. He passed first through the fertile but somewhat swampy plain, in which were many storks and duck and a few cranes. At 7¾ miles he reached the summit of the Lung-wang-miao Kou-tzu, 8400 feet, and then passed through cultivated valleys. On March 24 he reached Yi-ch'ê-hsün, 6800 feet, a busy market town of 850 families. Here he heard that a village he had slept in five days previously had

MIAO AT SHIH-MEN-K'AN.

face p. 198.

been raided by two hundred brigands on the following day.

On March 25 he followed down the Yu-ch'ê-hsün valley for 8 miles and then had a steep climb to the Ya-k'ou-t'ang Pass, 7100 feet, after which he followed down a narrow valley winding among hills to the Niu-Lan Chiang valley and crossed a stream by a chain suspension bridge to Chiang-ti-Kai, 5700 feet, a dirty village of seventy-five families, and here it was quite hot. Next day he had a very steep climb of 1600 feet to the top of the Hai-tzu Ya-k'ou, 7100 feet, from which the path lay along the hill-sides for some miles and then gradually descended through fir-clad red sandstone hills to T'ao-yüan, 6800 feet, a town of 280 families, on more level ground with paddy fields. On March 27 the way lay mostly across great fertile plains with occasional low hills.

Chao-t'ung Hsien, 6400 feet, has from 20,000 to 25,000 inhabitants. It is a small, dirty city but very crowded. The distance from Yünnan Fu was 226¾ miles, of which Pereira had walked 51¼. The weather on his arrival was fine and hot. There lived here Père Forten, a Roman Catholic missionary, and Mr. Hudderspith and Mrs. Hicks of the United Methodist Mission. From here Pereira made excursions out in different directions to see something of the Miao and Lolo tribes.

His first trip was on March 31 to Shih-men-k'an, 18 miles due east, and just outside the Province of Kwei-chow. Here he stayed with Mr. and Mrs. Parsons of the United Methodist Mission on Easter Sunday, April 1, and had the opportunity of seeing the large gathering of the Miao who come in for the service and also for medical treatment. Pereira describes Mr. Parsons as one of those apostolic characters who devote their lives to helping poor and down-trodden races; and Mrs. Parsons he describes as like a mother to the tribe. The famous Sam Pollard started the Mission about seventeen years previously with Mr. and Mrs. Parsons. He invented a writing for the Miao as they then had none, and the Mission now print books in Miao. Sam Pollard was the first to enter the Miao country about 1905 or 1907. Very few others have entered the country. Mr. J. W. Brooke was murdered in it in December 1908. Monseigneur de Guébriant and Vicomte d'Ollone and party are the only white people who have crossed it; but Père Walta and perhaps other Catholic missionaries have penetrated to Kia-kio.

Pereira records of the Miao near Shih-men-k'an that they are called the Ta-hua Miao on account of the large size of the embroidery which they fabricate. They are below the medium height and are considered to be the lowest in stature of the tribes. Mr. Sam Clarke was of opinion that the Miao were of the same origin as the Chinese and represented an earlier immigration whom the Chinese found in occupation when they reached Shensi and Shansi. Others think they are a distinct aboriginal race.

Pushed south, they retreated to the south side of the Yangtze, and about two centuries ago, when the Chinese pushed southward in Kwei-chow and Yünnan, the Miao retreated still farther west and

MIAO AT SHIH-MEN-K'AN.

face p. 195.

south-west. They are looked down on by all as a most inferior race; and without any powers of combining to resist and without any energy, they have fallen into the power of the Chinese and Nosu (Lolos). The last fight they put up was during the Mohammedan rebellion in Yünnan. They then fought both for and against the Mohammedans, but were finally crushed by the Chinese. In the north-west many have submitted to become serfs of the surrounding Nosu chiefs, and seem to have no power of resistance to the ill-treatment of their masters. Some 15,000 out of 20,000 of these Ta-hua Miao have become Church members or inquirer probationers of the United Methodist Mission.

Beyond these to the north-west are the Ch'uan or River Miao, who are so called from having come from the rivers of Szechwan. They are probably more numerous than the Ta-hua Miao, but so far only a few have been converted to Christianity. Some years ago they were raided by the independent Lolos and many were carried off as slaves. In the evenings, across the mighty waters of the Yangtze, voices singing the old Miao songs could be heard. But gradually the singing grew less and less as the slaves died, till it ceased altogether, and not one slave ever succeeded in escaping.

The independent Lolos in the old days used to be much bolder than they are now, and thirty or forty years ago they used to raid right up to Shih-men-k'an. When opium was prohibited in China the Chinese used to sell it to the Lolo chiefs, and through this they deteriorated. The serfs are become so numerous that they are rising against their chiefs.

A horn is worn by the men of both Lolos and Miao. The origin of this custom is unknown. Nor is it known whether there is any connection between the two races. The clothes of the Miao women are of white hemp. They wear quilted petticoats and sometimes coloured puttees. Both men and women wear the same short, finely embroidered cloak, sometimes thrown loose, sometimes sewn on to the dress. They either wear sandals or go bare-footed. The unmarried girls wear their hair plaited and coiled round the top of the head.

The Miaos are a gentle race, and after years of being ground down are at first suspicious, but once they have confidence in a stranger they are bright and smiling. They are very poor, and even in a good year only just make both ends meet. They live chiefly on maize, but are fond of oatmeal. The Mission started growing potatoes with great success.

They sing well, the hymns being adopted from well-known tunes. Pereira heard them singing a Miao hymn to the tune of "Auld Lang Syne".

Mr. Pollard's grave overlooks the beautiful field of his labours.

Pereira visited a Lolo village on his way back to Chao-t'ung Hsien on April 2. The people dressed like the Chinese. The men were if anything rather shorter than the Chinese and had the hooked Tibetan nose. The women were very shy. These were the subjugated and not the independent Lolos.

VALLEY NEAR CHAO-J'UNG

p. 197.

Pereira called on General Lung Yün at Chao-t'ung. He is warden over the Lolo borderland and is himself a Lolo (Nosu) though thoroughly Chinesified. He was very friendly, but he is not an energetic man. When his mother died the Governor sent an officer to represent him at the funeral, and this officer wore the Governor's uniform on the occasion.

Pereira's next excursion was north-west to the Nosu (Lolo) country—Ta-ching-pa, 48¾ miles, on the Yangtze. Leaving Chao-t'ung on April 6 he marched over the fertile plain and then down a valley to Sha-yü Ho, a village of three hundred families, at 10¾ miles. Next day the road lay among hills and there was a steep climb to the Leng-ka-li Shan, 7805 feet, from which there was a fine view over hills to the west and south-west, some of which rose to over 10,000 feet. There was now more fir forest on the hills and only a little cultivation and a few hovels. At 17½ miles he reached Hsin-tien-tzu, 7616 feet, with 125 families.

On April 8 he followed down the Nan-shui Ho for 3 miles and then had a steep climb to Ching-feng-k'ou, 9770 feet, at 7 miles. From there he had the first view of the Nosu (Lolo) country. It was a wild mountainous region with few trees. There were great ranges running in a southerly direction, some of which were from 12,000 to 15,000 feet high and partly under snow. From the top there was a long descent, in parts very steep. The path was very narrow and lay partly through a gorge between gigantic rocky precipices and partly along the hill-side. He was now in one of the deepest gorges in the whole course of the

Yangtze, and at 20½ miles he reached Ta-ching-pa, a village of 180 families, situated at an elevation of only 2411 feet on a small fertile plain by the Yangtze, which is here known as the Chin-sha Shiang or River of Golden Sand. It was here very hot and masses of flowers were in bloom on the way. Pereira especially mentions seeing quantities of a beautiful purple lily.

In this land every man's hand was against his neighbour's. Many houses have a tower to which to flee in case of Lolo raids. And every Chinese or Nosu who crosses the river requires a guarantee for his safety. The Nosu are also at feud among themselves, so a similar guarantee is required in passing from one tribe to another. Chinese merchants get a surety for protection and visit them for trade.

April 9 Pereira spent in Ta-ching-pa. In the morning he walked down the narrow street, which was now crowded for the market, and saw many of the Nosu who had come across the river. Unluckily he could not see the black Nosu, the pure bred, as they had committed a raid and carried off twenty Chinese, so were not allowed over. The Nosu Pereira saw were all of a white serf class, chiefly descendants of kidnapped Chinese and in features mostly like the Chinese. Some had trousers and some had skirts, but most wore over the shoulders the famous Nosu cloak made of felt and dark brown or black in colour. Some had cropped hair and some wore the queue tied round the head, with a piece projecting like the Nosu horn. They appeared to be a cowed race. Many were of the beaked-nose type and were probably of

REFUGE TOWER OUTSIDE TA-CHING-PA.

Face p. 1[illegible].

the same stock as the Tibetans round Jye-kundo, and perhaps, Pereira adds, of the same origin as the Red Indians. The Nosu, like the Tibetans, wear big ear-rings in the left ear.

In the afternoon, with four soldiers as an escort, Pereira made an adventurous trip across the Yangtze into Nosuland. He went down the river 3 miles to the north-east of the ferry. The village at the ferry, Kan-t'ien-pa, had some twenty Chinese families, who seemed to be fearless of raids and had not even protective towers. The Yangtze was here 80 yards wide, very muddy and running with a strong current. On the far side he stood on a rock, but though there was a farm with a tower just above him he did not see a single inhabitant; but there were glorious views up and down the gorges. Having accomplished his ambition to set foot in Nosuland (Lololand) he returned. He realised that even if everything had been arranged satisfactorily, the country of the Nosus would have been too steep for him to venture in with his bad leg.

Pereira heard from the chief Chinese merchant at Ta-ching-pa that a French priest used to come there and also that a Frenchman (Audemard) had gone down the river by boat. He was also positive that three Englishmen crossed Nosuland about 1905, coming from Chicu-ch'ang in the centre of the Nosu country to Ho-k'ou and on to Ta-ching-pa. Pereira thought that this was probably a French party.

The Chinese in these parts are miserably poor, living mostly in wretched hovels.

On April 10 Pereira set out on his return to

Chao-t'ung, which he reached on the 12th. The plain was now one mass of poppy in full bloom —mostly white, but also red and purple. The Governor was, however, quite unaware that any poppy is being grown!

Another excursion he had intended to make from Chao-t'ung to Wei-ning he had to abandon after the first day on account of brigands. So on April 16 he set out finally for Sui-fu on the Yang-tze, taking with him an escort of four men with single-loading Mauser rifles. The Chao-t'ung plain was fertile at first but gradually became poorer, and the villages consisted of wretched hovels. This poor country extends eastward into north-west Kwei-chow. At 9 miles the road led up a narrow valley to Chuang-k'ou Ya-k'ou, 6926 feet, at 11 miles. It then led down the narrow Wu-tsai Ho valley to Hsiao-si-tang, 6150 feet, at 18 miles, a village of twenty hovels. The day was very cloudy and chilly with much wind and a slight drizzle.

On April 17 the road lay down the same rather poor valley with hills from 500 to 1000 feet on either side; but at 9 miles there was a very steep rocky descent between clefts in rocks to a much lower level. The scenery was now magnificent, the hills rising to 1000 or 2000 feet in height and the valley becoming fertile again, with crops of wheat, barley and poppy. At 20¼ miles Ta-kuan Hsien was reached. It is a dirty, crowded town of 670 families, at an elevation of 4002 feet. Pereira heard a cuckoo for the first time this day.

Ta-wan-tzu was reached on April 18 after a march of 17 miles. It is only 2622 feet above sea-level. The scenery on this march was still fine. The valley was fertile and palms and bamboos grew here. At 10 miles the Ta-kuan Ho was crossed by a double chain suspension bridge. Ta-wan-tzu is about 500 feet above the river.

Next day's march was again amidst grand scenery, the hills often rising in steep precipices. At 4 miles there was a very steep descent down rocky zigzags and the path then ran by the river for some way, afterwards ascending to Chi-li-pu, 2660 feet, at 12¾ miles. On April 20 Pereira marched 12½ miles to Tou-sha-kuan, 2094 feet, a town of 350 families. The road still lay down the Ta-kuan Ho valley amidst grand scenery. There was much traffic, many coolies and strings of mules and ponies.

Lao-ya-t'an, now called Yen-ching Hsien, was reached on April 21. The road left the Ta-kuan Ho valley and ascended the narrow Hsiao-hu Kou valley. At 4 miles there was a steep ascent by a badly paved path to the Li-shan-ting Pass, from just below which there were glorious views to the east across a deep narrow valley bordered by hills 3000 feet high and beyond them ranges 1000 or 2000 feet higher still. The descent was very steep down a paved zigzag path, and at 9½ miles the Ta-kuan Ho was again struck. A quarter of a mile farther the river was crossed by a quaint covered wooden plank cantilever bridge supported on either side by eight chains. At 18 miles Lao-ya-t'an was reached. It is a city of 970 families, at an elevation of 1621 feet, and straggles along the right bank of the river in a deep valley. There were only some salt boats here and no regular passenger boats. This, therefore, must be the head of navigation for these parts. Most of the Chinese here wear a cloth like a turban wound round the head, and now their heads are generally shaved. A queue is very rarely seen, though the Miao and the Lolos often wear one.

On April 23 Pereira left Lao-ya-t'an and marched 20½ miles to P'u-erh-tu, 1258 feet. The road lay down the narrow valley of the Ta-kuan Ho still amid fine scenery, the hills of 1000 feet or more being covered with vegetation. P'u-erh-tu has 280 families. And here Pereira left the main road to Sui Fu, and on April 24 crossed the Ta-kuan Ho in three ferry-boats and made for Fu-kuan on the Yangtze, some distance above Sui Fu. At 8 miles from the ferry he passed through the Eagle-beak Gorge, and at 14¾ miles reached Lan-pa, a village of forty scattered farms, at an elevation of 3310 feet. The scenery was again beautiful. The hills were more wooded, and some wild yellow raspberries—rather sour—were picked.

A nearly uninhabited country was passed through on the next day. For 13 miles only four or five farms were seen. But after that there were more farms and patches of cultivation. The paved path led up the narrow Lan-pa valley, and at 7½ miles the top of the Ch'a-yen-so, 5360 feet, was reached. This is the divide between the Ta-kuan Ho and the Yangtze. The descent lay down the narrow Ta Ho valley, and the path, passing up and down along the hill-side, reaches Kuan-k'ou, 2720 feet, at 18¾ miles. This is a village of twenty-four families.

YANGTZE RIVER.

face p. 26.

Continuing all the next day down the Ta Ho, the Yangtze was reached in 21½ miles at Fu-kuan. The Ta Ho was only a small torrent, and the valley lay between steep, well-wooded hills often rising in great precipices to a height of 1500 to 2000 feet. The path was very narrow and poorly paved and led up and down the hill-sides. Occasionally villages or farms surrounded with vegetation were seen on the hill-sides. At 7 miles the way led through the beautiful Ma-t'ang-ssu gorge, in which were some picturesque waterfalls coming from a great height. Here was one of those small stone columns with a kind of devil's head which Pereira had noticed on the Tibetan border all the way from Kansu to this place. From here the path winds along the hill-side and through gorges till the Yangtze is approached. At 21 miles the Ta-wan Ch'i is crossed by a ferry, and half a mile farther on is Fu-kuan, a town of 3000 inhabitants, at an elevation of 1044 feet.

From Fu-kuan Pereira had hoped to have made a trip to Lei-po, but the Nosus had last May seized seventy Chinese on the road to it and sold forty of them as slaves in the interior. The Chinese authorities were accordingly fighting with these Nosus and travelling would not be safe.

Instead Pereira made a trip of 11½ miles on April 28 to Ma-yi-ssu (Ping-yi-ch'ang), which is the real head of Yangtze navigation. From Fu-kuan he ascended the right bank of the river, which is here about 100 yards wide, muddy and of a strong current with several small rapids. The going was easy and the scenery pretty, the red sandstone sloping hills from 500 to 800 feet high being fairly well covered with vegetation. At 11¼ miles he crossed the Yangtze by ferry to Ma-yi-ssu, a town of 550 families, where a busy market was in progress in booths on the shingly bank.

Though Ma-yi-ssu is the real head of navigation small boats do go another 12 or 14 miles higher up to Mao-shui-kung through some rather bad rapids. Pereira returned to Fu-kuan by boat in a hundred minutes.

On April 29 he left by boat for Sui Fu, which he reached the next day. His boat was 13 yards and 1 foot long by 2 yards 1 foot 3 inches broad, and it took seventeen persons—himself, two boys, five chair-bearers, and nine crew. He put his bed in the centre with the baggage underneath. That day he reached P'ing-shan Hsien, about 21 miles, travelling at the rate of about 1 mile in eight minutes. The hills soon became steeper, and he passed through some beautiful gorges for 11 miles. Then the hills became more sloping and were covered with vegetation and some trees. Occasionally a few farms and villages were seen. About a dozen rapids were passed, the chief being the Yao-T'an at 9 miles.

At P'ing-shan he called on the magistrate, and hearing he had some Nosu prisoners from Lei-po T'ing, he photographed them. Some were black Nosu and some were white. The former were slim and upright men with beaked noses, but the tallest was two or three inches shorter than Pereira. They wore their Nosu cloaks.

On April 30 he left P'ing-shan at 6.20 A.M. and reached Sui Fu, 51¾ miles, at 3.34 P.M., the boat travelling for eight hours and six minutes. The

THE WIND-BOX GORGE (FENG-HSIEN) ON THE YANG TSE RIVER.

Face p.

rapids were small and the river from 100 to 200 yards wide. At first the hills were high and covered with vegetation and some trees. At 20 miles the river passes through a beautiful gorge, and here in several places coal was being hauled down in baskets from the hill-tops by means of two ropes running in a pulley. At 25 miles the hills became much lower. At 28 miles was An-pien Hsien, 240 families, opposite which the Ta-kuan Ho, which Pereira had followed down for some way, joins the Yangtze. It forms the boundary between Yünnan and Szechwan. At 35 miles the hills were much lower and there was more cultivation.

Sui Fu is a big crowded city at the junction of the Min River with the Yangtze, and the Chinese consider the Min as the main branch because it is navigable up to Ch'eng-tu and Kwan-Hsien. From here Pereira travelled in a small Chinese steam launch to Chung-King, 277½ miles, leaving Sui Fu on the 3rd and arriving on May 4. The boat was crowded with passengers and very uncomfortable. There were low hills covered with vegetation all the way. On the river, too, there was still risk of brigands. Very few junks dared make the passage. Steam launches have a better chance. But Pereira's launch bore bullet marks on it, and the bridge for the pilot and steersman was protected by armour plating.

The first night was spent at Lu Chou, 94½ miles, but a start was made in the middle of the night to avoid the brigands. Thirty miles above Chung King the Mao-erh Hsia gorge in low hills was passed. This is the greatest brigand centre, but as the company who owned the steam launch had paid the subsidy of two hundred dollars a trip it was allowed to pass. These brigands are not of the ordinary unpaid soldier type, but are lawless desperadoes who are out for unlimited plunder.

On May 5 Pereira embarked on the s.s. *Alice Dolla*, a palatial steamer with airy two-berth cabins and every luxury, including electric fans. On May 7 he passed through the narrow and beautiful Feng-hsien (wind box) gorge, which had very steep precipices in parts, but the hills were not very high, and Pereira considered that neither this nor the I-chang gorge was as fine as the Ta-ching-pa gorges on the border of the Nosu country. Here the hills did not rise for more than 2000 to 3000 feet above the Yangtze, but in Nosuland they rose to 8000 or 9000 feet.

I-chang was reached on May 7, and on May 8 he left in the *Chang-sha*, the biggest boat up the Yangtze. On May 10 he reached Hankow, and on May 13 Shanghai. From there he sailed for Hong-Kong, where he arrived on May 27.

CHAPTER XVIII

THE LAST TREK

Pereira had now crossed China and Tibet to India. Starting again from India he had recrossed China from west to east. He had ascended the Irrawady, had traversed Yünnan to the highest navigable point of the Yangtze, and had journeyed down that river to its mouth. At Shanghai he might have boarded any P. & O. steamer and been taken straight back to London without any further effort. But the thirst for travel was insatiable for Pereira. Not even yet was it assuaged. There was still something left to be done on the Tibetan border, and return there he must.

So, in addition to his journey from east to west and from west to east across the Chinese Empire, he now meant to make a journey from south to north. Instead of proceeding to England, he sailed for French Indo-China, from whence he would go by rail to Yünnan Fu, and from there make his way to Batang and Kanze on the Tibetan border and thence to Lanchow Fu.

He spent a fortnight at Hong-Kong, and on June 9 landed at Hoihow and left it on June 25 for Pakhoi and Haiphong, arriving at this latter town on the 27th. This he found to be a fine city of 90,000 inhabitants and the chief mercantile town of Tonquin. The French Resident, Monsieur Krautheimer, very kindly sent on board an invitation to Pereira to come and stay with him, and in the evening took him for a drive round the city. The well laid out streets and fine buildings were a revelation to him. The city is built on marshy ground reclaimed, and is a monument of French capacity and infinite patience and ingenuity. There were nice French houses and small gardens, and a fine war memorial, and small, very well kept Botanical Gardens, with a few animals. Pereira had not expected to find such a flourishing place, and in many respects it impressed him favourably, even in comparison with Hong-Kong. The hotels and cafés were more attractive, though the buildings in Hong-Kong were larger and the natural surroundings were more beautiful.

Hanoi he reached on June 29 and called at once on Monsieur Monjuillot, the Résident Supérieur of Tonquin. And here again Pereira was struck with the genius of the French in building a city. He thought it the best laid out city in the East, and better than Saigon. Though it has not the huge buildings of Shanghai it has fine broad boulevards. The French, he thought, were better than we are in laying out a city.

To Yünnan he proceeded by night train from Hanoi. Lao Kay was reached the next morning, and here the railway crosses the Nam Ti in the Yünnan province. The railway ascends the mountains by a series of loops and many tunnels and is a wonderful feat of engineering. Ami Chou was reached at 5.30 P.M. The train halted here for the night, and Pereira had to put up in a rather poor inn kept by a Greek.

Yünnan Fu was reached on July 1, and Pereira stayed here with Mr. Sly, the Consul-General. It is now a kind of summer resort for people from Tonquin, from the heat of which it is a pleasant change, being 6140 feet above sea-level. He now had to make his preparations for the journey to the Tibetan border, and luckily this time he was able to secure the services of a companion, Dr. H. Gordon Thompson, whom he had at one time hoped to have had with him on his journey to Lhasa. Great difficulty was experienced in getting mules, but on July 17 all preparations were completed, and they set out with an escort of thirty-five soldiers.

A few miles out, from a hill-side, he had a last view back over the beautiful Yünnan plain. The paved road then led among hills and down a narrow valley to Erh-ts'un at 15¾ miles, a village of eighteen houses, but no inn, and Pereira had to sleep in the verandah of a house, for the inside rooms were swarming with bugs. The night was wet and there was drizzling rain as he left next morning for Che-pei, 21½ miles, 5394 feet, and in the afternoon there were two heavy downpours. At 10 miles he passed through Fu-min Hsien, a town of a thousand families, which should have been his first stage. Here there was a fine old covered bridge with shops on it. The escort was now reduced to ten. The road, partly paved but often very muddy, led up and down over low hills.

Pereira was now riding a mule instead of being carried in a chair as on his previous journey.

Pretty country, the hill-side fairly covered with pine and shrubs, was passed through on the next day, the road leading up and down over slopes rising to 800 feet at the highest. Wu-ting-Chow, a town of seven hundred families, at an elevation of 5664 feet, was reached at 21½ miles. Five miles to the north is a mission station at Sa-pu Shan, where Mr. Nicholls was working among the Lisu, Tahua Miao and tame Nosu (Lolos). Two Lisu boys brought by Mr. Nicholls to Pereira appeared to him to be very like Chinese, with almond eyes and snub noses, but they belong to a Tibetan group.

Ma-an-shan, 6366 feet, 25¾ miles, was reached on July 20. The road for a couple of miles led across a fertile rice plain and then up the narrow valley of the Hsi-ts'un Ho, in which rice and a little maize were grown. At 10½ miles there was a steep climb over the Yao-yin Ya-k'ou, about 7000 feet, and then down among low hills and rice valleys. The road was very muddy after the rain, and was often under water.

Yünnan, says Pereira, is a picturesque Province, but there is a great sameness. It is nearly all red sandstone hills with some pine and shrub. Between these are narrow valleys with rice cultivation, and where these valleys open out are large cities.

On July 21 he marched 22½ miles to Ma-t'ou, crossing at 7 miles the Kung P'o ridge, 8300 feet, the divide between the So-Ling Ho on the west and the Lung-kai Ta Ho on the east, both tributaries of the Yangtze. At 12 miles there was another rise to about 8000 feet, and the road then kept high up along the top of the Ch'a-fen Shan, with a deep valley on the left and beautiful views to the south and west over many ranges. At 17 miles there was a gradual descent with picturesque views over the broad fertile Ma-t'ou-shan valley, and at 19 miles came a steep stony descent down zigzags to the valley. Ma-t'ou-shan is a valley of forty families, at an elevation of 4964 feet.

Next day he made a short march of 9 miles to Ma-Kai, now called Yüan-mow-hsien, down the same fertile valley. It rained all the morning and the roads were very muddy. Ma-Kai, a town of eight hundred families, had been pillaged by brigands from Szechwan in April, and some houses in the centre of the city had been burnt. His escort was now again increased to thirty, and on July 23 he marched 13¾ miles to Wu-mo, down the fertile Sha Ho valley, 2 or 3 miles wide. It was a fine hot day and the going was good over an unpaved path. The cultivation was mostly rice and maize. At 6½ miles the Sha Ho joins the So-Ling Ho, which is the main tributary of the Yangtze, and drains the Kun-yang Lake, and is contributed to by the Fu-min Ta Ho, the Lu-feng Ta Ho and the An-ning River. At 8½ miles he left the road to Chengtu by Hui-li-chow and crossed the So-Ling Ho by a ferry. The river was here 100 yards wide and 8 feet deep. There was only one small boat, so the sixteen animals had to swim. He then left the So-Ling valley and crossed a low hill into a small fertile valley, and crossed the junction of the Wen-tao Ho and the Wu-mo Ho by another ferry. Wu-mo has seventy-five families and is at an elevation of 3660 feet.

Pereira had felt ill and worn out at Yünnan Fu, probably owing to the heat of Tonquin. But now he was on the march again he felt better. And as he looked down the So-Ling Ho valley he thought of the great journey he had made from Omsk to Kashgar, Urumchi, Lanchow, Chengtu and down by Ning-yüan Fu and Hui-Li Chow to this very spot where he had now crossed the So-Ling Ho, and then on to Yünnan Fu and Amoy. He now wore a big circular Chinese bamboo hat, like a shield, which served as a small umbrella in keeping off the rain. He also wore a green oilskin native mackintosh, which appeared to be designed for anything except keeping out rain, but which worn over a Burberry helped a little to keep him dry.

The so-called high road, though bad after rain, was no worse than other roads in China during wet weather, and was nothing like so bad as the loess roads of Honan or the clay roads of South Szechwan.

Ascending the Wu-mo Ho valley on July 24, there was a steep climb up the Ta-shao-Shan to the top, 4940 feet, at 8 miles, and then along the ridge for 3 miles. From here the most southerly bend of the Yangtze was only 6 miles off to the eastward. There was then an easy descent to Tso-ch'io, a city of 550 families, at 5071 feet elevation. The next day he marched to Ta-pa-kuan, 5502 feet, 13¾ miles, over low hills with higher wooded hills round. The Wu-mo Ho had to be forded four times. It was about 2½ feet deep. The country round is inhabited by Lolos. He saw some of the women in the fields. They had Mongol features and looked short and stumpy. Ta-pa-kuan has 120 families.

The path led over high ground beyond this, and on July 26 Pereira reached Ta-t'ien-kai at 15¼ miles. The first climb was to the top of a well-wooded ridge, the Ma-p'o Shan, 7510 feet. The country all round was well wooded, and there were beautiful views of high ranges. Along the ridge were many wild flowers, and the day was hot and fine. At 8¼ miles was Kuan-yin-ai Shan, 7490 feet, and a very steep descent to 5270 feet at 13 miles, and down a small valley to Ta-t'ien-kai, a place of ninety-four families, at an elevation of 5180 feet.

July 27 was another fine hot day, and the way lay down the valley of the Jen Ho all day to Jen-ho-kai, 18½ miles. It is a town of 450 families, at an elevation of 3789 feet. In the upper part of the valley cotton is grown, and in the lower part sugar-cane.

Here Pereira halted for a day to rest the mules; and Dr. Thompson was very busy with the sick, and saw more than 250 patients. The thermometer was 88° in the shade in the house and the weather was stifling. Some bananas were obtained here.

They heard a mother unmercifully beating her child next door, but when Thompson went to intervene, the child sided with the mother!

The Yangtze was reached on July 29. The path lay down the fertile Jen Ho valley for 2 miles, then over undulating country and down to the Yangtze, here called the Pai-shui Chiang. Nine miles lower down the Yalung joins it, and below the junction it is called the Chin-sha Ch'iang. At the point where Pereira struck it, the Ta-tu-k'ou ferry, it is 200 yards wide with a strong current. The boat had to make seven trips, and the crossing took four and a half hours.

On the opposite side of the Yangtze was Szechwan. Leaving the ferry, there was a stiff climb, and the path then led across level ground with some cultivation. It then runs by the river and afterwards by a small fertile valley to Hsin-chuang, 4107 feet, a hamlet of forty-three families, at 14¼ miles.

On July 30 Pereira marched 22½ miles to Hsin-kai. At 2½ miles he was again in the Yünnan Province. Two miles farther on there was some difficulty in crossing the Pa-kan Ho, which was 2½ feet deep with a strong current. At 14¼ miles was Ma-shang, a village of thirty families, where there was a Roman Catholic Mission under Pères Salvat and Durier. They have about six hundred Christians, and live in a nice little mission house with a courtyard, in the middle of which is a big acacia tree. They said the people round were a good deal mixed—Chinese with Shan and Lolo. Many looked like Shan. And here again people wore white turbans round their heads.

The road here leaves the Yangtze and ascends the Han-po Ling, 4500 feet, at 18¼ miles. It then descends over low hills, and passing up a fertile valley Hsin-kai, 4420 feet, is reached. It has fifty families.

Hwa-p'ing-hsien, a town of seven hundred

families, at an elevation of 4215 feet, was reached on July 31. The distance was 16¼ miles. There was a rather steep climb to Kan-chia-ya-k'ou, 5400 feet. The road then lay along fairly well-wooded hill-side, with pretty views over the fertile valley of the San Ho on the left. The trees were mostly firs. At 12 miles there was a steep descent of 1200 feet, and the road then lay across the fertile Hwa-p'ing valley.

The road on August 1 lay down the Hwa-p'ing Ho valley for 3 miles, and then gradually turned westward up the very fertile Hsin-chuang Ho valley. Here he saw rice being cut for the first time. Maize, millet, cotton, egg plant and oil-bearing plants were also grown, and he bought some very hard pears which were quite good to eat. At 12 miles was Hsing-Chuang, with twenty-five families, and beyond it the way led up a steep, beautiful little gorge and along a small valley to Pien-wu, 4696 feet, a scattered village of thirty-five families, among well-wooded hills. The thermometer was 93° in the shade.

The Lisu village of Ai-chüch was visited on the next day. It lay just off the road 7½ miles from Pien-wu, and consisted of about a dozen houses scattered among maize fields about half-way. The houses were built of logs without mud between, and they usually had penthouse thatched roofs. These Lisu are of Tibetan origin and occupy the surrounding hills, whilst the Chinese take the more fertile valleys. The men are very like the black Lolos. One man was 5 feet 4 inches. They all had Mongol eyes and very broad, beaked noses. They were dressed in a rather short blue gown with hemp rags underneath. They wore turbans and had bare legs. The only woman Pereira saw close had a blue robe extending to the knee, hemp rags underneath, a red sash round her waist, and her hair, dressed as a pigtail, was coiled round her head. Another woman, better dressed, had a turban, but fled before Pereira could get near her.

A log hut occupied by a bachelor was inspected. The bed was an inclined plank with a piece of wood for a pillow. For furniture there were a few wicker baskets and some cooking pots. The man and a friend were just starting on a bird-shooting expedition and were armed with old Chinese flint-locks. Their chief food seemed to be maize.

The road continued along the ridge above this village at $7\frac{1}{2}$ miles from Pien-wu. At $11\frac{3}{4}$ miles Wei-sha, fifteen scattered houses, was reached, its elevation being 6745 feet.

On August 3 Pereira marched $20\frac{1}{4}$ miles to Ta-Liu. After a short climb and a very steep descent there was a bigger climb out of a very steep and rocky ravine to the Wa-la-p'ung slope, where there was an easy road along the top with hills on the left and grand views over the valley on the right towards ranges beyond. At $4\frac{1}{2}$ miles there were some very steep rocky ascents up a beautifully wooded glen, and then an easier climb to the top of the Ping-chün P'o, 8080 feet, at $6\frac{3}{4}$ miles, and a farther steep climb to the top of Yeh-ya-t'an Ya-k'ou, 8520 feet, at $8\frac{3}{4}$ miles. From the top there were more grand views down the valley, which was bounded by high ranges well wooded and with patches of Lisu cultivation on the lower slopes.

Creepers like long streamers were hanging from some of the trees. Pereira had noted the same in Tibet and West Szechwan. His Tibetan boy called it Lao-wa-yen, or "Raven smoke". Some of the last of the rhododendrons were in bloom, and there were a good many ferns on the hill-sides.

Tsuan-t'ien P'o, 8670 feet, was reached at 13½ miles, and another grand view was obtained down the valley with (probably) the high range of the Yangtze in the distance. Beyond this the road wound along the hill-side, and finally there was a steep descent through a wood to Ta-Liu, a village of twenty houses, with ninety more scattered round, at an elevation of 7451 feet. The people round were partly Chinese and partly Lisu.

Keeping along the hill-side on the following day for the first 3 miles, Pereira then had half a mile of steep descent to a bridge over the Ch'u-i Ho, 6230 feet. The bridge was covered with a wood roof on mud walls. On the other side was a very steep climb and some bad pieces up steep rocky places among trees, chiefly fir, to the top of Ta-lo-han-sung-P'o, 7810 feet, at 5¾ miles. Then the path lay high up along the hill-side with a deep valley on the left to the top of Chi-tan P'o, the Egg Hill, 8200 feet, at 8½ miles, a pleasant spot with grass, some trees and a spring. Then after a steep descent of 450 feet the road rises to K'ou-tzu-chin P'o, 8050 feet, at 10½ miles, after which there are some steep descents; but the road passes along the hill-side among fir and bush till at 15 miles it descends to the very fertile

Yeng-peh valley, which is three-quarters of a mile wide and covered with rice fields.

Yeng-peh-hsien is reached at 17¾ miles. It is a city of 12,000 families, at an elevation of 6854 feet. Pereira stayed in the Roman Catholic Mission station, which is under the supervision of the priests at Ma-shang, whom he had seen five stages back.

On August 5 he crossed the fertile plain and then over hills with atrocious descents very slippery after rain. At 14 miles he reached Shui-ch'ung, where there were pears, plums and apricots. This place is also called Ho-tsung.

Next day he ascended the Ch'ing-shui Ho valley, climbing up the hill-side, which was fairly well wooded, with occasional farms and patches of cultivation. At 10½ miles he reached the Chi-ch'ing-kang Po, 8088 feet, and then slightly descended to Tawan, a village of forty-five families, at 13 miles.

From here on to Likiang Fu the people are mostly Mosu, a Tibetan race nearly resembling the Lisu and Nosu, with broad nostrils and beaked noses. Here they dress like the Chinese, but many had sheepskin clothes. The men averaged from 5 feet 5 inches to 5 feet 6 inches.

Making a bend to cross a stream which farther on makes its way through a deep gorge to the Yangtze, the road again climbs the hill-side, and at 16½ miles is the Chu Ya-k'ou, or Bamboo Pass from which there is a gorgeous view. The Yangtze, looking like a small muddy stream, is far below and runs between great steep mountains rising 5000 to 7000 feet above it. In front and around were deep valleys, and away to the north on the left bank of the Yangtze was the great Shao-chi Shan, rising some 7000 or 8000 feet, with sloping sides and the summit wooded, and patches of cultivation high up. Farther north the mountains look wilder, and there is one steep conical peak, and behind it, perhaps 40 or 50 miles away, is a high range. The scenery of the Yangtze here rivals that of Ta-ching-pa, west of Chao-tung, and quite dwarfs the well-known I-chang gorges.

A not very steep descent from the pass leads to Tzu-Liu, a village of sixteen families, in the Yangtze valley, where Pereira halted, and on August 7 he continued the steep descent and at 2½ miles reached what he believed to be the only bridge over the Yangtze. It was of the usual pattern, Chinese suspension bridge on sixteen iron chains, supporting a plank roadway 9 feet wide. There was an iron chain on either side as hand-rail. And the bridge is supported by stone piers on either bank. The bridge sags a good deal in the centre, and mules went over by driblets. It was 135 paces long. The height above sea-level at this point was 4321 feet.

The Yangtze, here called Tzu-li-chiang, dashed past in a wild tumult of muddy rapids. Pereira had never seen such a mighty torrent. Not even the Ngom Chu and other rivers in Tibet when in abnormal flood the year before could equal it.

On the far side there was a steady climb, partly by zigzags and a cobbled path through pine woods, with everywhere fresh views of glorious mountains and deep valleys. At 7888 feet was the village of Tui-neo-k'e with sixty-five families, mostly Mosu. The first part of the climb was very hot, and then it became milder. At 14¼ miles the top of the San-shen-miao P'o or Ch'ing-ming-k'ou, 9481 feet, was reached, a rise of 5160 feet from the Yangtze bridge. The descent led down a beautifully wooded gorge, and at 15¾ miles the great Likiang plain was reached, and at 22½ miles Likiang Fu.

Likiang Fu was one of the big stages on Pereira's northward journey. It is an unwalled city of some 30,000 inhabitants, at 7561 feet, and Pereira made the distance from Yünnan Fu 872 miles. Many pessimists at Yünnan had said that he would not be able to get through in the rainy season. The roads had certainly been very bad, but not worse than in other parts of China. And though there was plenty of rain, it fell chiefly at night.

Behind the city to the north rise great rocky, peaked mountains running north and causing the great bend in the Yangtze. They are partly snow-covered, and were the highest Pereira had yet seen in Yünnan. He estimated them at 17,000 feet.

Great excitement had been caused in this city by the capture of Mr. Weatherbe, an English engineer, by Chinese bandits twenty-two days previously at a place two stages south-west. He was trying to reach Batang from Burma and was making his way back by Yünnan Fu. Pereira called on the General and Magistrate to urge his release, and suggested that the bandits' demand for reincorporation in the army should be complied with while insisting on Weatherbe's immediate release.

There were living here Mr. Clover, of the Porte Costal Mission, and Mr. J. F. Rock, an American botanist. Pereira stayed with the latter, who told him that above the junction of the Chung Chiang and Yangtze, about two and a half days from Likiang, there are the most wonderful gorges, through which the river races in mad rapids, while the mountains rise 12,000 or 13,000 feet above it. Pereira was much tempted to go and see them, but time was pressing, so he gave up the idea.

There are a number of Mosu about Likiang. They object to being called Mosu and call themselves Na-hsi, which means black people. There being a festival, crowds of Mosu girls had collected. Many were walking together like in a girls' school: others were sitting out. The girls were in parties and the boys kept separate.

Small pandars, locally called huo-hu or fire-fox, are found near here.

Having collected mules for his next big stage, that is, A-tun-tzu, Pereira left Likiang Fu on August 11, marching 9 miles to Chi-L'o-ts'un. The road led across the plain and round the La-shih-Shui Lake. The next day he marched 16 miles to Shih-ku. At first the road led over rolling hills with plenty of pine trees, then it was less well wooded, and there was a gradual rise till at 5¾ miles the Mu-hsien P'o, 8400 feet, was reached. Beyond there was a steep descent, partly by zigzag, and below the Yangtze could be seen making its big bend to the north. The hills were high and partly covered with pine, but the scenery was not so grand as in other parts of the Yangtze valley. At 11¾ miles the Yangtze, here called the Chin-sha-Chiang, was again struck at an elevation of 5823 feet. Shih ku, 100 feet above the river, has two hundred families. The weather was now quite chilly at night, and even in the day only hot for a short time.

Following up the right bank of the Yangtze the next day, Pereira reached Hsia-ke-tzu, 19 miles. It has seventy-five families and is at an elevation of 6041 feet. The villages about here were a good deal scattered, and sometimes broken up into two or three clusters.

On August 14 Pereira continued up the right bank of the Yangtze. He had intended to go by the eastern route *via* Peng-tzu-ya to A-tun-tzu, but the magistrate objected, as there were no soldiers on it, and he had therefore no control. Pereira therefore took the Wei-si route. There were fewer villages as he ascended the Yangtze. Walnuts and chestnuts were grown in the low valley. Maize was the only crop, and no more rice was now seen. The hills were sloping and well wooded. There are many leopards in these woods, it was said. The rhododendron is locally called the Ch'a-shan-hua or Tea-hill flower. Wu-Lou-ting was reached at 17½ miles.

On August 15 he continued up the Yangtze valley for 8 miles and then left it near the village of Chü-tien. And now the first signs of Tibet appeared in the form of chortens, prayer flags and small mané stone heaps. At 10¾ miles he reached La-p'ien-Ku. The next day he marched up the pretty pine-wooded Pa-tsi-chi Ho valley, and at 6½ miles reached the top of the Hui-shao P'o, 7477 feet. From there he kept along the hill-side and at 9 miles reached T'ai-p'ing-t'ang, 7887 feet. Continuing up the valley but descending some 408 feet, he reached at 14 miles the open fertile Lutien valley, and at 16¼ miles reached Lutien, a town of 310 families. In this valley rice as well as maize was grown. Pereira saw a good many walnut trees and some wild plums and a wild peach. Some rhododendrons were still in bloom at altitudes over 7000 feet. Lutien, scattered among fields green with crops and clusters of trees and surrounded by high tree-covered hills, was very picturesque. Of the 310 families, roughly 60 were Chinese, 100 were Tibetan and 150 were Mosu. And three days' journey to the south were some Lisu. Maize is the chief food of the people, but they also grow wheat and barley for a first crop, and for a second crop buckwheat higher up and rice lower down.

The religious character of the people was exemplified by Pereira's host. Three or four times a day he would come to the loft where there was a Buddhist shrine and would kotow before it, say prayers and burn incense. It reminded Pereira of Tibet.

Rain fell heavily, so he halted a day at Lutien, and on the 18th marched 18 miles to Wei-si. Soon leaving the plain, he climbed 2600 feet through woods by easy zigzags to Ta-shih-t'ou P'o, 10,755 feet (Si-jam-bu in Mosu), which he reached at 5 miles. This is the Yangtze-Mekong divide. It is 4760 feet above the Yangtze, where he had left it at Chü-tien. From here there was a descent across undulating Li-ti P'ing grassy downs among trees. Three or four big flocks of sheep and goats were seen, and "a lot of small flowers"—Pereira evidently was not a botanist! It poured with rain during the afternoon and he got soaked. At 16½ miles was a small open, very fertile plain on which were grown maize, rice and tobacco. The Wei-si Ho was crossed by a high, open, wood bridge, and the road then ascended to Wei-si-hsien, a city of 250 families, at an elevation of 7016 feet. In the city the population was Chinese, in the valley Mosu, and in the hills Lisu.

Pereira stayed in the long loft or upper story of a clean private house. As there was a shrine in it, the Chinese were very particular that they must be allowed up to perform their devotions, though this is not a common feature of Chinese life.

Rain again compelled Pereira to stop for a day. It was raw and chilly, and he found a greatcoat very comfortable. He also had a charcoal fire. There were few mosquitoes and he slept without a net.

On August 20 he resumed his march, and at 14½ miles reached Ka-ka-t'ang, 6312 feet. At 4¼ miles he crossed the Wei-si Ho by a bridge to the right bank and continued down the valley, passing over the lower spurs. Ninety soldiers, mostly boys, were also going to A-tun-tzu, and passed him twice on the road. Some of the soldiers besides the officers were riding. The transport was coolie and a few mules, and often the coolies were carrying seven rifles apiece. After 8 miles the hills were more sloping and the trees more in clusters. The scenery was beautiful. Ka-ka-t'ang has thirteen Chinese families.

The Chinese occupied the villages in the valley bottom. The Mosu and Tibetans (who about here are called Lamas) live on the hill-sides; and the Lisu live behind in the higher ranges. Pereira notes how the milder Lisu have been pushed back at first by the more virile Mosu, who have assimilated more with the Chinese; and then how the Mosu in their turn have had to give way to the Chinese.

The Mekong was reached on the following day, August 21. The road along the hill-side was very narrow and wound up and down, sometimes well above the Wei-si Ho and sometimes close to it. There were beautiful views, and the hills were higher and steeper than before. At 5½ miles was the little hamlet of A-nan-do-t'ang of ten hovels, and at 8½ miles a side stream is crossed by a stone bridge. The road then leads down the narrow and beautiful Alando gorge between high, precipitous, rocky, wooded hills. And at 11 miles the Mekong is reached. It is here at an elevation of 5896 feet and is called the Lan-tsang Chiang or Dza Chu.

A tributary had to be crossed by a single rope bridge, which was a disagreeable operation, as the body was underneath the rope and the legs kicking up in the air. Beyond this the road ascended the left bank of the Mekong, which was here 150 to 250 yards wide. There were several villages by the river and the crop grown was mostly maize, but there was some rice. At 19¼ miles Hsiao-wei-si, 5610 feet, was reached. It has thirty families. Pereira and Thompson stayed at the Roman Catholic Mission with the Chinese Père Li.

Chinese soldiers passed on the way had no greatcoats or mackintoshes. They were probably not paid. No one takes care of soldiers in China, and they looked quite untrained. No wonder if these boys are attacked they get a panic and bolt. And it is not surprising, Pereira reflects, that they find it more lucrative to become brigands.

Continuing up the valley of the Mekong on August 22, he reached K'ang-pu at 17 miles. The going was easy all day, without any steep climbs. The hills were mostly sloping and well-wooded. The crops were maize and millet and, when the valley was more level, rice. The people were chiefly Chinese in the villages by the road-side and Mosu and Lisu higher up in the hills. The weather was mild and fine. At Ai-wa, 7½ miles, there was a ferry boat, but the road to A-tun-tzu continued up the left bank of the river, and three or four tributaries had to be crossed by rope bridges. In the hills there are leopards, bear, roe, wild boar, serow, but no pandars or tigers.

On August 23 he marched 14½ miles to Yeh-chih, still up the Mekong valley. The country gets wilder and the path leads alongside the river up narrow gorges between steep well-wooded hills, with only an occasional farm or patch of cultivation. At 4½ miles is a steep climb of 800 feet, and fine views to the north are obtained. Three streams are seen breaking through the mountains, the eastern stream piercing through a great wall of red and grey rock, showing high hills beyond with patches of cultivation, the work of Lisu. At 5½ miles the road descends to the river again and passes by the wonderful La-p'u-Lu rapid, which Pereira thought the wildest he had ever seen. Here the mighty Mekong, restricted to less than 40 yards in width, thunders through the gorge, the muddy waters in their wild career dashing against the rocks and being churned into great white waves.

The hills again open out at 10½ miles and the going is easy to Yeh-chih, a village of fifty-five families, Chinese and Mosu.

Pati was reached on August 24 after a march of 20 miles. There were the same sloping hills with a good deal of cultivation, and there were more flat belts with rice fields. Pati has twenty families, of whom eight are Mosu. It is at an elevation of 6095 feet.

These Mosu Pereira found to be a nice quiet friendly people. He stayed in a Mosu house. The kitchen showed that his host was in comparatively opulent circumstances. It was a big room with planks projecting from the wall on two sides like a guard-room at home. On these the natives sleep in hot weather. Part is covered with flat stones for the cooking. Three large copper tripods for supporting the ovens or cooking pots stood on these stones. The centre of the room was supported by a beam, round which were tied boughs and branches of trees. This Pereira's Tibetan boy said was to propitiate the spirits of the kitchen. The whole family with their fourteen children seemed to collect in this room.

The Lisu from here onwards become more and the Mosu less numerous. The Lisu girls wear a cotton hood with rows of cowrie shells—sometimes as many as seven or eight hundred. These shells are brought up from Burma at a price of seventy for a dollar.

On August 25 Pereira marched 19 miles to Lan-lu-k'a or Na-lon-k'a. The country was now wilder. The hills were steep and well-wooded. And the road passed through some grand gorges—the river breaking through rocky cliffs 500 to 700 feet in height. At 17½ miles the trail from the Salween comes down to Tzu-ku, where there was formerly a Roman Catholic station, but it was burnt by Tibetans about a dozen years before, and there is now a new station 1½ mile higher up at Tzu-chung. There was rain during the night and light showers during the day.

Pereira paid a visit, the next day, to Père Ouvrard, whose mission station was on the opposite side of the river. The crossing had to be effected by a double rope bridge, which is an especially troublesome matter for any one with a bad leg, and he found it exciting looking down into the foaming river below. Professor Gregory, Weatherbe, and many other travellers had crossed by the bridge.

Père Ouvrard was suffering from malaria. He said his parish extended some 89 miles to the south to Yeh-chih and on the north nearly to Yakalo. He had 622 baptized Christians, of whom over 400 were Tibetans and the rest mostly

Chinese. A few were Mosu. He said the tendency in these parts was for the Chinese to become Tibetanised. When the old mission had been burnt two French priests were decapitated. Forest, the botanist, after eight days' wanderings in the mountains among the Lisu, escaped to Hsiao-wei-si.

One of Pereira's muleteers died during the night of malignant malaria. Père Ouvrard said that this disease was very prevalent in these parts.

Regarding burial Père Ouvrard said that the Tibetans usually bury the corpse temporarily, and when decomposed dig it up, burn the bones in a vase and bury them again. The poorer either take the corpse on to the hills to be devoured by wild animals or else dump it in the Mekong. If it sticks on the rocks they push it off again lest the Christians would take it up for re-burial.

The rainfall in normal years occurs in July, August and September. But in the present year there had been very little rain, and the maize crop, on which the people rely, had failed, and there would in consequence be a famine from here to Hsiao-wei-si, about 70 miles farther south, and the people would either have to go west to the Salween, where the harvest was good, or else depend upon buck-wheat.

Slaves are kept by the Tibetans and Mosu of these parts, but they are well treated. There are no Lisu north of Tze-ku, but the Mosu extend nearly to Yakalo, where they are mixed up in separate villages with the Tibetans. The Mosu are born soldiers. Two or three hundred years ago, when they were a powerful independent race, the Tibetans attacked them near Tze-ku, but they repulsed the attack and drove the Tibetans back nearly to Yakalo. Afterwards they came to terms and each occupied separate villages in the same country. Most of the Chinese troops in these parts are recruited from the Mosu, and only very few from the Lisu.

In the afternoon of August 27, after burying the mulcteer and arranging for his effects, Pereira marched 5 miles through gorges between high hills to Huan-fu-p'ing, 6144 feet, a village of sixteen families.

On August 28 he marched 16 miles to Yang-tsa (in Tibetan La-dze). The hills were more sloping and the villages were high up, and there were only hamlets by the river. The villages were now all Tibetan with flat mud-roofed Tibetan houses. At 5 miles was the narrow and fine Hsiao-yen-chai gorge. The path was very narrow, and there were steep precipitous drops to the river. In places the Mekong was not more than 100 feet wide. Yang-tsa, 6366 feet, has five families, all Tibetan. Pereira stayed in a clean square plank Tibetan room, but fleas were very troublesome.

A wild country with steep hill-sides was passed through on the next day's march. The path winds up the steep hill-side rising at 4½ miles to 7643 feet. It then keeps along high up with very big steep drops to the Mekong, which rushed in rapids through deep gorges far below. At 9 miles is Kunia, a village of ten Tibetan houses. At 12 miles the Chia-pieh Ya-k'ou, 7980 feet, was reached. From here there was a grand view back down the Mekong valley. All round were great hills with a partly snow-clad range running north and south to the west. It is the Mekong-Salween divide. In it is the sacred mountain Ka-ga-bu, which means "Snow White". It is said to be 20,000 feet in height.

From here the path descended to Chia-pieh, a village of eight families, mostly Tibetan. Its elevation is 7234 feet, and the distance from Yang-tsa 12½ miles. The Tibetans of the lower classes in these parts were very friendly, though somewhat obsequious and timid. Most of them met on the road-side would greet one by holding out one or both hands. At night the Lama, having lighted his sacrificial fire in the room which Pereira was occupying, lay down by the door and began mumbling his prayers.

A-tun-tzu was reached on August 30. The country changed on this last stage. The hills were wilder and were practically treeless. They had on them only shrub, and only occasionally could two or more houses with patches of cultivation be seen. But the path was better and broader. A mile west of Chia-pieh it led down to the Mekong valley at 7020 feet, and led up it for 3 miles, where it left the Mekong and ascended the narrow Yung-chu valley between bare hills, and at 16 miles A-tun-tzu (in Tibetan Gyu) was reached. This was the 16th stage from Li-kiang-fu and the 37th stage from Yünnan-fu.

CHAPTER XIX

THE END

A-TUN-TZU is a town of four hundred families, half Chinese and half Tibetan, at an elevation of 10,810 feet. The country is nominally under Tibetan princes to whom the Chinese have granted the rank of t'u-ssu. But they have no power. The northern prince rules the country from Yakalo to Dong, the next stage north. According to Monsieur Perronne, a French musk merchant who had lived here for twenty years, the Tibetans of these parts prefer Chinese to Tibetan rule, as the Chinese at any rate pay something, whilst the Lamas pay nothing. Also the Lamas are constantly fighting among themselves, and there is a vendetta between the chiefs, whilst the Chinese do keep some sort of order. The southern prince rules some way south down the Mekong. A third t'u-ssu is a Mosu who resides at Yeh-chih.

Trade was very bad. The Chinese were gambling and letting things go. Chinese rupees were current here. Pereira found among the rupees one of the East India Company of William IV., 1835. There was a bad habit here of cutting the rupees in half, and often people would not take what they considered the smaller half.

Monsieur Perronne said that the Mekong and

Yangtze in these parts do not freeze, though there is sometimes an ice fringe on the bank of the Mekong. At Chamdo the Mekong is frozen from January to March.

On September 5, having hired fresh mules and Dr. Thompson having recovered from an attack of fever, they set out again on their march to Batang. They had a steep climb for 2½ miles to the top of Chula, 11,480 feet, then an easy winding descent to Dong at 9 miles. It is a Tibetan village of forty families situated deep down in a valley. The next day they marched 13 miles to Ku-shih (Go-hsieh). There was a rather steep descent for 6 miles down the Dong-lung Chu valley between very high steep bare hills. High up on a ledge was a monastery. At 3½ miles the path leads through the wild Ru-wa-shou gorge between high rocky precipices. Then there was a climb of 500 feet to the Ma-pa La, 7890 feet, from which there was a steep descent. On the opposite side was Ma-pa-t'ing, from which there is a trail between A-tun-tzu and Chamdo. After two stages this trail leaves the river, crosses the wild Shu La and proceeds on to Pi-t'ou monastery, which has always been notorious for its anti-foreign feeling, and which pays little attention to the Kalon Lama at Chamdo.

The Mekong on this march was of a dark reddish colour, showing that it had been raining lately in Tibet. The path continued to wind up and down along the hill-side and was often very narrow with steep drops to the river. Ku-shih, a village of ten families, is situated on a small fertile ledge 300 feet above the river. Its elevation is 7018 feet. The weather was fine and hot.

On September 6 Pereira marched $19\frac{1}{4}$ miles to Sung-shih. The Mekong flows through a deep valley between bare desolate hills. There was a steep winding climb for $2\frac{3}{4}$ miles to the top of Ku-la, 8655 feet. Then the path wound up and down along the hill-side. At $7\frac{1}{4}$ miles is Jung, a scattered village of about sixty-five houses. From there a well-graded path led to Tang-ku-güng at $10\frac{1}{2}$ miles. The Ka-go-bo mountain could be just seen from here bearing 198°. There was some snow on its sides, but the peak was not visible. Farther on there was a steep descent to a gully, then a slight rise to Sung-ting at $17\frac{3}{4}$ miles, and down to cross a torrent and a short rise to Sung-shih, 7126 feet. Here many villagers came out to meet Pereira, bringing presents of fruit and cakes.

The hills were now higher, and many spurs had sharp razor blades. They were mostly bare in the Mekong valley, but there were sometimes trees high up in the side valleys.

Pa-mei (Chinese Pa-mi), 14 miles, was reached on September 8. The path was fair and lay near the river. At 3 miles was Na-pu. At one point there was a good piece of scaffolding to support planks for a roadway against sheer rocks. At 12 miles there was a very steep climb to Pa-mei, 8381 feet, which was hidden in a small fertile fold high up on the hill-side. It is a village of twenty-five families. The weather was fine and hot in the middle of the day, but windy in the afternoon. Pereira noted a number of beautiful little blue flowers growing out of small bushes. There was a snow range visible not far back on the opposite bank. It was only partly covered with snow. The people here are Mosu, but they have become Tibetanised.

On September 9 he marched 15¼ miles to Pai-yung-güng. There was a very steep climb by zigzag for three-quarters of a mile, then the path wound along the hill-side to Ta-key-no, 9687 feet, at 8¼ miles. At 8 miles there was a grand view of the Mekong winding among spurs and of a partly covered snow range not far off on the opposite bank. The path then descends by steep zigzags with the deep Shih-ti Chu valley far below on the left. At 9¾ miles this river is crossed by a plank bridge. Then there is a very steep climb by zigzags to a shoulder of the Mu-chia-gong slope. Pai-yung-güng, 10,088 feet, has twelve families. There is a small lamasery here, the monks of which had cartridge belts and swords. Here it was very cold.

The clouds lifted and there was a glorious view of a partly covered snow-peaked range to the west, which was probably the Salween-Mekong divide, and of the snow-covered Ka-ga-bu, which is estimated by Handel-Mazetti at about 20,000 feet, perhaps 38 miles to the south. The bearing to it was 178°. A still more imposing snowy peak was the Da-mi-yung, perhaps 15 miles off, and bearing 322°. This Pereira saw again from near Batang and estimated it at about 18,000 to 19,000 feet. It is on the Mekong-Yü Chu divide. Farther back could be seen the Dong-jia, partly covered with snow, probably on the Yangtze-Mekong divide.

Yakalo was reached on September 10 after a march of 13¾ miles. The path winds down bare hills with shrub. At 2¼ miles there is a steep descent to cross a side valley at 8700 feet. Just beyond a rock marks the Yünnan-Szechwan boundary. The path then again ascends to about 10,000 feet at 9 miles, and soon after is a steep descent to Yakalo on the small fertile Yen-ching plateau.

This is a town of about seventy scattered families. Its elevation is 8655 feet. Pereira made it 84¾ miles from A-tun-tzu and 715¼ miles from Yünnan-fu. It is the residence of a magistrate, and there is a salt industry here, the wells being about half a mile off on both banks of the Mekong. The Tibetan name is Tsa-ka (place or wells of salt), to which is sometimes added the Mosu name, Pei-ting, which is also used by itself.

Yen-ching is 2 miles south of Yakalo, and the two places are separated by a ravine 50 feet deep.

Père Gorè entertained Pereira during his stay at Yakalo. He has three hundred Christians—all Tibetans, except five or six Chinese.

The heaps of stones with Tibetan prayers engraved on them which are frequently passed by the road-side are called, according to Père Gorè, Dobourg, meaning a hundred thousand stones. Pereira's boy pronounced it Mbembong. This word is also used for the stone piles, with prayer flags stuck in, on the top of every pass in Tibet. But as they are somewhat different it is best to keep the Mongol word "obo" used by Huc for these. The small mud white-painted pyramids on the roofs of Tibetan houses are for burning incense and not to ward off sickness.

The Mosu are called Diong by the Tibetans.

Their ruined towers may be seen nearly up to Yakalo. Two or three centuries ago they extended their conquests beyond Yakalo up to Garthok, Batang and Litiang, but none are now found north of Yakalo.

The wild lawless tribes south of Litiang are the Hsiang-ch'eng (Tibetan Sia-chera-wa). They have their headquarters farther south at Sang-pi-Ling on the Lamaya River. The tribes who hold up the road north of Batang to Kanze are the Leng-ka-shi. They are under a Lama. North of the Tibetan frontier, which is some 10 miles south of Sama, the country is peaceful.

Chinese soldiers did not venture more than a dozen miles north of Batang. There were no Chinese soldiers west of Pa-mu-t'ang on the Batang-Yakalo road. The Batang garrison was about three hundred strong. Of these one hundred were employed on the road east towards Litiang, some twenty at Batang, and the rest were scattered along the road south and south-west up to Pa-mu-t'ang (Bum). But these soldiers could effect very little, and the Nanka (Lanka) Lama's bands were raiding across the Yangtze. The Gunka Lama had again recently come to terms with the Chinese and was practically independent at Tsong-su (Chung-ai). The official at Garthok, the Mark-ham Ti-jei, had twice sent his soldiers across the frontier. About a fortnight previously fifteen Tibetan soldiers came to Yakalo and greatly alarmed the people, as they did some looting. The magistrate suggested to Pereira that he should ask the Garthok official to stop sending men over the border. There was a band of twenty brigands in the Pa-mei, but they were "friendly" brigands and not likely to trouble Pereira.

The postal arrangements at Yen-ching were of a primitive description. The postmaster was a Tibetan. Pereira found him in bed in a small dark evil-smelling room. He sat up half naked in bed to register the letters and Père Goré did the stamping, while a number of dirty children clustered round the door.

The salt pans were visited on September 13. There is a very steep descent of 1367 feet to the Mekong river bank. The salt on the west bank is reddish. The pans consist of small mud squares on logs supported on piles. The brine is poured on to these and the water evaporates in the wind and sun. The wells, which were now in the rainy season below the level of the river, could not for the time being be used.

Dr. Thompson was taken ill at Yakalo and feared he was being attacked by cholera. However, he recovered and was able to continue the journey.

But the country ahead was very unsettled. While they were actually at Yakalo a band of the Nanka Lama's had raided a village near Tsong-en on the road Pereira would be taking to Batang. On the other hand, the Markham Ti-jei, in reply to a letter which Pereira had written him, had asked Pereira to meet him at Lhandum, just over the border near Pa-mu-tang.

So on September 15 Pereira set out on his next main stage—to Batang; and he had now to get back from the valley of the Mekong to the valley of the Yangtze. After descending the ravine between Yakalo and Yenching he proceeded easterly up a narrow gorge, passing the fine Drag-shih canyon, where steep precipices rise on either side to a height of from 500 to 600 feet. At 5 miles the country is more open and there is some cultivation. Then there is a continuous gradual but steep climb till at 6¼ miles Lha-da-ting, 11,312 feet, is reached. From here the great mountain Da-mi-yung could be seen bearing 263°, but it did not seem so high as when first seen some stages back.

The divide between the Mekong and the Yangtze was crossed on the following day and Pereira marched 13¼ miles to Ngu-chao (Chinese Yao-ch'ao). Soon after starting, cultivation ended and the path climbed along well-wooded hills, fir trees predominating. At 2 miles the ascent became steep, and at 3¾ miles the Chia La, 14,310 feet, was reached. This is on the Mekong-Yangtze divide. West of Jye-kundo the height of the pass across the divide is 15,724 feet. And farther south the height of the Shung La, the pass crossing the divide, is 10,755 feet. From the pass there was a steep descent among fir-covered hills to 5¾ miles, when the descent became easier and lay down the narrow Durashi valley. It was stony and often muddy, and would have been bad after rain, but luckily the weather was fine and warm, though it had been rather chilly and windy on the top of the pass. At 9 miles the path crosses to the right bank and ascends to the Chu-chih La, about 12,500 feet. It then winds down and ascends again to the Chih-ru La, 13,111 feet, at 11¾ miles. And from there the descent to Ngu-chao was easy. This was a hamlet of five houses in a small valley with some cultivation. Its elevation is 11,984 feet.

A gentian, which Pereira had found so common in Tibet at 13,000 feet, he saw again on the Chia La. It is the gentian nubigena. There was also a little yellow flower, rather pulpy, which grows in marshy places.

There was considerable fear among the Chinese escort of raids on the next day's march, and they wanted to get ten men as escort. The Gunka Lama's men had fled into the hills and might be dangerous. But Pereira thought two additional men would be sufficient, and proceeded on September 17 to Chia-hi-ting, 16¾ miles. The road lay down the valley, joining the Chung-tsa stream at 3¾ miles, and crossing it by a poor bridge on two piles at 4½ miles, at an elevation of 9978 feet. Half a mile beyond is the village of Chung-tsa, consisting of twelve dilapidated houses, with another twenty scattered about. This is the Tsong-en on the maps—in Chinese Chung-ai. The Gunka Lama lives at the Sogong Gompa, lower down the river. The road continues up a small valley between low shrub-covered hills to the watershed at 14¾ miles, and then along level ground amid fir trees with open grass spots, and farther on an open plateau with the Mai-ya stream below flowing south among grassy fir-covered hills. Chia-ni-ting, 12,209 feet, consists of thirty scattered houses on a sloping hill-side.

Here a representative of the Markham Ti-jei was awaiting Pereira. He said the Ti-jei was sick at Lhandu Di, just over the border, and asked

Pereira not to go there as he had intended. The illness, of course, was a sham, and Pereira, when he was told that no messenger had yet been sent to the Kalon Lama at Chamdo to obtain leave for him to proceed from Batang to Kanze by Tibet, said that if he did not get a reply at Batang in ten days he would write to Lhasa to complain.

Pa-mu-tang (Bum), 15¼ miles, was reached on September 18. Pereira's caravan had swelled from his seventeen animals and eight extra for the Batang Mission to sixty-eight animals, besides some pedestrians. The road lay over high rolling grassy downs. There were few trees and the path was stony. At 3¾ miles the Dong-ti La, 12,998 feet, was crossed. It is an open pass on the top of the downs. Beyond it is a slight drop and then a rise to the Bum La, 13,054 feet, at 5½ miles. At 7½ miles the descent becomes steeper to the Tamba-Larji grass valley, where there were some nomad tents. This open grass country and nomad tents and flocks reminded Pereira of North Tibet, and it was now cold enough for a greatcoat to be worn. At 9 miles the road lay down the Bum valley, which is a half to three-quarters of a mile wide, with some crops among the grass and shrub. Pa-mu-tang, or Bum, has twenty-four scattered houses at an elevation of 11,090 feet. There had been fifty Chinese soldiers here, but they had retreated a month previously after their trouble with the Gunka Lama.

Continuing down the Bum valley on September 19, Pereira, at 14¾ miles, reached Ganra on the Yangtze. At 2¼ miles the valley narrows to a gorge. The river is then crossed twice by log bridges. At 6¼ miles is Kum-tzu-ding, a village of fourteen families, where fifty or sixty Chinese soldiers were quartered. At 7 miles the top of the Kung-tzu-la, 11,090 feet, was reached. The descent was steep by a stony path leading among firs down a narrow valley. And at 13½ miles the Yangtze valley was reached, and the road led up it for another 1¼ mile to Ganra (Chinese Kung La), 7997 feet, about 150 feet above the river. It is a village of eight houses, and seventy Chinese soldiers were stationed in it. It had been chilly on the top of the pass, but down below it was quite hot and fine.

The history of the feud between the Nanka Lama and the Gunka Lama was this. In the month of May the former attacked the latter in the Tsong-en district, but the Gunka Lama, with the aid of Captain Wong, drove him off. Later the remaining Chinese companies from Ganra and Drubanang joined the Gunka Lama. But in August he and the Chinese had a quarrel and the men fired at but missed the Lama, who then fled with his people to the hills; and the soldiers, having in consequence nobody to furnish them with supplies, had to retire to their old quarters. Thereupon the Gunka Lama returned and went to Lhandum to see the Markham Ti-jei, who advised him to make it up with the Chinese. About September 13 the Nanka Lama, keeping his feud with the Gunka Lama, raided the villages of Konpu and Botsa, 6 or 7 miles below Chung-tsa village. And this is how matters stood when Pereira passed through. The Sogong monastery, the headquarters of the Gunka Lama, is not on the Chuntsa River, but in the mountains about 3 miles below on the east side of the river.

Following up the right bank of the Yangtze, which here runs between hills about 2000 feet high and covered with shrub and grass but no trees, Pereira, on September 20, marched 6¾ miles to Drubanang (Chinese Chu-pa-lung) ferry, and another 3 miles to Drubanang Druka. The river at the ferry was 150 yards wide and was 7690 feet above sea-level. Just below the ferry the Si Chu joins the Yangtze. Drubanang Druka is a village of thirteen houses and has a garrison of sixty men.

Batang was reached on September 21 after a march of 20½ miles. The road lay up the left bank of the Yangtze, keeping low down not far from the river. At 8 miles the Lamda stream, where Père Brieux was massacred in 1881, was forded. At 10¾ miles is Lei (Chinese Shui-mao-kou), where there is a Chinese garrison. At 11½ miles is Nyu-shu, a village of five families, where there is a ferry of coracles, then a rather steep climb to the spot—12½ miles—where Dr. Shelton of the American Mission was murdered by Kei-mu-wa tribesmen in February 1922. This tribe are a pastoral race who had been plundered by the Sia-chern-wa people who live to the south-east, and being reduced to dire straits had turned brigands. The murderers were known, but the Chinese at Batang were too feeble to arrest them.

Continuing to climb out of the Yangtze valley, Pereira at 14¾ miles reached the top of the Ku-yu La, 8985 feet, which is a favoured haunt of brigands, and then descended to the pleasant green fertile Ba Chu valley, which is formed by the Kan Çhu coming from the north-north-east from Dam, and the Ba Chu coming from Batang. The road then ascends the Ba Chu valley to Batang.

Batang, 8271 feet, is a regular little Tibetan town with two-storied Tibetan houses. It was formerly a great centre of industry, but, under the present chaotic rule in China, trade is at a standstill.

There were resident here Dr. Hardy, Mr. Macleod (a Canadian), Messrs. Duncan and Morse of the American Mission, and Père Nussbaum. Missionaries could not venture in safety more than 2 or 3 miles each way up the valley, and no outsider had been here since Major Magruder, Military Attaché, and Mr. Bucknell, American Vice-Consul, had visited it in 1921.

Pereira was told that the Tibetans here preferred Chinese to Tibetan rule. The people are very superstitious and it is almost impossible to convert them.

Respecting the geography of these parts Pereira was able to collect some information. Among the great mountains there are (1) two mountains, one 15 miles S.S.E. and another three or four stages S.S.W. of Ta-chien-lu; (2) the Ngemda, slightly south-east of Batang; (3) a great range visible to south from Kanze and forming the Yangtze-Yalung divide.

The frontier between Tibet and China was said to extend from north of Chamub'ang on the Salween up the Salween-Mekong divide to north-west of Yakalo, then turning E.N.E. across the

Mekong it passes the Do-tse La on the Yakalo—Garthok road (a little south of the old border as shown on Davies's map) and then crosses the Bum La (in Chinese Chesun-ling-Ch'ing-shan), between Lhandum and Pa-mu-t'ang, and follows the divide between the Yangtze and Tsong-en rivers as shown on Teichman's map, turning to the north-east, as shown on the same map, to take in the province of Derge and passing some 10 miles south of Sama, south of the Ngu-pa La.

All inside the Tibetan frontier, which extends 10 miles south of Sama, was peaceful, but the Leng-ka-shi tribe, with whom Teichman had trouble, were holding up the Batang—Kanze road, and Chinese soldiers could only occasionally venture as far as Dam.

The Batang monastery had at this time 250 monks, though all did not live in it. The abbot is the Laka Lama. He belongs to the red sect.

On September 26 there were rumours that the Leng-ka-shi, annoyed by the arrest of some of their people, were going to attack the Chinese at Litang; that the Chantui (or Nyarong) people were threatening to attack Ta-chien-lu from the north-west, and that Kanze was disaffected and wanted to be rid of the Chinese garrison. In addition to all this the Chinese feared that the Nanka Lama was going to attack Batang. Pereira did not put very much faith in these rumours. Nevertheless, there was the fact that within the last fifteen years there had been fierce attacks of Tibetans on Chinese and Chinese on Tibetans with wholesale massacres — and also murders of Europeans. The possibility of further conflict could not therefore be ruled out.

The Chinese garrison at Batang consisted of some three hundred soldiers, who were mostly stationed on the road south up to Kung-tzu-ting, 39 miles off. Only twenty or thirty were in Batang itself. There was a garrison to the east at Litang, and to the south there were some eighty men at A-tun-tzu. The officers of these troops were practically all opium-smokers. The men apparently did nothing and they were all married to Tibetan wives. Before the present extreme chaos resulted the Chinese soldiers wanted wives. The Tibetans brought the old women. The Chinese said they wanted young girls. The Tibetans under compulsion brought the young girls, but swore to be avenged when the occasion arose. They lay outside Litang capturing and killing every small Chinese detachment and carrying off their rifles. In this way they killed over seventy Chinese.

Eastern Tibet under Chinese rule comprised kings (debo) at Dergc and Tachienlu, prefects (deba) at Batang and Litang, the five tributary races of Horpa, namely Changko, Berim, Chu-wo, Nyarong or Chantiu. The governor was appointed from Lhasa till the country was subdued by Chao-Erh-feng. Chamdo was under the (?) papa Lama, Draya was under another Lama, Markham, that is Lower Kham, was, as at present, under a sub-governor or ti-jei. The other states north and west, *e.g.* the king (debo) of Nangchen, were under the Koko Nor administration.

Pereira had now to prepare for the most difficult and most risky part of his present journey—

the stage to Kanze. It would be difficult, because he would have to cross high ranges with the winter now approaching. And it would be risky, because there was no kind of rule or order in the region he and Thompson would have to traverse. So risky was it that the Chinese magistrate tried to make the Wa-shi muleteers whom Pereira had engaged give a guarantee for his safety. This they naturally refused to give, and after much dispute Pereira accepted the responsibility himself, and both he and Thompson sent letters to the magistrate and the general relieving them of all responsibility. After various threats these Chinese officials allowed Pereira to proceed. But, as Pereira remarked, this was bad for him and Thompson, as it left the brigands free to do what they liked with them. The fact that the Chinese had refused to be responsible would doubtless become known and trouble might be expected. However, that risk Pereira determined to face, and on October 5 left Batang, the American Mission kindly making up his deficiencies in such stores as cocoa, kerosine, baking powder, etc.

His first march was a short one—9½ miles—to Meliting. He ascended the valley by the Litang road and then had a steep stony climb up the narrow Ba-chu—a smaller branch—between high bare hills. At 2½ miles he passed a rock, with an inscription in Chinese, at the place where the Amban Feng was killed by Tibetans in 1905. The small torrent had to be crossed by four log bridges. At 6½ miles the valley became more open. At 9 miles is the hamlet of Ba-chiang-hsü with eight families. Meliting has only two houses.

Its elevation is 9536 feet. There was light rain all day. He got very chilly riding and was glad to have a house to stop in. The last European along the road (with the exception of Père Nussbaum going up the valley to Yargung) was Teichman, who went about one and a half stages up. So far as he knew, no Europeans had been along the road to Litang for nine or ten years.

His miscellaneous collection of transport animals—donkeys, mules and ponies—were now changed for yaks, and he made another short march of 6½ miles to Pongdramo (Pang-chra-mo). There was first a steep ascent up the stony hill-side, the valley narrowing between high fir-covered hills. At 1¾ miles he passed the scene of a fight a few days previously between Chinese soldiers and the Nanka Lama. The path then descends slightly and crosses a side stream full of boulders, and afterwards continues up the valley with the Ba Chu, a small raging torrent, always on the right, to Pongdramo, two or three ruined houses on a clearing. The day was cloudy in the morning, but the sun came out in the afternoon. The yaks were quite unsuited for this enclosed country. They were constantly running in all directions and shedding their loads. Long delay was caused by them in crossing a small torrent, into which they deposited two of Thompson's boxes.

About twenty-eight Wa-shi men, some of Pereira's own and others taking the opportunity of his presence to return to their own country, a few marches north, accompanied Pereira and formed an escort, as they were armed with Mauser rifles. And from here onward to the Wa-shi country Pereira would be passing through a danger zone, as it was all infested with brigands, though it was said that these brigands were only in small bands. He would have to encamp, too, as there would be no houses. He had two tents made at Batang—one for himself and Thompson and one for the boys. But these tents, with only a single fly, were bitterly cold, and the cold would be increasing, as not only was winter approaching but they were rising higher. Pongdramo was 12,231 feet elevation.

Next day's march was the most anxious as regards brigands. The path continued up the Ba Chu, ascending a steep narrow valley between high hills. At 4¾ miles the limit of trees was reached and a steep climb over stony open ground followed. The main Litang road, which was at that time closed on account of brigands, was then left and Pereira followed the small more northerly Litang track, and at 7½ miles reached the summit of the Ta-so-shan (Tsang-bung-a La), 15,610 feet, the divide between the Ba Chu and the Ding Chu. This was the highest point he had reached on his present journey from Yünnan. At the top forty or fifty Chinese soldiers returning to Batang after going up the valley for the Litang convoy were met. The descent was steep, leading down open slopes. Some pretty small emerald and blue ponds, probably the source of a branch of the Ding Chu, were passed. Then the path lay down a deep narrow valley between high rocky peaks, some of which were covered with snow. At 12 miles he encamped at To-sumba-ala, 13,903 feet, in a part of the valley where there was some shrub about.

Being in the region of small bands of brigands, Pereira's party and the rest of the Wa-shi kept close together, and in certain places two or three of the men went on ahead to reconnoitre. But besides the Chinese soldiers Pereira did not see a single house or person since he had left Meliting. It was very cold at the start on this march. But at 8 A.M. the sun appeared and it was warmer. Again in the evening it was cold and windy.

From the camp he got a bearing, 120°, to a high snowy peak 8 to 10 miles away, which he thought could not be Bacot's Pic Desgoudins (in Tibetan Ga-mu-ni), as this must be farther south.

On October 8 he marched 13¼ miles and encamped on the Ding Chu. It was chilly getting up at six o'clock in a tent at nearly 14,000 feet elevation; and even when the sun rose and it was warmer it was also windy. He followed down the same valley, climbing 300 feet up a spur and then dropping some 800 feet to the Ding Chu valley. From the spur downward there were grass valleys, and in the Ding Chu valley the hills were grassy and formed excellent pasture. On the lower slopes were fir and spruce. But owing to the brigands there was not a living soul in these parts—except a convoy from Litang with rice and money for the Batang garrison which Pereira met in the valley. The road then lay up the Ding Chu valley and was easy except in a few rocky places. The stream was forded three times. It ran in a stony bed and was 30 yards wide and 2 feet deep. He camped on an open grass slope.

A narrow valley leads from here to the Gungrei La, with the snow-clad Chei-gung-tung-sei, which must be some 20,000 feet in height, on the north side of the pass and about 10 miles off. A path leads over the Gungrei La to a point near Teichman's Sodong on the road north from Batang to Bei-yu. The grassland starts from the Ding Chu valley, and Pereira surmised that it might extend northward all the way to Mongolia.

His next march was 15 miles to camp on the Shara Chu. Fording the Ding Chu at half a mile to the right bank, he continued up the grassy and often rocky and marshy valley for 7 miles to the Chago La, 14,981 feet, the divide between the Ding Chu and Li Chu. This is quite a low saddle on a spur from the Pic Desgoudins range. The main range is farther east, and Shara Chu takes its rise between the main range and the side range and so starts in a N.N.E. course.

This pass is also the boundary between Batang and the Wa-shi country. So after five days of anxiety in the brigand-infested area of Batang he emerged into what he believed to be a peaceful country, and having got through the worst part in safety his mind was greatly relieved.

On the far side he continued down another grassy valley between bare grass hills with a tributary of the Shara Chu on the right. At 12¾ miles he had a fine view of the snowy Nai-ya on the main Ga-mu-ni range, about 6 miles off to the south-east. Like all these Batang and Mekong mountains, it appeared to be about

20,000 feet high. At 13½ miles he reached the pleasant grass valley of the Shara Chu, a tributary of the Lí Chu. It was about half a mile wide, and the river itself was 25 yards wide and 1 foot deep. Here for the first time for four days there were signs of life. There was a Wa-shi nomad camp of several black tents and three white tents (for a Lama), and near by were some 600 yaks and 300 sheep and goats. Pereira halted half a mile farther up at an elevation of 13,450 feet. His yaks since the first day had gone very well and were, he considered, the finest he had seen. The weather had been good—being mostly sunny and warm.

Only a very short march of 3¾ miles was made on October 10, as the yaks needed a rest. They cannot go for more than five or six days without a halt. So Pereira stopped for the day near a Wa-shi encampment. He was still on the " small " Litang road, but on the next day's march it crosses to the right bank and later runs down the Li Chu valley.

On October 11 Pereira marched 14¼ miles to Rei-mu Chu camp. The pleasant grass Shara Chu valley was from three-quarters to a mile wide, lying between grass-covered hills from 400 to 600 feet in height. At 3¾ miles he struck north over a rolling grass plain with low hills. Here he saw many gazelle. Away to the north-west was a fine snowy range forming the watershed on the far side of the Li Chu. At 9½ miles he forded the Li Chu (Litang Ho), here 25 yards wide and 1 foot deep, and emerged on to the Mo-nia plateau, 1¼ mile wide and running for some 10 miles by the Li Chu, bearing 115° before it turns southerly in the hills. It is covered with Wa-shi tents and herds; and here Pereira changed yaks. Crossing the plateau, he ascended the narrow Rei-mu Chu valley in a northerly direction between grass hills, and soon leaving the nomads, camped higher up at an elevation of 13,790 feet.

Troubles began the next day. He marched 14¾ miles to Ta-chi-ku camp, but it was a bitterly cold, windy, snowy day, and the cold began to tell upon him. He continued for 3¼ miles to ascend the narrow Rei-mu Chu valley and then crossed the Ram-bu La, about 14,400 feet. It was the divide between the Li Chu and the Ho Chu. Most of the march after this lay up and down a narrow grass valley between bare grass hills. At 6½ miles the Guo-chen Chu, about 13,600 feet, was forded, and here were met the only nomads seen this day: they belonged to the Dei-yung tribe of the Wa-shio—the other tribes being the Mao-ya or Mo-nia, and the Tsong-hsi. From the ford there was a steep, stony climb up the narrow Bei-lung valley till at 10 miles the Bei-ling La, about 14,800 feet, was reached. From here there was a fine view to the east of a snowy range, probably the Yangtze-Ho Chu divide. Then the path wound down and up to the left round an amphitheatre, and at 11½ miles the Ta-chi La, about 14,800 feet, was crossed. On the other side the path descended the grassy Ta-chi valley and Pereira camped on a ledge 14,471 feet elevation.

The night was very cold and windy and the tent only just stood, but on October 13 Pereira marched 15 miles to Jou-ri-ku camp. For 2¾ miles he continued down the valley and then crossed a plain and ascended the Hara-gu La, about 14,300 feet, at 5¼ miles. Then he descended a valley and at 6½ miles struck north up the Tze-ku Chu valley, 2 miles wide and grassy, but rather marshy, where a few gazelle were seen. Following this was a gradual rise till at 13½ miles the Crei-tay Nya-ra (Nya-ra = Ya-k'ou = pass), about 14,000 feet, is reached, on the other side of which was a descent down a small valley to Jou-ri-ku camp, 13,563 feet. Not a human being was seen all day, but there was a small chorten near the camp. Though cold, this day's march was not so disagreeable as the previous, as the way was sheltered from the north by a side valley.

Snow fell during the night. It cleared with the morning's sun on October 14, but there was a sleet storm before the end of the day's march of 14¼ miles to Jara-güng, and Pereira writes in his diary this day : " Prospects very wretched, besides I had nausea and indigestion, and the sight of my boy's food made me feel sick ". Dr. Thompson says that on this day Pereira took practically no food, but they opened some tinned stores and Pereira was persuaded to take some hot milk and dry biscuits. In spite, however, of his sickness he still kept up his detailed description of each day's march.

The road continues down the Jou-ri Chu valley for 1½ mile, when the river turns north and apparently flows into the Yangtze, in which case the Crei-tay is the Yangtze-Ho Chu divide and it continues in a high snow-peaked range running N.N.E. The road then ascends a side valley, and at 5¾ miles the Jya-rei La, about 13,650 feet, is crossed. After which there are rolling grassy downs, and at 8¾ miles is the Sa-ma La, about 13,750 feet. Then there was a descent to the great Jara-güng plain, some 5 or 6 miles wide, on the north-west corner of which Pereira camped at 13,450 feet.

"I felt seedy and wretched", he writes at the end of his diary for the day.

On October 15 he marched 8¾ miles to a camp in the Chao-lung valley. The way lay up and down over grass downs. At 5¾ miles was the Chao-lung La, about 13,500 feet, on the far side of which the way lay down a narrow valley, in which he first met the Nyarong (or Chan-tui) nomads, the Wa-shi having ended at the Jara-güng plain. The elevation of the camp was 12,885 feet. It was slightly warmer here, and Thompson says that an attack of vomiting seemed to give him relief, and some bismuth and other drugs with which he treated Pereira eased him slightly. But he was more disturbed than he usually was at the rumours of brigands ahead which they heard here. It was said that the brigands had killed two men and driven off some animals. Pereira asked Thompson's opinion, and the doctor voted for pushing on, as they were then only a few days from Kanze, and he was anxious to get his patient into some kind of shelter where food could be cooked in some better way than by rough camp-fires; for all this time he was eating very little. Milk, biscuits, Bovril and cornflour was all Thompson could get him to take; and even these only in very small quantities.

A gale blew during the night and there was more snow. But they pushed on and marched 13½ miles to Na-lu Tso camp. All day the road lay up and down over high grass downs with streams flowing south-west, presumably into the Yangtze. After fording the two branches of the Druga Chu they climbed to the Dru La at 3¼ miles, and then descended to more open country and, after fording the Tsai-mo Chu, climbed to the Tsai-mo La, about 13,500 feet, at 9½ miles, beyond which they descended a nice grassy valley about a mile wide, and after fording the Chu-gu Chu, flowing W.S.W., followed it up and camped beside the lake, some 1½ mile long by three-quarters of a mile broad, at an elevation of 13,111 feet.

On October 17 they marched 16 miles to Lung-ni camp. At 2¾ miles they came across a big camp of nomads who said they were Jyade and not Nyarong people. After this there were alternately very stony ascents or ascents up grassy valleys to Momu Nya-ra, 14,244 feet, at 11¼ miles, which is the Yangtze-Ho Chu divide. They then crossed a great slightly undulating very stony plateau extending some 15 or 20 miles to the north-west and north. The path then descends to a small lake 200 yards wide and 2 feet deep. And beyond this is a descent down an open rocky valley, in which they camped at an elevation of 13,790 feet. This evening he was, if anything, a little better.

The same utterly desolate country—" a great gloomy country, especially as I still felt seedy " —was passed through on October 17 as they marched 17 miles to Raju-sumdo camp. The way led down valleys for 8½ miles, and then they had to cross a ford over the Asei-Yindu Chu (the Ho Chu), 15 yards wide and 1 foot deep, flowing in a direction 120°. The elevation here was about 12,500 feet. Then there was some steep climbing up grassy, stony valley to the Lu-mu La, 15,152 feet, at 12¾ miles. This is on the Ho Chu-Yalung divide. They were here in the midst of snowy peaks. One range continues south as the divide. Another side range runs north-east with the gigantic Na-shi peak, just to the east of the pass, perhaps 20,000 feet high. Leaving the pass the path leads down a valley between high ranges to Raji-sumdo camp, 13,337 feet.

The end was now very close at hand. This is the last entry in the diary, though he continued to make the map right up to the last. He seemed to be better on the 18th, and even on the 19th he said he had enjoyed his breakfast of biscuits, milk and a little jam. And each evening he worked out his map immediately after arrival in camp. On that morning Dr. Thompson took a thermos with hot chocolate in case they might be delayed at the Kanze ferry. They now rapidly descended towards the Yalung River. But about noon Pereira had a sudden attack of abdominal pain and got off his pony and lay down. Thompson covered him with rugs and sent the transport on to cross the river. They were now at about 10,000 feet altitude, and it was much warmer, with no snow on the ground.

After fifty minutes' rest and taking some hot chocolate he seemed easier. And as they were only about 2 miles from the Yalung and 4 miles from Kanze, their destination, he wished to go on. Thompson suggested that he should put up in a Tibetan house which was near by, but he would not hear of it. Thompson thereupon agreed to go on if he would tell him at once if he felt that he could not proceed. Pereira's one idea was to reach Kanze because of his bearings, times, etc., and he was relieved when Thompson said he would take these for him.

So the pony being led along slowly, they made their way down to the ferry. Here Thompson gave him some stimulant to help him tide over the rest of the distance. They crossed the Yalung in a coracle, and on the other side Thompson hastily arranged his own camp-bed for Pereira to rest in, while he sent on a man with Pereira's bed to be put up ready in Kanze. He tried to get bearers to carry Pereira on his bed for the remaining $1\frac{3}{4}$ mile, but none could be persuaded.

After two hours' resting Pereira said he felt easier, and as it would soon be dark he was lifted on to his pony again, and the boy supporting him on one side, he was brought into Kanze, where everything was found ready on arrival. He was soon undressed and made snug in bed with hot-water bottles, and for the first time for fourteen days he was now under a roof instead of in a flimsy tent.

But he had only arrived to die. The pain in the abdomen and between the shoulders became very severe, and after trying various remedies Thompson gave him a small hypodermic injection. This eased the pain and he was very grateful. At about nine he asked for the light to be put out and said he would try and sleep. But he was very restless and was moaning in a dull way. Later he wanted a drink of water and apologised for causing so much trouble. He then dosed and wandered in his sleep, sometimes talking in Chinese and sometimes in English. At 1 A.M.—that is in the early morning of October 20 —he wanted to turn over on his side. Thompson helped him over, and again Pereira thanked him and talked quite rationally. But a few minutes later a sudden change came and he became unconscious. About ten minutes later he passed away quite peacefully, resting in Thompson's arms.

He had died of gastric ulcer, and the sudden collapse on the road twelve hours before his death was probably due to perforation. He was already in such a weak state that he had no chance. And this trouble must have been going on for some time. His friends at Yünnan had noticed how extraordinarily small was his appetite. He did not eat enough to keep a child alive, Mr. Sly said. And to all inquiries he replied that he was upset if he ate very much, but that he would be all right once he was on the road again. He was very impatient, too, of any objections being raised against his making another long journey in the middle of the rainy season. In short, his passion for travel wore his frail body to death.

Kanze has a population almost entirely Tibetan, but Dr. Thompson was able to get from the Chinese magistrate permission to bury Pereira in an enclosure reserved for special Chinese. His grave would thus be ensured against desecration. The spot selected was on the east side of Kanze, under the shadow of the great Lamasery on the hill. A coffin of the best wood was made, and, with his sword and military cap laid on it, it was carried up the steep hill-side by twenty Tibetans. Dr. Thompson himself read those beautiful words: "I am the resurrection, and the life", and Pereira's Chinese boy read parts of 1 Corinthians, chapter xv. After prayer the sword and cap were removed and the coffin was committed to the earth. A temporary wooden cross was placed over the grave, and as there was a Roman Catholic priest two marches away, arrangements were made with him for a more permanent memorial.[1]

So in the scene of his great endeavours his body is laid at rest. But his spirit lasts on. To the very end he was true to his self-imposed duty. His iron will forced out of his frail body its last possibility. But it was not only his inflexible will and fidelity to purpose that impressed those who met him on his journeys. They speak of his essential goodness, his lovable nature, his faculty of endearing himself to all he met. French, American and British, Chinese and Tibetan, alike esteemed him in the highest regard. This spirit which animated his work will remain as an inspiration to all who follow after him in that distant borderland, and to many a lover of travel in every quarter of the world.

[1] This has since been done, and he is now buried in the cemetery at Ta-chien-lu.

The honour which every explorer covets and which geographers would most surely have conferred on him had he survived never was his. But his name is secure in the heart of every traveller, and those whose praise he would most have prized will always do reverence to him.

CHAPTER XX

THE PRESENT SITUATION IN CHINA [1]

In 1900 the Chinese people were in a state of unrest, partly caused by a failure of the crops and partly by the recent introduction of European education and a feeling of the necessity of reform. The movement was primarily anti-dynastic, but the Court, realising its danger, managed to divert the Boxer Movement to an anti-foreign outbreak. At that time the country was united under one rule, and enjoyed the benefits of individual security and prosperity under a mild form of autocracy, the only form of government suitable for Asiatic nations in their present undeveloped state. Therefore, whilst the anti-foreign movement was more dangerous owing to the better organisation under a united government, still it was greatly lessened and localised, thanks to the Provinces being swayed by an exceptional number of eminent and capable viceroys and governors, such as Liu Kun-yi at Nanking, Chang Chih-tung at Wu-ch'ang, Li Hung-chang at Canton, Yuan Shih-K'ai in Shantung and Tuan Fang in Shensi.

In 1900 those who prophesied trouble, before

[1] Written by General Pereira in December 1921.

the Boxer outbreak, were stigmatised as alarmists, whilst those who pooh-poohed the chances of trouble were afterwards abused for their want of foresight. The same will happen again at the present time, the fact being that prophets fail to realise that there are such thousands of unforeseen circumstances that none can foresee, which will divert popular feeling and action into unexpected courses. This makes it wrong to make definite prophecies, as their fulfilment is a pure gamble, and it is only the irresponsible man, with a limited local knowledge, who ventures to do so. If he turns out to be right he can say "I told you so," whilst if he is wrong his prophecies are too unimportant to be remembered. At the present time it is universally admitted by all who know China that the country has never been in such a rotten state, and that the experiment of a republic has proved a most dismal failure. The people, especially the upper classes, are not educated up to the requirements of a liberal form of government, and it will be many years before they attain to it. Not only do all the evils under the Imperial regime still exist, but they are multiplied, owing to there being many heads instead of one. In the old days millions poured into the Court at Peking, and a good deal of the money was spent in the service of the State, whilst smaller sums, more or less regulated by precedents, and in a sense recognised as legitimate perquisites for underpaid officials, were received by officials. At the present time the millions go into the pockets of the bigger officials, such as Chang Tso-lin in Manchuria, Wang Chan-yüan, late governor of Hupei, and

Hsiung K'o-wu, lately the ruling spirit in Szechwan, and little or nothing of this comes back to the State. In the same way the minor officials, with no restraining influence from Peking, or fear of public opinion, are out to make what they can, and as quickly as possible, whilst their day of power lasts. In the old days public opinion had much influence over the officials, and if one tried to overstep the recognised limits of squeeze, the people rose and there was trouble. Now the soldiers have increased so enormously in numbers and power that they keep the people in subjection and a state of terrorism. The merchants and peasants long for peace and security in vain.

The break-up of the Central Power has been the chance for adventurers, and now Provinces are divided against each other and often a Province itself is split up into factions.

In the old days the army was despised as an inferior profession and a restraining influence kept on it, but the rise of innumerable factions has given the soldiers their chance. Each petty leader is dependent on his men, and the men themselves now thoroughly understand their power. Very few military officers trouble about discipline, or take any pains about securing a regular payment for their men. As a result, the soldier is generally owed a large amount of back pay, which is sometimes made up for by encouraging looting. If this is not sufficiently profitable, the soldier deserts and joins a brigand band.

The students are, to my mind, an even greater source of danger. It must be remembered that, whatever his failing and lack of education, the student of to-day represents the future ruling class of China, and that the ideas he now imbibes will later be developed. The spirit of unrest is increased by secret societies, which have always existed in China and have now increased in numbers and power. Though primarily they may be organised against the Chinese Government of the day, still there is often the watchword of "China for the Chinese", which tends to an anti-foreign feeling. This, at times, may only require a few foolish actions by one or two irresponsible foreigners to fan the spark, and produce a local and totally unforeseen combustion which, once started, may easily spread.

Probably the two Provinces that are in the greatest state of chaos at the present time are Shensi and Szechwan. Both Provinces are torn by contending factions, especially Szechwan, which is hopelessly broken up into countless parties. Brigandage is rife in both, though the European traveller should have no difficulty if he takes the trouble to warn the officials of his proposed route, and uses an intelligent discrimination as to what routes are safe. The fever of gambling is probably more fully developed in Szechwan; but the chief difference between the two Provinces is that whilst the students were kept in subjection under the late Tu-chün of Shensi (Ch'en Shu-fan), the soldiers were more aggressive in that Province. Whilst I have had no trouble from the soldiers in Szechwan, I have found from all accounts that the students in it are far more troublesome.

Szechwan is indeed probably the most faction-split-up Province in China. With apparently no commanding figure to restore order out of chaos, there is of course a certain amount of safety for the foreigner whilst the factions are fighting amongst themselves, and the leaders may feel that one day their only chance of escaping may be through the assistance of the foreigner. On the other hand, owing to the lack of any stable form of government or dependence on any central authority, a sudden anti-foreign rising by a mob, or engineered by secret societies, would be more dangerous than in any other Province, owing to its inaccessibility.

Through the collapse of Russia, and in a lesser degree of Germany, the power of the foreigner to command respect in China is much less than it used to be, the more so as the remaining Powers are more engrossed in restoring order in their own countries. Luckily they still can demonstrate against Peking, Canton, Wu-ch'ang and Nanking, the four most important centres of influence in China, whilst with its long coast-line other important points can be threatened. Yünnan, too, with the railway to Hanoi and its neighbourhood to Burma, can feel the power of the foreigner, but the Western Provinces are generally isolated and beyond the reach of a foreign expedition. In the case of Kansu this does not much matter, as long as the Mahommedans and Chinese are more or less equably divided and engrossed with their own rivalries. Shensi and Kueichow and Kuangsi are unimportant Provinces, dependent on and influenced by their more powerful surroundings. The only inaccessible Province that matters is Szechwan, which is secure in its own isolation and possibly could only be brought into subjection by a boycott of its exports.

As my recent experiences are connected with Szechwan, I feel that this Province requires the most delicate handling; the feeling of restlessness may pass away with the struggle of contending factions and the rise of the strong man to power. There is always, however, the danger of some imprudent action by a foreigner diverting the unrest to a movement against the white man, and causing a trouble which no one can foresee.

As regards the all-important question of the state of the students in the model Province of Shensi, I formed a poor opinion of the model governor as a man, because he truckled to the students and allowed them to invade his yamen and force him to comply with their demands under fear of threats of a general strike. On the other hand, I realised his sterling merits, as a kind grandmotherly being, for his kindly wishes for the welfare of the people, for the excellence of the platonic vapourings which he caused to be posted on many of the houses throughout the Province, for his good intentions, and for some minor useful reforms. On the other hand, in the otherwise lawless and divided Province of Shensi, Ch'en Shu-fan (the late Tu-Chün) took a strong hand in keeping the students in subjection, notwithstanding all the difficulties of his position. Though probably his past life has not merited for him the hope of beatification after death, nevertheless he struck me, from the accounts of qualified foreigners who had met him, as being essentially a strong man with a will and mind of his own. So far he has never had a fair chance, as when in power only a limited part of the Province acknowledged his rule; but if he succeeds in reasserting himself, as seems at present possible, I hope he will be given the chance of proving that he is an efficient ruler, and capable of re-establishing order in this distracted Province.

Szechwan is so broken up by the number of contending factions that a return for it to a state of peace and prosperity seems at the moment remote. Possibly Hsiung K'o-wu may decide to return to political life. He appears to be the most popular figure in the Province, is still young (35), has a reputation for capacity and might develop into a strong man.

To sum up, poor China, torn by contending parties, in which everybody is fighting for his own hand, overwhelmed by an unexampled series of catastrophes in the shape of famines, earthquakes and floods, has never been in such hopeless straits before. The honest, law-abiding Chinese, as represented by the bulk of its population, and also by the merchant, longs for peace and security, whilst the soldiers (a term at present synonymous with brigands), whose numbers are far in excess of all legitimate requirements, see they have the upper hand, and make use of their power to tyrannise over the wretched people. At the same time the students, seeing the weakness generally of their officials, and particularly of the foreigners with whom they come most in contact, are daily becoming more anti-foreign. History may be repeated, as in the case of the Boxer Movement in

1900, and they may succeed one day in diverting the overwrought feelings of the wretched people against the foreigner, as the cause of all their woes.

To make matters worse, some ill-advised foreigners go home and give a roseate and absolutely false impression of an imaginary wonderful improvement in China under the beneficent rule of a republic, and even, which seems incredible to any foreigner who has any extensive experience of the interior of China, advocate the abolition of extra-territoriality. As far as I know, these men are all foreigners who have spent their lives in security in China in the midst of foreign communities such as Peking, Tientsin and the coast, and who have no first-hand experience of the interior. One can only regret that these advocates of putting the foreigner under the jurisdiction of so-called Chinese justice cannot be forced to live for six months in some remote village or city in the interior, far away even from the restraining influence of a consulate, and made liable to be publicly and ignominiously dragged to a yamen, forced to kneel on chains to extort a confession, liable to the ignominious and cruel punishment of the bamboo, or, even putting aside the risk of torture which still goes on in some places, liable to die from cold in the winter in the wretched dens which do duty as prison quarters . . . only last winter I heard of such a case. Such a degradation of the foreigner would mean his loss of prestige, and, when this comes to pass, the interior of China will only become attractive to those wearied of the vanities of this life and aspirants for the martyr's crown, a noble band, whom I admire, but among whom I have no wish to be enrolled as a member.

The state of chaos in China will not be improved until

(1) The strong men get control, and combining together gradually put each prosperity in order;
(2) The students are kept in check;
(3) The soldiers are reduced to legitimate requirements and kept under a proper state of discipline, whilst brigands are relentlessly hunted down.

It is impossible to forecast what combinations of strong men will eventually bring back peace and prosperity to the country. I should like to see a combination of such men as Wu Pei-fu in the centre of China, Ch'en Shu-fan in Shensi, Ch'en Ching-mei at Canton and possibly Hsiung K'o-wu in Szechwan. Other Provinces, of which I have no recent experience, might be able to add to the number. These combined should be able to put an end to the effete puppets of the Peking Government, that visionary impossibility Sun Yat-sen and the wind-bag Wu T'ing fang of the Canton Government. As regards Chang Tso-lin, who rules supreme in Manchuria, I do not know whether he has improved and is a reformed character from what he was twelve or thirteen years ago, when I visited him. He had then recently retired from the leadership of the Hung-hu-tzu of his district, and had a reputation for cruelty. He disgusted me by bragging about a recent triumph over an enemy, another ex-robber chief, the fact being that he had invited him to a feast of reconciliation, and after the feast had seized the opportunity to have him crushed to death between two of the big stones used for crushing grain.

CHAPTER XXI

THE CHINESE STUDENT[1]

FORMERLY I considered the want of discipline and unnecessary number of soldiers was China's chief trouble ; I have now come to the conclusion that the students are an even greater evil, certainly from the point of view of the foreigner.

The student, usually a wretched half-baked creature who argues like a small child without fear of correction, has no solid basis of education to help him. He picks up a smattering of foreign learning, which enables him to pose without difficulty as a superior being among his own people, who therefore fear him, whilst before the foreigner he realises his inferiority, causing him a loss of face and turning him to anti-foreign feelings at heart.

If the students were under a strong foreigner, not afraid of them, the foreign trained student in China would, no doubt, benefit, but, when he is under weak foreigners, afraid to stand up to him in a fight to a finish, the student gets the upper hand and the prestige of the foreigner sinks. He judges that all foreigners are weak in the same way, and the more this feeling takes root, the more anti-foreign and dangerous he becomes.

[1] Written by General Pereira in 1923.

Unfortunately, from my own experience, by far the greater number of foreign teachers I have met, in native or foreign-run schools and universities, have proved to be weak. They are handicapped by being generally poor and dependent on their salaries from Chinese officials or foreign societies. If onus put up a fight to a finish in a Chinese-run institutio they will probably be forced to give up their jobs, whilst in the foreign-run institution there is the danger of the students going out in a body, with the onus to the teachers of being made responsible for the collapse of the school.

The Chinese are past-masters in the art of asserting themselves by combination, and, as a result of successful strikes and threats in the past, they have gradually got to realise their own strength and the weakness of Chinese officials and foreign teachers in the face of organised opposition, the only thought of the latter being to check the evil by temporising and concessions.

The Chinese student is the result of the zeal of the foreigner for bringing the Chinese up to modern requirements, and, I think, the very large bulk of foreigners now regrets his arrival.

It is curious how the Chinese mind is diverted into the wrong channels. China rose to its highest prosperity under the Han dynasty, roughly from 200 B.C. to A.D. 200; they themselves look upon this as their most glorious epoch, and even to this day speak of themselves as the men of Han. Since then they have gradually gone downhill except for brief flashes of advancement, such as the glorious reigns of the great Manchu Emperors, K'ang Hsi and Ch'ien-lung.

Some of the students sent abroad have done great things, such as T'ang Shao-yi, who went with one of the first batches sent abroad to America; others sent to our Navy have signalised themselves and done good work in the Chinese Navy, but unluckily they have not had the chance of proving their worth in a more extended field of action.

The chief failure, however, has been among those educated in China, especially among those under foreign instructors in Chinese universities. Here the unfortunate foreign teacher finds he has no real authority, he himself is under Chinese officials, who are afraid of the students and cringe to them.

This is one of the extraordinary anomalies of China, where respect for ancestors and elders has been one of the chief characteristics of the middle kingdom, so called because it is supposed to be the centre of the universe. Perhaps it is because the older official, educated in the old system of education, at last recognises the superiority of foreign teaching and gives the student credit for being a superior being.

The result is that the student finds himself pampered, and the more he asserts himself the more the higher authorities knuckle under to him, and the more he becomes a popular idol and leads public opinion.

Affairs have reached such a pitch that he finds that he can assert himself with impunity. Under the autocratic rule of the old Dowager Empress, the first ebullition of unruly students would have been put down with a vigorous use of the bamboo, but those days are past, and now no one can cope with the student except the soldier. The student has been quick to realise this, and he is now very chary of interfering with the military.

Huc's theory of the Chinese being strong to the weak and weak to the strong is thus again exemplified, and this accounts partly for his antipathy to the foreigner. There is generally a latent feeling of dislike to the foreigner in every Chinese who has any education, chiefly because he realises in his heart of hearts the superiority of the foreigner.

The student therefore finds he is a popular idol if he goes for the foreign devil. His chief weapon of offence is of course going on strike or organising a boycott, a form of passive resistance for which the Chinese are unrivalled.

If only they could organise their internal affairs with the same ingenuity and thoroughness they would soon rise from their present state of chaos, but unluckily Chinese ingenuity, which is great, always seems to be diverted into a wrong channel.

Official corruption is the curse of China, every one is out to make money, the foolish people in power often playing with edged tools and raising soldiers far beyond the needs of the country and neglecting to pay them. This is the chief cause of the present state of brigandage throughout the country—and yet against these crowning evils the voice of the student is never raised.

Though the lot of the tribes or alien races who have fallen under the power of China has not been a happy one, this is never thought of.

The Mahommedans of Kansu, the finest fighting race of China, have been oppressed for ages, and it is only since the advent of the Republic that they have been able to assert themselves, and now they are beginning to retaliate on the Chinese, to whom they bear no love.

In the south, the fierce Nosu (Lolo) have been oppressed in the past by many corrupt officials, they have lost their best lands, and a branch has been driven into the wild mountains of southern Szechwan, where they have maintained their independence and bear an undying hate to the Chinese. Here they have not remained passive, but year after year they have seized harmless Chinese families of the farmer class and driven them as slaves into their mountain fastnesses, from which they generally never return.

To the eternal disgrace of China this has been allowed to go on, and never a word of protest is raised by the wretched students of Szechwan and Yünnan.

One can imagine what a howl of indignation would be raised in any country if such a state of affairs were allowed to continue. One cannot imagine what the state of public opinion would be if it were possible and an announcement made that a small alien race was in the habit of raiding the surrounding country, kidnapping British farmers and their families, and bringing them and their descendants up as slaves in the heart of our own land, and yet these things have been happening for years within less than 200 miles of Cheng-tu, and never a word of protest has arisen from the Cheng-tu student.

When I looked over the bleak, forbidding hills of Nosuland and thought of the thousands of patient suffering Chinese hearts who had trodden those paths on their way to slavery, which has utterly crushed them down, I could not help but feeling, although a foreigner, a bitter indignation against the Chinese in general, and the students, as the leaders of public opinion, in particular, for their apathy and allowing such things to be.

Again as I passed by Lu Chou on the Yangtze and heard how brigands had been allowed to pillage the city recently with impunity and how it had previously suffered from soldiers, I thought of the countless harmless citizens of towns and villages who had suffered in the same way, and yet never a word of protest has been raised by a student, for they know it is the work of the soldiers, and their patriotism does not go so far as to risk falling out with one who would administer a beating in return for their protest.

Yet this same student, so silent when matters vital to the happiness of his country are at stake, is ready to raise an outcry against the foreigner at the slightest provocation.

One of the chief of these grievances is the British occupation of the very important village of Pien-ma on the Burma frontier. It is immaterial that the Chinese claim arises from their ignorance of the difference between a watershed and a valley, or that the lucky natives of this village are far happier under British than under Chinese rule, or that the Chinese trader, if he visits this out-of-the-way spot, gains by transacting his business under British rule instead of under

Chinese misrule; these considerations never occur to the student; he only knows the British are in possession, and when nothing better offers, this old grievance is again trotted out as a popular cry, whilst his suffering countrymen nearer home are forgotten.

CHAPTER XXII

A TENTATIVE PROPOSAL [1]

THE Shantung Railway outrage has at last roused people on the China coast to the state of China, as it happened in their midst, whilst the far worse state of some of the internal provinces was too distant to cause any interest. Some of the optimists at home also seem to have had a shock, and are now realising among other things that the curse of the poppy in China is now far worse than it has ever been before.

China is the country of anomalies, and whilst the foreigner is more likely to be kidnapped and held up to ransom at the present time, yet there are fewer cases of foreigners (generally missionaries, as they form the greater number of white men living in the interior) being killed, and of foreign buildings and mission stations being looted. So far one bright spot, in the constant pillaging of cities and towns, has been that mission stations and foreign property have either always or generally been spared. This is a point that I have not seen noticed in the papers, and may perhaps show that in many respects the anti-foreign feeling is not so strong as it used to

[1] Written by General Pereira in July 1923.

be, even in what may be called (in comparison) the palmy days of the Manchus. The one disturbing case is that the Chinese student is more outspoken in his denunciations of foreigners. With an ancient race like the Chinese, reforms should be brought in gradually, and I think the foreigner is to blame for trying to force his ideas of education too rapidly on the Chinese. The result has been that too much education has been crammed into the rising generation, and he has only got a smattering of Western learning, without a proper grounding. The first idea of sending Chinese boys to foreign countries for a long and systematic course of training was sound, but when it came to establishing schools and universities broadcast throughout the land, the evil has far exceeded the good. The youths were taught to realise the superiority of Western education over their own antiquated ideas, and whilst it has made them realise their own superiority over their parents, they also have awakened to the fact that they are still far behind the foreigner, and this has aroused a feeling of jealousy against him. In the old days respect for their elders was one of the virtues of the Chinese, but this is now rapidly dying out. In the old days, too, the power was in the hands of the older men, but now it is generally the younger men, between thirty and forty, who have control of the country. Another difficulty is that in many cases the foreign teachers are poor men, to whom the loss of their posts would result in serious financial embarrassment. As long as the Chinese student feels he can force his superiors by threats of boycott to do what he wishes, this state of affairs will continue. The only remedy is to have Chinese officials strong enough to enforce discipline, and to have foreign professors who can feel they are strong enough to see their orders are obeyed without the risk of losing their posts. Unluckily, nothing is done, the scholars get more and more out of hand, and the foreign instructor becomes more and more an object of unpitying contempt.

Of course, the worst evil of all is corruption. This has always existed, but under the Manchus it was generally organised on fixed rules. In those days every one, excepting the highest, was underpaid, and he made up for it by recognised system of "squeeze". Sometimes new and ingenious forms of squeeze were invented by more enterprising and astute men, but generally if an official exceeded the recognised rules there was a riot, and the culprit suffered. Under the Republic, corruption has increased beyond all bounds of decency, the country has been broken up into countless factions, and each leader of a small faction has generally only thought of enriching himself. To carry out his orders each leader has had to raise soldiers, and these have at last realised their power. In many cases the leaders have committed the blunder of not paying their men, whilst thinking only of making their own fortunes. Sometimes, to remedy this, they have led their men to pillage a rich city or town to make up their arrears of pay or to keep them in a contented frame of mind. Sometimes when they found there were no such hopes, the soldiers have gone off with their rifles, driven by necessity for a means of livelihood to turn brigands. Sometimes the defeated army has been forced to play the rôle of brigands, so that it often happens, as the varying factions obtain the upper hand, the soldier of yesterday changes rôle with the brigand. Then, if the successful candidate is not strong enough, he may come to terms with some of the leaders of the vanquished force and get them to join his force. This, for example, has happened recently in Yünnan, where the brigand chief who seized the Hudson Taylors last year with a view to political eventualities is now an honoured General on the side of the victorious Governor. However, matters vary in different provinces. Szechwan is probably in the worst state of any province, as there are so many different factions, none of whom are strong enough to establish themselves in power for any length of time. There the various Generals are constantly making new combinations and it is impossible to keep track of what is going on. They are totally engrossed with their own affairs, and none of them have any time to cope with the brigand trouble, beyond sometimes calling in a band of brigands to help them as a temporary measure. As a result, organised bands of brigands hold the Yangtze, especially between Lu Chou and Chung-king, and perhaps the worst spot is Miao-erh-hsia, only 30 miles west of Chung-king, where the owner of the Chinese steam launch on which I travelled told me he had agreed to pay the brigands a subsidy of $200 for every trip from Chung-king to Sui Fu and back. It is not surprising, therefore, that these brigands are becoming more arrogant as they realise that nothing can be done, and that they can act openly and with impunity within 30 miles of a treaty port, where there are foreign gun-boats. The brigands, too, I was told, have opened an office in Chung-king, where the oppressed merchants can buy brigand protection at a fixed robber rate.

Cities, like Lu Chou on the Yangtze, are plundered, sometimes by soldiers and sometimes by brigands, and one wonders how the unfortunate merchant can carry on at all, whilst all over the country luckless coolies are seized and forced to work for nothing.

If there were any gleams of honesty in the officials there might be some hope, but they seem to be going from bad to worse. Matters have got so bad that it looks as if it would be a long time before things can again become normal. The only hope appears to lie in foreign intervention or in the advent of a Chinese Napoleon. The latter would be the better solution, but unluckily there is no sign of the advent of any commanding personality who can enforce discipline and gradually bring corruption at any rate within bounds. No doubt such a man will eventually be found, but this may not be for years. On the other hand, if the Powers decide that the breaking-point has been reached and that they cannot wait indefinitely, the result may be some sort of foreign intervention. If they could work with some sort of unanimity the prospect might be hopeful, but after the fiasco of the Versailles Conference, where friends found themselves hopelessly divided by conflicting interests, it hardly looks as if they could work in harmony in China, where interests clash in every direction. One solution, to give one country, which can only be Japan, a mandate to act, would probably not be agreed to, and probably, after their experience in Siberia, the Japanese themselves would not be willing. Even supposing the Powers were unanimous, they could not act without a force to carry out their reforms. The question is, Where is this force to come from ? The tendency is to scrap ships, reduce the number of soldiers as far as possible, and economise in every way. Intervention therefore would mean a big increase of expenditure, which might and probably would be opposed to public opinion. It is easy enough to call for foreign intervention, but will the taxpayer at home submit to paying the bill ? Under the Manchus there was a definite Central Government, and after the Boxer troubles an allied force of between 50,000 and 70,000 soldiers was able to coerce the Manchus by occupying Peking, Pao-ting Fu and Tientsin, but this state of affairs no longer exists in China. If effective intervention is impossible under present conditions both at home and in China, the only thing is to try and reform very gradually and to move very slowly.

Some people advocate the disbandment of soldiers, but they do not suggest what provision is to be made for the men when disbanded. Previous efforts have shown that men so disbanded have gone off with their arms to swell the number of brigands. It is an undoubted fact that there are far more soldiers in China than are necessary, and that they have an unlimited supply of rifles of all sorts, Mauser pistols, etc., whilst the brigands are often as well armed as the soldiers. In theory, disbandment would be the right course, but who is going to enforce it, and how can soldiers be prevented from going off with their arms as brigands ? Another sound theory would be to insist that no recruits should be enlisted, but how can this be enforced ? Now that the foreign communities on the coast have at last woke up to the gravity of the situation, they will clamour for things being put right without considering how it can be done, or the difficulties to be faced.

I think the best thing would be to raise a small model army under young and energetic foreign officers, starting in some more or less isolated place, say at Tientsin, and to enforce Chinese agreement, this force to be paid regularly out of fixed sources of revenue in the hands of the foreigners. At the same time Manchuria might be handed over to the Japanese, who could cope single-handed with Chang Tso-lin. This model army would be increased gradually according to circumstances until it could be extended all over the 18 provinces.

But this would mean a very slow beginning, and might also meet with opposition from the nation generally and the local chiefs in particular. It would therefore be advisable in particular to secure the co-operation of the best man who can be found. The man who appears to be the most suitable is Wu Pei-fu, who might be willing to act with the co-operation of the " Christian " General Feng Yu-hsiang. Wu can be classed as the best General in China ; as far as I know, he has retained his reputation for honesty, and his troops are very nearly the only disciplined soldiers in the country, and paid regularly, whilst Wu himself, judging from the accounts of the fighting at I-chang on the Yangtze some two years ago, appears to be possessed of personal courage. Against him as a soldier is his inexplicable neglect to crush Chang Tso-lin early last year in the neighbourhood of Shan-hai-kuan. The reason for this fear to push on, when success lay open before him, has never been explained. It may have been due to his realising his own incapacity to take over the burden of government, but this hardly seems likely in view of his present extensive activities, extending to Szechwan in the west and Kwangtung in the south. Possibly there may have been some secret reason, such as fear of clashing with the Japanese if he took over Manchuria. Whatever the cause of his inaction on that occasion, he appears to have been unable to handle the political situation after success.

It is of course a risky undertaking backing one faction against the rest, and could only be done with the unanimous consent of all the Powers, but in the present chaotic state of the Republic it is only a choice of the lesser evil. The only candidate appears to be Tuan Chi-jui, who some sixteen or seventeen years ago enjoyed the reputation of honesty when commanding one of the old Lu-chun divisions. I do not know whether he still enjoyed this reputation when, as the head of the An-fu party, he ruled the country. He was a protégé of the Japanese and his nomination would be acceptable to them, but for this reason he would probably not be popular in the country, and he has not a trained army behind him.

After the Japanese War of 1894, Li Kung-chang realised that it was necessary to model an army on Western lines. His work was interrupted by the Boxer Movement, but later Yuan Shih-K'ai carried on the idea, and, with the help principally of German officers, brought the Lu-chun to the greatest state of perfection that has ever been attained by a Chinese army. It was far from being perfect, but from 1905 to 1907 or 1908 it gradually improved. Then unluckily, owing to jealousy, Yuan Shih-K'ai was removed from the command, and it slowly began to deteriorate. With the advent of the Republic it rapidly declined, and with the division of Provinces this national army has now long since ceased to exist.

The best solution, therefore, seems to be to come to an arrangement with the least incapable of the many leaders in China, to induce him to start a model army under foreign guidance, and to assist him in every way until he is able to stand on his own feet. It is not by any means a perfect solution, but it appears to be the best; there are many obstacles in the way, but obstacles only exist to be overcome.

I speak as an outsider, who, after twenty-four years' experience of the country, is thoroughly disgusted with China, and determined never again to revisit it under any circumstances.

These reforms must take a long time to work out, and they require young and energetic officers at the head of affairs who are prepared to devote their future to the work.

Map to illustrate

THE JOURNEYS OF B. GEN. G. PEREIRA IN CHINA AND TIBET, 1921 TO 1923.

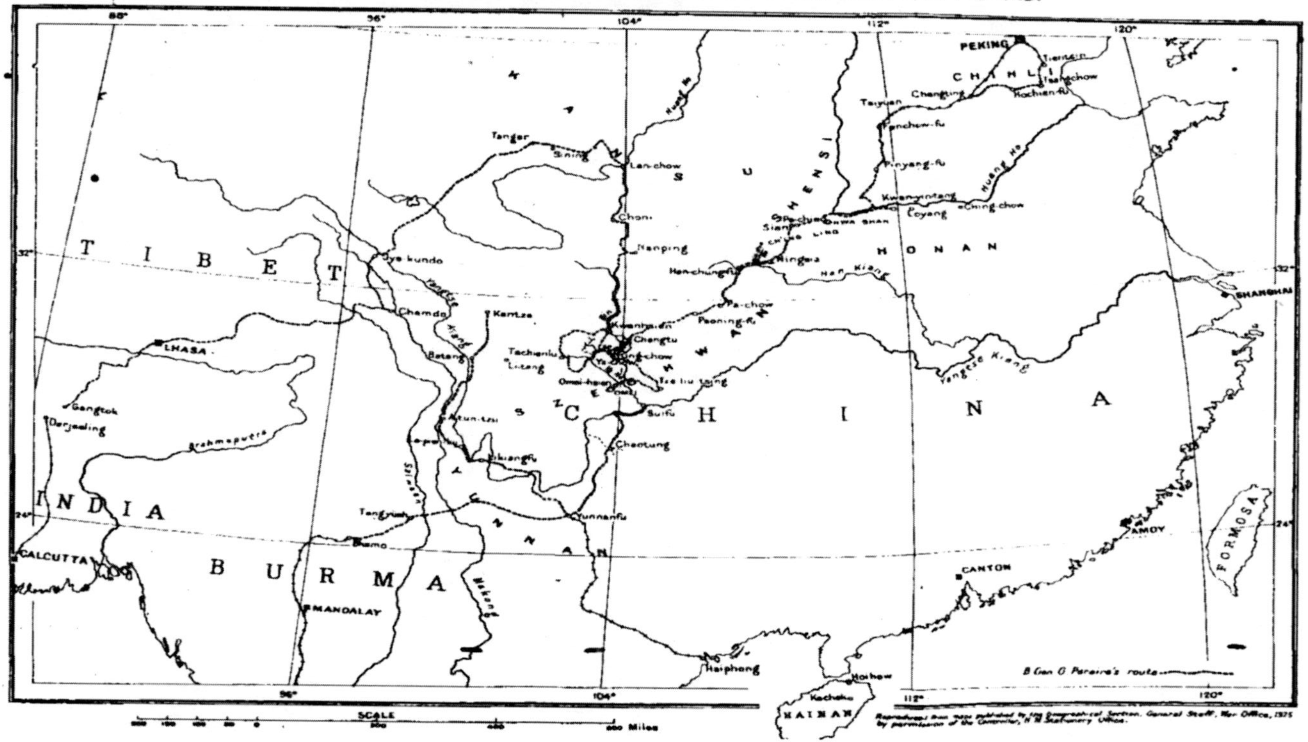

INDEX

U

THE END